GW00992305

BRIEF GLORY

... if one was ever over the Salient in the autumn of 1917 and saw an SE5 fighting like Hell amidst a heap of Huns, one would find nine times out of ten that the SE was flown by Rhys Davids.

James McCudden VC.

BRIEF GLORY

The Life of Arthur Rhys Davids,
DSO, MC and Bar

ALEX REVELL

Pen & Sword
AVIATION

First published in Great Britain 2010 by
Pen & Sword Aviation
an imprint of
Pen & Sword Books Ltd
47 Church Street
Barnsley
South Yorkshire
S70 2AS

ISBN 978 1 84884 162 8

A CIP record for this book is
available from the British Library.

First published in 1984 by William Kimber & Co Ltd, London.

Typeset, Printed and Bound by
CPI Antony Rowe, Chippenham, Wiltshire

Pen & Sword Books Ltd incorporates the imprints of Pen & Sword Aviation,
Pen & Sword Maritime, Pen & Sword Military, Wharncliffe Local History,
Pen & Sword Select, Pen & Sword Military Classics and Leo Cooper.

For a complet list of Pen & Sword titles please contact
PEN & SWORD BOOKS LIMITED
47 Church Street, Barnsley, South Yorkshire, S70 2AS, England
E-mail: enquiries@pen-and-sword.co.uk
Website: www.pen-and-sword.co.uk

To the memory of a remarkable family.
Thomas
Caroline
Vivien
Nesta
Arthur

Contents

List of Illustrations

Introduction

To those interested in the history of aerial warfare the name of
Arthur Percival Foley Rhys Davids is well known – almost a legend.
Yet, like so many legends when closely examined, few hard facts
were known about his brief life. What little was known was almost
solely due to his being mentioned in four books: *Five Years in the Royal
Flying Corps*, by James McCudden; Maurice Baring's *Flying Corps
Headquarters 1914-1918*; *Scarlet and Khaki* by T.B. Marson; and that
superb evocation of another time and place, *Sagittarius Rising* by Cecil
Lewis. These books were published after the First World War, the
authors all knew Rhys Davids during his service with 56 Squadron
and their memories and knowledge of him mainly relate to his
meteoric career as an airfighter during the summer of 1917. Apart
from these glimpses of Rhys Davids, plus a few photographs, little
more was known.

In the spring of 1982, author and journalist Ralph Barker was
commissioned by a popular newspaper to tell the story of one of that
lost generation of young men who were killed in the Great War of
1914-1918. The brief was that the subject should have shown
exceptional promise of a future career and have been killed while still
a teenager. Barker immediately thought of Rhys Davids, who was
killed a month after his twentieth birthday, and knowing of my
interest in 56 Squadron and Rhys Davids, Barker contacted me for
possible source material. During research into the history of 56
Squadron, Vivien Rhys Davids, the elder sister of Arthur Rhys
Davids had been traced, but Barker found that she had since died.
However, he established that the Rhys Davids family papers had
been left to the Pali Text Society and were housed at the Faculty of
Oriental Studies, Cambridge University. Ralph Barker arranged to
view them and asked me if I would care to accompany him. We were
both astonished at the wealth of material contained in the papers and
Barker suggested that I write this book. The sheer extent of the
material precluded working at Cambridge, but owing to the
kindness of the Board of the Pali Text Society, and in particular its
President, K.R. Norman, the material was made available on loan.

The Rhys Davids papers are the copyright of the Pali Text Society and have been quoted with their permission.

I should also like to acknowledge and thank the following for their help. The late Vivien Rhys Davids; Ralph Barker; P.M. Quarrie, the librarian of Eton College; P. Strong, Keeper of College Library and Collections; E.F. Foster and D. Kasher of University College, London; Mr Haysom, Ministry of Defence; Dr Gustav Bock; Miss F. Archer; Mrs N. Marshall, née Eadon; Q.Y. Stevenson; B. Grey; B. Schmaling; B. McKay; N. Eadon; A. Imrie, and H.E. Hervey.

Alex Revell,
Hatfield

CHAPTER ONE

Boyhood

In the last decade of the nineteenth century, Forest Hill, south of London, was still a pleasantly rural area. Although the expansion of the railway from the metropolis in the 1870s had led to the building of a number of houses at the foot of One Tree Hill and the development of large, double-fronted houses for the Victorian professional and middle classes was gradually spreading – particularly to the higher ground of the district – the overall aspect of the locality was still that of scarcely disturbed countryside. Honor Oak Road was just such a development, the road rising steeply to afford magnificent views of the distant Weald of Kent, and it was here, in 1895, that Professor Thomas William Rhys Davids brought his wife Caroline, pregnant with their first child.

Thomas Rhys Davids was born in 1843, the son of a Congregational minister. After schooling in Brighton he refused an opening for training as a solicitor and enrolled at Breslau University to study Sanskrit, taking a Ph.D. In 1864 he entered the Ceylon Civil Service, acting as secretary to the governor, and while in Ceylon an event took place that was to set the course of his career and dictate his life's work. Serving as a magistrate in a local court he presided over a case of dispute of land ownership between a Ceylonese and an Englishman; the case involved questions of canon-law and a document was produced in evidence which was written in a language unknown to any in the courtroom. The language was Pali, in which the sacred books of Buddhism are written, and Thomas Rhys Davids, his interest aroused, resolved to study Pali and the interpretation of Buddhism. His first teacher was a Buddhist monk, Yatramulle Unnanse, and the young student made rapid progress; learning Pali, exploring the Sigiri Rock and the site of the Anurashapura, copying inscriptions and studying the history of Buddhism in Ceylon.

Rhys Davids' finding against the Englishman in the land dispute case had been viewed unfavourably by his superiors and led to his almost complete ostracism by the British community on the island, and in 1872 he resigned his position, came home to England, read for the Bàr and was admitted to the Middle Temple in 1877. He practised little law, however, for his interest in Buddhism had become all absorbing and in 1881 he founded the Pali Text Society, to translate and study the treasure trove of early Buddhism literature which was lying unedited and unused throughout the universities of Europe.

In 1882 Rhys Davids was appointed Professor of Pali at University College, London and it was here that he first met his future wife. Caroline Augusta Foley had been born in 1859, one of the ten children of the Reverend John Foley BD, Vicar of Wadhurst in Sussex, and Caroline Augusta Windham. Caroline Windham was one of the thirteen children of Vice Admiral William Lukin who had assumed the name of Windham in 1824 on inheriting Felbrigg Hall, Norfolk – and his wife Ann, née Thellusson.

At the time of their marriage Professor Rhys Davids was a 'young fifty-two', Caroline Foley thirty-six, a not uncommon age difference in their class and time. It was an extremely happy marriage, for both, although individualistic, had similar academic interests and backgrounds. Caroline had entered University College, London in the 1885-1886 session and gained a BA in 1886. She was awarded an MA in 1889, later gained a D.Lit and was elected a Fellow in 1896. It was while reading economics and philosophy at University College that Caroline was advised by her tutor, Professor Croom Robertson, to further her interest and understanding of Indian philosophy by learning Sanskrit and Pali. Croom Robertson sent her to Professor Rhys Davids. A romance quickly blossomed and led to their marriage in 1894.

After living in rooms in the Temple for some months, the Rhys Davids moved to Honor Oak Road, naming the house 'Nalanda' – 'after a beautiful spot in Ceylon' – and in July 1895 their first child was born there: a girl, Vivien Brynhilda Caroline Foley. Just over two years later, on 27 September 1897, Vivien was taken into her mother's room to see her brother for the first time, born the previous evening. She was held over his cot as he slept and her mother recorded that she touched his features 'with a face aglow with tender smiling interest and murmured, *'Bruder klein. Bruder klein.'* The boy was named Arthur Percival Foley.

Unlike many parents of their social class during the late Victorian and Edwardian era, Caroline and Thomas Rhys Davids devoted a great deal of their busy lives to their three children – a second daughter, Nesta, was born in 1900 – and they were an extremely close-knit, happy and affectionate family, demonstrative in their love for each other. The household at Honor Oak Road was small, with a cook and parlourmaid to attend to the family's needs and a nanny, Minna, for the children. Minna was German and, ironically in Arthur's case, the first words and sentences the children uttered were in German.

As she had with Vivien, Caroline Rhys Davids kept a detailed account of her son's birth and first years:

> Arthur was born at 10.20 pm September 26th 1897. He arrived in the fullness of time and well nourished after three months of vigorous movement. His skin was from the first of a healthy pink without blemish or wrinkles. His head well covered with fairly long dark brown hair. His eyelashes well advanced and his eyes are large and of a dark greyish blue, becoming bluer in a month. The nose was remarkably well formed for a new born and the shoulders of great breadth.

By his first birthday he was 'a bright jolly baby, an infant Bacchus: strong, sturdy, energetic, all curves and dimples, but with a face that promises sturdiness and seriousness for all its dimpled roundness.' Only one crisis in his first year had threatened his steady growth. At nine months he caught a heavy cold which turned to acute bronchitis, with severe congestion of the lungs. The doctor was called after midnight and prescribed a hot bath, bed, a bronchitis kettle and a garngee jacket. Arthur slept through the remainder of the night, throughout the next day, Sunday, and by 4 am on the Monday morning was pronounced out of danger.

At the end of his first year, after a summer of recovery at Aberdovey, he was again healthy and strong. His favourite game was now with a ball, 'with or without a bat', and he would call out 'good s'ot' when wielding his sister's golf club.

> Words now come fast, for he imitates everything he hears. Ergo, most are English, a few German. He is very imperious, very dogged. Cannot bear opposition, but will fling his arms around one's neck at times. He is eager to get out. 'S'oes, S'oes. Townstairs, garden, want to go.' What more is there to say? He shows no fear of *anything*.

At two and a half his mother again summed up his progress and character.

It's odd that it is so much more difficult to give particulars of the development of his intellect, heart and will than in the case of his sister. He is every bit as interesting and satisfactory, but the growth isn't so much on the surface, is not so tangible. Moreover there's the sister as fugleman in everything, marring his beginnings and attainments, this way and that being thrown into relief. Less precocious, if anything than she, he will very likely go further and is the antithesis of a stupid, mulish child. But whereas his little ways are delightful they need to be seen and heard. Description is difficult. Some quaint efforts of fancy, humour and criticism might be properly described. Once, on being troubled, he wept and called (in the nursery) for his usual solace: 'Minna, love me, love me'. Then, consoled, he murmured, 'Sunshine again'. 'Where?' asked Minna, seeing none without. 'In my eyes' was the reply. The same year, in the autumn, his sister admonished him, 'Say thank you, Mother'. 'Too young' he retorted with affected artlessness. . . .

He has two crazes on: to play cards with me and golf. I play two or three patiences and beggar-my-neighbour with them after dinner to keep them quiet during the nurse's meal and give them prizes in sweets if they win. But the taste for cards, mixed with the child's fancy for some of them 'Kings and Boys' has survived the sweets. As to golf, he will go into the garden, on the hill or to the golf club with me and wang away with a little brassey and a short putter until the 'good s'ot' comes off. He is naturally rather lefthanded, which hinders just a trifle.[1]

*

At three years old Arthur started kindergarten at the Manor Mount High School for Girls, Forest Hill. He went reluctantly, but was quite content once he was there and his teacher, a Miss Clare, reported that he was: 'Excellent when he chooses to be interested, but given to dreaming fits from which he will suddenly awaken'. His first school report, for the autumn term of 1901 sums him up as 'a good, quiet boy. He shows good capabilities in nearly all his lessons and is already very eager in school.'

His mother's journal is full of Arthur's first drawings and attempts to write and one drawing is of unusual interest. Under the coloured drawing – a very creditable effort for one not yet six years old – his mother has written, 'Arthur's memory sketch of looping the loop at

[1] Caroline Rhys Davids was a golfer of tournament class.

Crystal Palace. July 14, 1903.' This was, of course, before the advent of powered flight and can only refer to the 'Topsy Turvy' machine in the fun fair at the Crystal Palace. The 'Topsy Turvy' was a crude forerunner of the present day roller coaster and was situated opposite the aquarium, near the watershoot. The structure was wooden and four people in wooden cars were propelled around and into a loop some twenty feet high. It evidently impressed the young Arthur Rhys Davids.

As was her husband, Caroline Rhys Davids was a prolific author. Arthur was now taking an interest in his mother's writing and his bedtime questioning would include enquiries as to how many pages of proofs she had corrected that day, eagerly checking her progress. His affection for his mother was now taking the form of addressing her as 'Belle' or, in Pali, '*Amma tata*'. Words fascinated him. At five or six he had developed a craze for spelling games and riddles, and he now made frequent puns and plays on words. Vivien (still called Brynhilda by the family) having read a magazine of short stories, declared that her favourite story was one called 'The Well Maiden'. 'Huh', commented Arthur slyly. 'I should choose the "Well-made Maiden".'

Caroline, anxious that he should grow healthy and strong, made sure that he was in the fresh air as much as possible and took plenty of exercise. As soon as he was old enough he was taken to the local swimming baths for a swimming lesson, but became entangled in the rope support, rolled over backwards and sank. 'He got frightened and cross and I did not repeat the experiment.' He was also taken to the London Hippodrome to see one of the early wild west shows, then very popular: 'but he got into a state of anguish and misery when the redskins were pursuing the palefaces.' On his birthday his mother took him and his sister to Hayes Common and Keston Ponds. 'We picnicked there and I took stolen snapshots of my narcissus naked and of Brynhilda as a bather, while no police were around. A donkey ride towards the station was much appreciated.' Caroline and Thomas Rhys Davids were much against the false prudery of the Edwardian age and the children often played naked together in the garden of Nalanda.

The summer Arthur was seven years old his mother took him to Wales: 'to the Snowdon country'. He was still 'clumsy, not deft, and incurs frequent bruises; but sturdy, swift of movement and eager'. Arthur was taken to the top of Snowdon and for a moment was near danger.

He leapt out of a standing train to pass into another as the former began to start. A stoker lifted him as he fell. But he accomplished his first mountain pass well, in fine heart, between two valleys, and flung himself into farm life, where his clumsiness was replaced by great deftness. 'I must do all that mother did' was his reply to praise. Meanwhile mother felt pangs.

Caroline Rhys Davids ended her journal detailing her son's progress during his first years with an entry on 23 September, three days before his eighth birthday:

He is outgrowing the passionate stage and scarcely stammers, except when speaking under excitement. His great rage now is geography, and map drawing one of his pastimes. He is very winning and quickly on friendly terms with strangers. His other favourite study is French, which he sings and croons over out of school. Games he is keen about, developing a craze for chess and craving games with his father.

In late 1904 Professor Rhys Davids had accepted the post of Professor of Comparative Religion at the Victorian University of Manchester and the family reluctantly left Nalanda in October 1905. Their new home was Harboro Grange, in Ashton-on-Mersey, a suburb of Manchester. Arthur was now eight years old and his last report from the Manor Mount High School for Girls for the summer term of 1905 shows him sixth in the class with consistently high marks in almost all subjects. Strangely enough for a future brilliant classics scholar, he had resisted the idea of taking Latin.

He tried to get out of this with his favourite cry 'too difficult'. But when I caught them up coming out of school, he hailed me with joyous shrieks – Latin was lovely – I know all the cases – Nominative, etc. Now it's Mensa etc.

The summer of 1905 had been spent in Switzerland, at Champéry, staying at the Châlet Walker and the Hôtel de la Poste on Lake Champex.

He was in splendid health all the time there, growing passionately to love the mountains, the individual creatures, climbed rocks fearlessly, plumped boldly into torrents and pools and tried hard to talk French. He took great fancy to only two men who helped him as guides – Paul Exenry and Alexis Berthod, and won the hearts of both.

Vivien was now away at boarding school and Arthur spent a great deal of time with his younger sister, Nesta. 'But his great need is school. That awaits him at The Sale, Brooklands and Ashton-Upon-Mersey High School for Boys, where I hope to take him on September 27. Last memoir from Nalanda.'

At his new school Arthur began to show the first signs of the exceptional scholar he was later to become. He was one of only three boys in the school as young as eight, but put into the most junior form he found the work too easy and, although quickly moved higher, still found the work well within his capabilities. By the end of the Easter term of 1906 he was in Form 11, whose average age, at nine and a half, was a year older than himself; despite this age difference he was seventh in the form and third in the mathematics set. By the summer term he was top of the form, first in mathematics and had gained further praise for his mark of ninety-two per cent in French.

On the more personal level he had settled in and adjusted well to his new environment, although he had suffered a certain amount of petty persecution from the older boys. By the end of his second term he had 'won over' his foes, but dreaded being 'slapped in the face' by bigger boys and evaded fighting whenever he possibly could.

In fact I scolded him for his pliancy when he told of two boys pushing a little girl into a ditch, he having looked on, and ordered him to bring home a scalp. He soon after reported having one – viz, he had turned on a pursuer and tripped him up.

He was now playing football and cricket, keenly envying Vivien her hockey and tennis, and he seems to have got into the usual boyish pranks – including the breaking of a window: 'he simply confessed with sobs and asked to pay for it from his savings bank'. He bought his first bicycle from this savings bank, but found it 'curiously difficult to learn', showing no wish to take it out on to the public roads. But it was a happy time. 'He is full of happy energy. Latin, French and geography he devours, declining and conjugating anything and everything and taking constant pleasure in his work.'

By the summer of 1907, in a form whose average age was now two years older than himself, he was third in class and sixth in the mathematics set. It was obvious that he needed a greater intellectual stimulus and he was shortly sent to Doctor Summerfield's Preparatory School near Oxford. It was while Arthur was at Summerfields, with his mother and Nesta at home, and Vivien at school at Monmouth, that their four-sided correspondence began. As an affectionate and devoted family, it was hard for them to be separated and they compensated by writing regularly and later, when Nesta was also at boarding school, sending their letters to each other, circulating them between themselves. From her very earliest letters it is evident that Nesta had a great sense of fun and style. She loved writing to her brother in the local Manchunian dialect, and he answered in the same vein. His first letter from Summerfields to Nesta starts with 'Dear Boiby, Oi 'opes uz yer is well' and, after telling her of his latest football match, he goes on, with a keen sense of irony for a twelve-year-old. 'This morning the Arch-Deacon of some place with the most terrible name I have ever heard preached to us about the spread of Christianity in the mines of Johannesburg, and very interesting all together'.[1] He finally ended: 'Good boi, me looving boiby, moind uz yer roite ter me soon, afore oi chops yer 'ead orf! Love to all. Arthur.'

His letters home during his time at Summerfields are full of riddles, puzzles and scraps of Latin, French and German. His academic work was progressing, but sport was not neglected. He was in the gymnasium eight, coached by Sergeant Morley, and in February 1910 he wrote to Vivien: 'I have started golf, am driving well and can carry about a hundred yards with my cleek. I like mother's jigger a bit better than my old mashie, I think.' After telling her of the triumphs of the Rugby XV and detailing with evident relish how his friend, one Griffiths major, had broken his arm in two places, illustrating it with a graphic drawing – 'lucky it wasn't me, eh?' – he wrote: 'I was equal top in French this week and three marks behind the two top (equal) boys in Greek. But next to bottom in Latin, and second in Latin comp.'

Summerfields was a school which prepared boys for the scholarship examinations for the public schools and in September 1910 Arthur and Dr C.E. Williams stayed at the White Hart in Windsor while Arthur took the scholarship examination for Eton. These lasted for two and a half days, ending with a viva on the last

---

[1] Rhys Davids' spelling and punctuation has been retained throughout.

morning in which the candidate was questioned by a formidable array of Eton notables. Successful candidates, usually about ten in number, are known as Collegers. There are seventy Collegers at Eton, while the Oppidans – the fee-paying boys – number around a thousand. It has been said that the Collegers have two obvious distinctions: that they are, on average, poorer financially but more scholastically talented and inclined than Oppidans. Collegers tend to look upon Oppidans as philistines and hearties, while Oppidans have a similarly derogatory view of Collegers, thinking of them as a lot of swots and 'unwashed saps', and referring to them in general as 'tugs'.

Arthur was elected with two other Summerfields boys and the following May entered Eton as a Colleger. He was now a King's Scholar – the scholarship endowment stems from Henry VI – and the letters KS were added to his name, to stay with him throughout his days at Eton.

CHAPTER TWO

King's Scholar

Caroline Rhys Davids left her son at Eton on Wednesday, 3 May 1911. On the following Sunday evening Arthur wrote the first of the hundreds of letters he was to write to his mother and sisters while at Eton.[1]

> My Darling Mother,
> How awful I felt for the next five minutes after you had gone! I felt as though I was left alone in the middle of some entirely unknown desert or something of that sort. I will tell you as far as I can remember what has happened since Wednesday. After you left, I went back to my stall and read a book or talked to other boys, and so on till tea time. On Thursday I got up about 8 and fetched the water for my bath and dressed (no mishap with white shirt) we then went down and had breakfast, and at 9.15 we four new boys went to be 'gowned' by the Provost. This was a most wonderful ceremony, we had to kneel before him while he read out the paper I enclose. We then went to Lower Chapel, not College Chapel, as we had not got our suplices. At 11.00 we had our first school, only I think I didn't go to it. I can't quite remember. Then we had Hall (that's dinner) at 1.30. During the afternoon I read in the field. We had absence (that's our names are read out and we have to answer) at 2.30 and 5.30. Then at 7.30 was lock up, and 8.30 was supper in Hall, and at 9.00 prayers, as we all had to be in bed by 9.30 and so we have to hurry to get into bed in about fifteen minutes or so. On Friday we had early school at 7.30. This was Maths and we just had to do a paper, for which we got no marks, to see what we could do. Then we had breakfast and Chapel the same as on Thursday and at 11.00 we had our first Greek lesson (construe it's called, you prepare out of school and say it in school). We are doing Aristophanes' 'The Knights'. At 12.00 we had to go to Mr Crace, but I thought it was Saturday we had to go so I went after lockup instead. Dinner was as usual and at 3.45 to

---

[1] It was 7 May, exactly six years before his first combat in the air.

4.50 was school again. I forgot to say that in the morning we did not actually do the construe, but he told us all about Aristophanes, and what we were going to do during the half. So we did the construe during the 3.45 school, then at 5.00 it was school again till 5.45. Then we had tea. At 7.30 I went to Mr Crace, as I said before, and when I got back to College I went to grace practice, which is all in Latin and rather fun. Then the rest was the same as Thursday. Yesterday we had early school at 7.00 and it was science, then at 8.00 we got our fagmaster's breakfast ready.

I'm fag to the Captain of the School, Haldane, a nephew of the War Minister, I think. I had to do two pieces of toast and get one plate of porridge. Haldane and three or four others mess together, so we each do a share. Haldane has three fags, about 4 other chaps two, (all VI formers) and some have one. Yesterday was a half holiday and the rest was the same as Friday, except the lessons were different. We break up on August 2 and go back on September 20. We break up so late as there are such heaps of holidays this half. My new trousers (Eton) are much too light, they ought to be dark. I have got cricket shoes and cap. I hope Viv's confirmation has come off alright. I hope Nesta will look after our garden and the 'wurms'. Huge love to you boo's.

Arthur.

PS. Overcoat arrived, thanks very much for pen, I like it immensely. No sign of shirts!

As a junior Colleger, one of the bottom fifteen in the school, Arthur was living in Chamber, a long airy room divided into fifteen stalls by wooden partitions ten feet high, liberally carved with the names of their former occupants – the partition of Arthur's stall contained his uncle's name who was at Eton in the 1870s. Halfway down the Chamber an open space between two stalls contained a round table of some antiquity, a large fireplace, and bootlockers forming benches. This space was the centre of communal life in Chamber. Magazines and papers were left on the table and in winter chairs were brought from the stalls and set in a semi-circle around the fire. Each stall contained a small bureau – known as a 'burry' – a chair, a bed which folded away into a cupboard, and a wash basin with cold water. The remainder of the furnishings was left to the taste of the occupier. For privacy, curtains could be drawn across the entrance of each stall and unwanted visitors could be driven out by a cry of 'Stall Curtains'. Two warnings were given to intruders. If the first cry of

'Stall Curtains' had no effect, it was repeated, followed up with a shout of 'Siphon'. If a boy really meant business the cry of 'Stall Curtains, Stall Curtains, Siphon' could be made in a second and a half.[1]

By his second letter home, on the following Sunday, Arthur had settled into the life in Chamber and Eton in general, although still a little bemused by the number of rules, official and otherwise, which regulated the daily life there.

> It's quite extraordinary the number of special little rules about clothing there are here. You aren't allowed to wear your gown without a topper unless you are in 'liberty' (that's Sixth form and a few other people just below) you mustn't wear flannels without a cap, and you aren't supposed to say a word to anyone who isn't in your election except on special occasions such as fagging.

The coronation of King George V was to take place on 22 June and Arthur's letters are full of the plans for the coming celebrations. The boys were allowed only three alternatives.

> First, we can go on Wednesday evening, see the Thursday procession and come back on Thursday evening. Second, go on Thursday evening, see the Friday procession and come back on Friday evening, or, thirdly, go on Saturday morning, see the Naval review and come back on Monday morning. In the first two you can go to any relation (or Godmother) but in the last you must go with your parents and no long leave is allowed for the Eton and Harrow match. So the last is quite impossible.

Boys at Eton were allowed long leave, as the breaks during the half were called, only on written evidence from their parents as to where they were staying while away from school. The question of where to stay on long leave – his parents being in Cheshire – was a constant source of worry and planning throughout Arthur's time at Eton and various aunts and uncles were mooted as possible hosts for different days and events.

During his second week at Eton, Arthur tried glass-blowing – 'I only succeeded in burning my fingers, which greatly annoyed me' –

---

[1] 'Siphoning' was seven strokes with a length of rubber hose.

and Chapel, the essence of life at Eton, seemed to be a source of annoyance and amusement.

> I am rather unfortunate in Chapel as the Oppidan who sits in front of me usually has his hair soaked in hair grease, which I can hardly call pine, and the air around me becomes a bit oppressive. The same chap is also rather fond of talking to his neighbour during prayers and so I can't hear whether the person who is reading the prayers has got a cold in his big toe or not. I expect you think this rather rot.

Arthur had already been picked to sing in the choir on Sundays and had introduced chess to his fellows in Chamber.

> Before and after Hall we sing a long Latin Grace, with various responses and things. Only a selected choir sings, I, of course, being one, and also of course wanting to clear my throat at one of the most important amens. I seem to have introduced a mania for chess into Chamber (that's the bottom 15 in College) but I think I can beat anyone in it. Work's going on all right.

He also wrote to Vivien on this second Sunday at Eton, thanking her for sending *Punch* and telling her that he had read *Stalky and Co*, which, although he thought very funny, not as much so as *Three Men in a Boat*. Vivien, now almost sixteen, was having her first contacts with the opposite sex. She could confide in Arthur because he had assured her that at Eton, unlike her own school, nobody else read his letters. She wrote:

> I'm very fond of Claude (ahem). He's such a sensible sort of boy, none of your silly flirting about him! He and I have shooting matches in the cellar nearly every time I go there and my record is 22 for 7 shots, counting the bull as five, the next as four and the outside as two – not bad is it? He and I are very even so it is great fun. What do you think is the latest? Geoffrey wrote me a letter asking why I didn't kiss him goodnight instead of shaking hands!!! So I wrote him a sort of maternal letter and told him I didn't want to, or something like that. And he's quite decent now. Of course it isn't a light and silly thing when a boy gives you his whole hearted affection like that.

As yet there was little sign that Arthur would develop into a classics scholar; in fact he seems to have leant more towards science. In one of his early letters home he explained to his mother that although he had not chosen to take science – 'as everybody, at least the upper boys, learns science now' – if given the choice he would still have picked science as a subject: 'I am now fairly well settled to take up science and maths when I get higher up.'

Arthur's first 4 June at Eton – a day celebrated annually by the school in honour of the birthday of George III – was spent in the company of his Uncle Harry, who visited Eton for the event. Arthur wrote: 'We all had to wear special white waistcoats (mine will be big enough for two more years, I think) and buttonholes and frightfully loud socks etc.' After lunch with Arthur's housemaster, Arthur and his uncle watched the cricket – Eton versus Liverpool, which the school won by seventy runs – then had tea with Miss Ward: 'after absence Uncle Harry shoved a sovereign into my hand . . . so I shalln't want my second instalment of pocket money as the sovereign will last me nicely to the end of half.' When his uncle had left Arthur watched the customary procession of boats: 'with the cox of each dressed in a cocked hat, epaulettes, dirk etc while the rowers had striped shirts and straw hats with sham flowers on.' After Hall there were fireworks: 'There were two acrobats made of fireworks which spun round, and the King and Queens were drawn in lights. Of course, there were rockets innumerable and things which jumped about in the water.'

The remainder of Arthur's first term at Eton, apart from his normal work, was taken up with complicated arrangements for seeing the Eton v Harrow cricket match at Lords and the rowing at Henley; the fact that his favourite cricket bat had split in two – disaster – and the 'glorious' victory over Winchester due to the excellence of one Boswell, the only Colleger in the Eton First X1. 'The best all round man at Eton, having his fives, field, wall and cricket choices (caps) being in 'Pop', or the Eton Society, which consists of the 25 most popular or best chaps in Eton, and also being fourth in the school in work, also being awfully decent and all that to us smaller chaps.'

A master from Summerfields was down for the Winchester match and took the three ex-Summerfields boys of Arthur's election to dinner at the White Hart in Windsor. Arthur wrote:

My word, how I have enjoyed these last three days. Thursday *'non*

dies' (which means no work at all) Friday ditto and the beginning
of the Winchester match. Saturday, whole holiday (which means
only early school at 7.00) and the glorious victory over
Winchester, plus tea and ice, plus dinner enough to last for
months. Add up, reduce to teaspoons, divide by four carrots and
add 4/11¾ worth of Gorganzola cheese and there you are! (Quite
mad, suppose the excitement of the last few days has done it).

To give a slight check to this euphoria, Trials were looming on the
immediate horizon, to begin on 26 July, but Arthur's letters are full
of the approaching holidays and of seeing his family again: 'think of
it, only eight more days until I see you again . . . and then eight whole
weeks of your darling company.' The last few days of the half were
blighted by having half a sovereign stolen from his stall, but the
culprit was soon found.

Arthur left Eton at the end of his first half, happy in the knowledge
that he had done well. In the classics papers he had obtained 530
marks out of a possible 700; and in maths, French and science he had
gained 966 marks out of a maximum of 1350. These results earned
him a 'Well done – first rate' and he was 'sent up for good'. His
classics master, Chitty, was pleased with his first showing. Although
his marks were only 'fair', Chitty wrote: 'I consider that he has made
an excellent start and that his place does him great credit. A sensible,
hard-headed boy, who extorts respect for his determination. I have
found him very pleasant to deal with.'

The summation by Arthur's tutor, J.F. Crace, of his first half at
Eton, was in a personal letter to Caroline Rhys Davids:

The boy has made a capital start: he didn't take long to find his
way about the place and has taken to the life of the place with zest
and vigour. He has shown himself much better able to keep a
steady head in the independence and freedom of Eton life, than
some of his contemporaries. He is businesslike and careful and
quite well able to get his work done thoroughly in the midst of all
the many distractions which we have had this half. That seems to
me a very creditable thing, and it means a good deal of sturdiness
of character in a little boy, to keep a cool head thus. His work in
itself is decidedly promising: he is alert and vigorous in mind and
likes being occupied, and trying experiments, and even if the
experiments in classics are not always successful, I think they
show promise. He seems to me a capital boy, wholesome and

straightforward and thoroughly trustworthy: and I think he promises to be a most satisfactory Colleger. You will see that for school work he is top of the election. This is a very creditable place.

*

Arthur returned to Eton in late September for the Michaelmas Term. Football now replaced cricket and rowing, and he played his first Field game, 'but Association (football) is by far the best game, as field is all speed and weight and practically no science'.[1] During October he joined the school Officer Training Corps Recruits – he would have to wait until he was fifteen and five feet tall before being allowed to join the Corps proper – and sent home the form to be signed by his mother and local doctor. He was weighed and measured on joining the Recruits and found to be '4ft 11¼ high, 29½ round chest, and 6 st 11 lbs in weight'.

In this second half he was also to sing in Chamber, thought by some as being somewhat of an ordeal as it was obligatory to sing a solo with all looking on, but Arthur had no qualms and decided to sing 'Men of Harlech', requesting his mother to send him the words of the first two verses. School work in his second half he found more intense:

> Our Division master is a regular brute, he gives us so much work to do that we are forced to hurry over it, and if we do it badly he makes us do it again. Both my other masters, for French and maths, set a great deal of work, so I find myself absolutely swamped in work compared with last half. I suppose it's only good for me, only it makes you feel so like a slave, though you are supposed to be free at a public school. Even on Sunday you have hardly any spare time, what with Sunday Question, Sunday private business with Crace and Chapels.

Long leave in November, although elaborately planned, with his mother giving detailed instructions as to what train to catch to London, what time to arrive at his aunt's – 'jump into a taxi at Paddington, it's only 10d and you can give the driver a shilling, 2d for himself' – was at the last moment found to be against the school rules and had to be abandoned.[2] Only one other boy besides Arthur

[1] Field is a game peculiar to Eton, a cross between Rugby and football.
[2] One shilling is 5p in decimal currency. Twopence, the driver's tip, under 1p!

was left in Chamber, but thanks to the kindness of the Eton Bursar, Halway-Calthrop and his wife, who took them to the Follies at the Apollo Theatre, for lunch to an Italian restaurant in Soho and tea at Stewarts, returning to Eton in the evening, their long leave was not wasted.

At this time, November 1911, Caroline Rhys Davids had just completed her current book and had sent off the manuscript to her publishers.

> I feel so relieved. The book will be called simply 'Buddhism' and there are nine chapters . . . about 250 pages of print in all. Father read it through and was very pleased with some things. In fact the conclusion fairly made him choke and sob a bit – though this would not happen to anyone who had not given his life so devotedly to the one cause and to truth, as father has done. But it made me very proud to have moved him so. If only he can live till *you* can do something to move us both equally! There are no more lovely moments in life than the thrill of discovery and intellectual creation – and the emotion of reading something that seems true and finely said.

At the end of the Michaelmas term of 1911, Arthur was again sent up for good, and Crace again wrote to Caroline that he was thoroughly satisfied with his work and progress. 'He is sensible and thorough in his methods and has a good humoured sensible way of taking things that makes it very pleasant to work with him. I trust him thoroughly and believe he is going on just as we should wish.'

Lent term, 1912, started badly for Arthur. The journey from Manchester was 'very bad . . . the jolting in Derbyshire was awful and I had a headache or felt queer inside nearly the whole time'. On arrival at Eton he was told that he was now Captain of Chamber but was saddened to learn that Villiers, 'my only decent friend,' had died of meningitis during the Christmas holidays. Two days after arriving back Arthur was sick in bed himself, but sent a postcard to his mother. 'I am still in bed and feeling dizzy when I sit up. I have been starving myself so have no ballast in me. I am in staying-out rooms and am very slack and comfy'.

The feverish cold soon burnt itself out, however, and his next letter was more cheerful. He was not yet back in Chamber, but had been allowed up and was 'sprawled in an armchair in front of the fire, doing jigsaw puzzles', illustrating his letter with a sketch of one, a view of Grenada. He was evidently feeling much better, made several puns in the letter, expected that his mother had seen that Wooley had made 308 not out in the MCC v Tasmania match, and told her how much he was looking forward to the next test match. He had just finished reading Kipling's *Kim* and had noticed several Indian and Pali words in the text. He ended: 'It also spoke of Pali-speaking priests in Ceylon – so long (rather far-fetched) yer loving Arthur'.

His mother's reaction to this letter was typical. 'Well I'm blowed! Sprawls in armchairs and dreams of Grenada vistas. And makes, oh, such puns! I'll jigsaw tha' ma lad.'

From the general tone of Caroline Rhys Davids' letters, the family, although by no means poor, – the house at Ashton had a staff of three – needed to watch its expenditure carefully, with both Arthur and Vivien at boarding schools and Nesta's education to be thought of. In March, Caroline wrote that his father would be going to Athens in April. 'Auntie would come here if I went, but father thinks it too costly, so you and I must go there one fine day when there's some cash flying around. In fact I think I shall put the £50 for my book, which I hope to get out this year, aside for that purpose. But to go to Athens and back alone costs, for two, £40. Father will be repaid by the Ceylon government.'

She ended this letter by castigating the authorities at Eton: instead of posting Arthur's bills for the last half they had put them in his trunk, where they had lain undiscovered. This had annoyed Caroline. 'Fancy saving themselves penny stamps. Well they can wait a bit before I pay.'

The January of 1912 was bitterly cold, with floods and high winds, and at Windsor the river froze over and conditions were safe enough to allow the boys to ice-skate. Arthur jokingly wrote to Nesta: 'Most people have been skating during the last few days, but as I have no skates, don't skate and have got rather flexible ankles, I have not been doing so.'

The cold and influenza of the first week of half had evidently undermined Arthur's health more than realized. On 17 March, only two weeks before the end of half, he wrote to Vivien:

On Thursday we had Extra Books, which is an examination on a piece of Virgil and piece of Homer set. As it happened on Wednesday night I had a bad headache and queer eruptions and gurglings and feelings inside. During the night I was sick, and in the morning I didn't feel much better. But I was determined not to miss them, firstly because they count in Trials – the exams at the end of Half – and could make a lot of difference to my marks, as you get no average if you miss them; and secondly I had been preparing them and learning them up for the last fortnight, so it would have been rather sickening (as I was in the night) if I had been forced to shirk them. So at 7.30 I went into school and worked hard for an hour and a quarter and then came out and had some breakfast, which cheered me up considerably, and I managed to get through the 1½ hours of Greek much more easily.

Arthur collapsed after this examination and as soon as he was fit enough to travel it was decided to send him home. The matron of Eton wrote to Caroline to explain the travel arrangements, disclosed that the doctor had found that the pupil of Arthur's right eye was larger than the left, and that he had complained of abdominal pains and a tenderness on pressure. 'However,' she ended, 'Arthur seems well, and has had a little walk today in the lovely Spring sunshine. He is still pale and changes colour a great deal, but does not complain of anything.'

This letter brought a horrified reply from Caroline, but the matron assured her that Arthur was quite fit to travel: 'He is taking a quinine tonic. He requires a rest from brain work – plenty of *sleep*, especially early to bed and plenty of open air. He ought really to sleep the clock round if he can.'

This collapse had been brought on by overwork and a desire to do well. Despite his illness the papers on Virgil and Homer were marked at 90 and 81 and earned the comment 'two excellent papers'. But he had been forced to miss Trials. John Crace wrote to Caroline that he was sorry that Arthur's last half should have had such an unlucky end, hoped that her own doctor would find nothing seriously wrong and asked to be kept informed of Arthur's progress.

Miss Ward mentioned to me the possibility of a little trouble with eyes, which I hope is not the case. He had done splendid work all the half – was it that he had done too much? – he certainly more than satisfied all his division masters. He has a quick and eager mind which is ardently busy the moment it has material to work on – only the other evening when he was sitting up in bed playing patience I was almost horrified to see how quickly his thought went. And he is eager to learn and enjoys work: and so, where competition too is keen, there is danger of his doing too much: but I very much hope that no harm has been done. He is of course a most delightful boy to teach, if only because he is so eager to learn. But Arthur is more than that, he is a thoroughly trustworthy high-minded lad besides.

At home, surrounded by the people he loved best, Arthur soon recovered and Grace wrote to thank Caroline for the good news, but adding a note of warning:

We must not forget that he *did* have this collapse and that there must be a cause for it, and I hope you still find the opportunity of putting the question of the possibility of overstrain to his doctor, both in reference to his eyes and to his general health. The keen competition in College and the boy's own eagerness and his loyalty to what he knows we expect of him are all driving him on, and he is without that protection of instinctive idleness which effectively guards many young brains from overtaxation. But I am delighted to hear of him being so well again.

While Arthur was regaining his strength an event took place in the outside world which was ultimately to shape his destiny. In the late autumn of 1911 the Committee of Imperial Defence had instructed its standard sub-committee to consider the future of aerial development in respect to military and naval purposes and to discuss what measures would be needed to set up an efficient aerial service for the country. The committee recommended the setting up of an aeronautical service, to be known as the Royal Flying Corps. The Committee of Imperial Defence approved the recommendation and the Royal Flying Corps was constituted by Royal Warrant on 13 April 1912.

Back at Eton in May 1912, Arthur wrote jubilantly:

How fine it is not to be a fag! No need to drag yourself up at some unearthly hour of the morning – we get up at six in the summer – thinking 'Oh law, I've got to go and call that flat faced dust heap my fagmaster.' Also these Aertex shirts are a blessing. No more struggling and swearing in a stiff shirt for half an hour before one can get one's stud in properly.

He now also had a room of his own.

> It looks very bare at present, but I soon hope to make it comfy. Please ask Nesta to take the Meccano Warehouse to pieces and put it away, as it will get rusty.

While on holiday he had created a Professor Tosh in a story he had made up for Nesta. Nesta wrote to ask if he would send her the further adventures of the Professor each week and suggested that, in continuation of the story started in the holidays: 'the Professor takes the officials in an aeroplane to taste the brandy and then he flies off with them. This I accordingly put down on the machine, but with more details.'[1]

With a present of ten shillings from his father, Arthur furnished his new room: 'I have got a deck chair and six pictures, which altogether came to 7/3.' But Caroline, financially conscious as always, replied:

> I hope you have the chair (easy or armchair) from your stall moved into your room. *We paid 10/6 for that.* We also paid for a new rug, jug and washbasin. I shall send you a list of what was charged us for furniture. We had to buy everything except the bed and bureau and I have no intention of making the College a present of all that!

Arthur's health was still of some concern. In late May he wrote:

> Darling Mother,
> It appears my left hand gland was a bit swollen because my tonsils were a bit cockeyed. However, a little painting soon put that right. By the way while I was out I saw an aeroplane go over the fields. It was so high I could only see it was a monoplane.

This was Arthur's first reference in any of his letters to anything aeronautical and he seems not to have been particularly interested in aeroplanes, as were so many of his contemporaries. He explained further about his swollen gland, only having discovered it while he was washing his neck.

> I thought it was rather funny so I conveyed the alarming news to

[1] Caroline's typewriter.

that dear gentle old bun-faced baboon who chooses to call herself 'Matron in College'. She is the only matron who lives in College, but as for looking after the boys when they are ill or not she takes the biscuit unopposed.

A letter to Nesta shows that he was still interested in mechanical things, although leaning more and more towards the classics in his school work:

I have been thinking that if I could only get my vertical steam engine – the one that drives the flywheel round and has a whistle – to act properly we might somehow manage a connection between it and the Meccano set. I *must* have that 4A set.

The 4A set cost 38 shillings but with the state of his present finances – 'I now have only 3/6 left but that will do me nicely till about June 16 (end of half)' – plus his pocket money due then, and an advance on his birthday money, he thought he could just manage it. That engineering and science still interested him is plain in a letter to his mother in June:

Mr Goodhart, my division master last term, has given me a prize for being top of his division last half. I have chosen Corbin's 'Engineering Today' a very good book with lots of photographs and diagrams. I am hoping for two more prizes at the end of this half, one probable, the other possible.

Caroline was delighted to hear of his prize and the possibility of others. She was very busy, she replied, but managing to play a great deal of golf. She was also arranging their summer holiday, a cycling tour of Scotland.

I have a cycling book giving inns, all at modest prices. I shall have to decide about yr bicycle. Shall I have one made for you, man's size? Will you send me your height and length from 'fork' to bottom of instep. Or shall I hire one for you in Perth or Edinburgh?

Arthur replied that he did not think he was big enough to manage a man-size bicycle. 'I am 5.1" high, or very nearly, and I think it would be rather a long reach for me.' Of far greater importance were the arrangements for Long Leave which leave, would enable him to see the Eton v Harrow match at Lords in July. Could he stay at Accini's house, conveniently near Lords; or at Guildford with Uncle Harry who had definitely asked for him to stay. Guildford was definite, but so much further from Lords than Accini, who was not, however, certain whether or not she could have him for the weekend. Meanwhile the day of the match drew near and Caroline had still to write to his housemaster nominating one or the other as his guardian for the weekend. Decisions! Meanwhile there was Eton scandal to relate:

> My Darling Mother,
> Thanks so much for your cash, which is now all except 1/6 locked up in my hat box underneath my hat and stowed on top of my bed behind a curtain. As I carry my keys about with me, I don't think that [even] the cleverest of College thieves will get at it. That fellow Mendel is advancing like lightning on the way to being sacked. He certainly smokes cigarettes – which of course is forbidden – and almost certainly drinks whiskey, at least people in Chamber say he often comes out of his stall smelling of whiskey. He'll get sacked someday, I'm sure.[1]

Arthur did get to see the Eton v Harrow match of 1912, travelling up each day from Guildford, the pleasure being compounded by an Eton victory but a little negated by having to journey to and fro from Lords to Guildford in 'that awful get-up which nowadays is called decent dress. One looks more like a pantomime clown than an Etonian'.

Trials were successfully negotiated and he was again 'sent up for good.' Only his French seems to have been below standard, his master commenting: 'his prose work is weak and his free composition only shows a moderate knowledge of grammar and idiom'. Maths and classics were still good, however, and Crace was again pleased with his work and progress:

> Arthur has done a first rate half's work and has in every way earned a thorough holiday which I hope he will have, and as complete a rest as may be for I think he takes his uttermost out of himself over his school work, from sheer eagerness and appetite

[1] One wonders what did become of the disreputable Mendel. Did he survive Eton and become successful in life or was he too swallowed up in the holocaust of the Great War?

for learning. He is an excellent little fellow and in every way gives me the utmost confidence in him, and he only needs to go on as he is doing. I am more than contented.

Arthur's division master, however, perceived a problem. After commenting that: 'in a very agreeable division he was quite the nicest, and also I believe, the ablest. Everything seems to interest him and nothing affords him much difficulty. Certainly he shaped better than any of his fellows at the Greek tongue.' He continued with a warning note: 'But I fear he has been far from strong and it was only too clear that his energies flag now and again.'

When Arthur returned to Eton for the Michaelmas term this lack of robust health was still apparent, despite the bicycling holiday in Scotland with his mother and the long summer holiday. During the summer he had had several attacks of asthma and no sooner was he back at Eton than he contracted a severe cold. Caroline had left for a holiday in Italy in September and she begged to be kept fully informed of his state of health. His stammer had also become much worse and was causing problems. He was now in 'B', or upper division, and the work was getting 'decidedly harder – Plato and Theocritus instead of Aristophanes and Thucydides.' But most of the 'rotten fellows' in the sixth form had left, and he now had a particular friend in Brown: 'Much bigger and older than I am.' He also wrote to his aunt – standing in for his mother for a while. 'I am going to be confirmed this half, I hope Pa and Ma will not object.' He wrote to his mother on her birthday, 27 September, that he was beginning Plato's *Apology of Socrates*. 'We have only done two pages of the first one (Socrates' speeches in his defence against the charges of corrupting the youth and bringing in new gods) but even that is frightfully good.' Nesta and Vivien had given him a penknife for his birthday – 'well, I call it a knife but I think it ought to be called a twobladecorkscrewpincerneedlewalnutcrackerborerscrewdriver' – his mother and father a watch, 'which keeps excellent time'.

Despite his mother's worries about his health, he was playing football and made light of an injury:

I got a hack on the shin, which had the impudence to bleed and get raw and rude in other ways. So after dinner I marches off to Miss Ward and says 'Please Mum, can I have a bandage round this 'ere blooming little leg o' mine?' Says she 'Right'o me boyhee.'

The injury was on the bone, the bruise large and painful, and Arthur was laid up for two days, thoroughly enjoying himself by having no work and playing bezique and piquet.

Arthur's letters to his mother and Vivien, throughout this Michaelmas term, were cheerful: full of spoonerisms, puns and news of work done. Those to Nesta, full of jokes, drawings, puzzles, and explanations of the various types of railway engines she had seen at Sale, plus episodes of 'Tosh'. But in November he was again ill with a heavy cold, and although he reassured his mother that it had 'practically gone', she was determined to take positive steps to promote his health. She arranged for him to see Sandow, the renowned physical culturist and, during the holidays, a Miss Ward in Manchester, 'a well known trainer for voice and throat', to help cure his persistent stammer.

Arthur did well in his Trials in his first half in a new and higher form and Crace wrote to Caroline:

> Indeed the only change I can wish in him at present is for him to *grow*! and gain in robust physical health, so that he has more of a margin of vigour and vitality than one can now be sure of. In every other way he gives me complete satisfaction and I rejoice to have him as a pupil.

In this letter Crace also discussed Arthur's plans for the future. He saw no reason why he should not win a scholarship to Oxford or Cambridge as he had made 'first rate progress in his classical work' and 'was well able to distinguish himself in mathematics.' Arthur had mentioned his wish to take up engineering as a career, but Crace seems not to have been too keen on this; the choice, as he saw it, was first Oxford or Cambridge. He also was concerned with the worsening of Arthur's stammer. 'It certainly did in the middle of the half and I feared it might be due to overstrain'. He was gratified that he had been able to prepare Arthur for his confirmation:

> . . . he took the matter with all the seriousness and sincerity which I knew I could expect in him. He is a good lad, and gives us every reason to feel confidence in him as a boy whose influence will always be on the right side among his contemporaries. He has a strong sense of duty and a sensitive conscience, and he is sensible and straightforward and quite free from any sort of priggishness.

Arthur started the Lent half of 1913 with another troublesome cough, but with high hopes that the sessions with Miss Ward had helped his stammer. 'Dearest of My Heart' he wrote to Caroline in January. 'I really can't say anything about my stammering yet. I haven't been put up to construe in school yet. I have had one thing to say off by heart, and got through that much better than before.' By February he was writing to Nesta that the stammering was 'streets better – both Mr Crace and Mr MacNaughten have noticed it as well as some of the boys.' Caroline wrote to Miss Ward, telling her of the success of her exercises. Miss Ward replied that she was delighted. 'I think Arthur a very, very splendid boy. I saw of course that he quite understood what I wanted him to do, but I did not think that he would overcome the stammering so quickly.'

Arthur also wrote to Vivien in February, with a slight note of censure under the humour:

> I object to you calling me sonny. I am not a thing of three feet high with socks and shoes and blue knickerbockers with buttons, and HMS Thingimmebob on my hat, nor are you a benevolent old gentleman or lady with an enormous ... and spectacles like saucers and hundred of shawls and coats and muffs and fluffs and- and- camisoles and corsets and kicksees and stays and braces and all the other little bracelets etc.

Vivien had had a schoolfriend named Aileen home for the Christmas holidays and she and Arthur had become close friends, writing to each other when they had returned to school. Vivien was jealous of sharing her brother's affection with anyone outside the family and censured him a little. He replied:

> Dear Buzzage,
> I'll jolly well say what I jolly well like about Aileen, and you'd better shove your head through the middle of your tennis racket if you're going to be jealous, as you call it. I had my second Communion today and Aileen is very right about realising its marvellous mystery the second time more than the first. Why does Aileen have the stupendous rippingness to write me enormously long letters in reply to my grubby little missives? I dunno. Probably a good-natured feeling of pity for my crass ignorance, stupidness, clumsiness, gaucherie, forgetfulness, rudeness and making her absolutely bored. She's a downright brick!! So there,

my jealous Buzzage. No, that's beastly. If she's a downright brick, you're an upright jolly good sport. All square on the home green. Phew! quite exhausted after that emotional and boorish display.

In February 1913 all England was shocked to learn of the death of Captain Scott and his companions at the South Pole. Caroline, in a letter to Arthur, showed her logical attitude to the news:

You will have read about poor Scott and Co. Oates's going out voluntarily to end it all if happily he might save the rest is the finest part. I guess that prolonged hardship had so worn them that death came as a restful sleep. Tragic to be so near the end as they were; yet how far *more* tragic is *any* fatal railway accident, let alone the Titanic business. Those men knew they had their lives in their hands *all the time*, but the others have good reason to believe they will arrive safely and the shock is far more cruel. How I think of it everytime you go or come by train; everytime too when I think of that fire (thro' electric wire fusing) at Eton some ten years ago and you sleeping there now.

Goodbye Darling.

In February it seems that Arthur's interest in engineering as a career was given fresh impetus by a lecture given at Eton by Sir Francis Fox, the renowned civil engineer:

My word, it *was* a lecture. All about radium mining in Cornwall, also tin mining, with lantern slides to illustrate. Then about working with compressed air under Winchester Cathedral and other places, how to dig in quicksand, bridge building in central Africa on the Cape to Cairo railway, sea diving at Constantinople, with a fully equipped diver on stage to explain all the arrangements. Wouldn't have missed it for the worlds!

Long leave was spent at his Godmother's house in Maida Vale. He wrote home to say he was having a splendid time. He had met a 'charming young lady friend of Accini's, by name Miss Pamela Bird – weirdest of weird christian names.' and they had both been to the Playhouse to see the play *The Headmaster* starring Cyril Maude – 'frightfully good, awfully funny'. He was also taken to the Zoo, where friends of Accini 'knew all the keepers, every blessed man jack of them! I had rather a good time.' He was taken behind the scenes, allowed to pet the cheetah and Emperor Penguin, and saw the pigmy hippo. He held a baby alligator and had a six-foot long snake wrapped round his neck. 'It was beautifully soft and smooth.' The only black spot was the elephant: 'it was rude and spat at me. Got me in the face – filthy beast!'

Caroline was arranging an Easter holiday at Budleigh Salterton for the family. Professor Rhys Davids had also been ill, with recurrent malaria and influenza and she herself had been troubled with a series of colds. She hoped that a short holiday in Devon would restore their health. In the meantime she wrote to Arthur: 'Don't for goodness sake overwork and break down this year. I couldn't bear it this time. Hope breathing keeps good and the stammering curse is quite got under.' Arthur replied that he was well and that he felt sure he would be in the top three in Trials:

> Godfrey and I are tremendously equal. We are both intending to be engineers, Summerfieldians future mathematic specialists, nearly the same age and very equal in classics – perhaps I'm a bit better, and he's a bit better at French. The first three will almost certainly be he, I and Nichols, but in what order? That's the problem.

In the event, in the mathematics division, it was Nichols first, then Arthur, but Godfrey was sixth. Arthur was first in Division, comfortably beating Godfrey at ninth place and Nichols at thirteenth.[1] Despite Arthur's assurances to Caroline, however, his Classics Master reported: 'My only regret this half is that the stammering has grown distinctly worse – and this has probably lost him a few marks. But at Greek and Latin he excels the rest.'

Just how well Arthur had done in Trials was not known until he returned from the Devon holiday. On 1 May, on arriving back at Eton, he sent a jubilant and proud postcard. 'Find I am top of my election in Trials, and got Trials prize, also prize for three distinctions, bringing up last half's prizes to five (record)'. He had travelled down to Windsor with two Frenchmen, 'who gabbled most of the time about the price of matchboxes of various sorts, during which one of them pulled out six different kinds, a specimen of which was minutely examined by his companion.' He had not yet chosen

---

[1] Far from having been sacked, the blacksheep Mendel had moved from last to tenth place.

his Trials prize – 'value 30/-' – but was very tempted to get Whymper's *Climbs in The Andes*: 'lovely pictures, including cocopotan kettle – I mean Popocatapetl.' He had had a little adventure on the way back. He had missed his train to Windsor, arriving at Paddington just in time to see it leaving the platform:

Halt, swore. Booking Office shut. Swore again (sub spiritu) Head Usher arrives on platform and goes through exactly the same process. Swearing doubtful. Both adjourn to bar. I have a ginger ale and a sausage roll, as I know I shall get no supper. Head Usher has – well I'm blowed! The beggar has a glass of water and marches out. Stalks up and down platform to stem tide of wrath.

Caroline was evidently puzzled by this reference to the 'Head Usher'. Who was he? Arthur replied:

Dearest Mother,
The Head Usher is not a pet name for the Rt.Hon. The Reverend Edward Lyttleton MA. DD, BUN. It is his ordinary name. At Eton an usher means a beak, otherwise a master, therefore the Head Usher equals the Headmaster, which is the ordinary denomination for the boss of the caboodle.

Arthur then regaled Caroline with the story of the Headmaster of Harrow preaching at Eton at Matins:

I've never seen such a performance. I could hardly hear a word of what he said. He bobbed about like a jack-in-the-box, nearly fell out of the pulpit and nearly knocked all his books on the heads of the congregation below. One of the few sentences I heard was 'Out of every 23 persons, only one gets beyond the ordinary stages of reading writing and elementary arithmetic. That is less than 4%.' Read that through and examine it carefully and you'll see the joke. *His* elementary arithmetic was not good!

Arthur finally decided against the Whymper book as his Trials prize:

The book was 22/6 which would have left 7/6 to the firm of Spottiswoode and Co., which should be mine. So I got a 20/- book, 'The Royal Navy' and a 10/- book, Stevenson's novel, 'The Master of The Ballantrae'.

Caroline was horrified to hear of his 'adventure' of missing the train. She cautioned:

> There's a lot of human vultures, you know, in every big town; some would know quite well that London was full of schoolboys that day, going thro' with plenty of pocket money and might tempt the unwary to jump into a taxi to be 'stood' some fun, chloroform them and take all their money; if girls, kidnap them. There's been a lot of this lately.

The weather by the end of May that year was extremely warm. Arthur wrote: 'The heat's something terrific. Oh for this weather all the holidays.' He was worried that the summer holiday arrangements would enable him to see Vivien for only one week of the seven, especially as King George V was to visit Eton on 16 June, 'and last time the King came down we had an extra week's holiday from him. That was two years ago.' He was confident that his stammering was not due to breathing, as his mother had thought. He had experimented and was convinced that it was due to nerves. 'It will go in time with confidence and practice.'

Arthur seems to have been disenchanted by the festivities of 4 June that year. He wrote to Nesta:

> June 4, thank goodness, is past. You have to dress up in beastly uncomfortable clothes, no games allowed, not even bathing, and for me it was made worse because I had no people down like everybody else did, except for a very few who were in the same miserable state as me. Fancy watching a cricket match for five hours wearing a top hat, a white waistcoat and no overcoat!

But 4 June 1913 was marked by an unusual event:

> An incident occurred which served to pass the time. The Army Airship Beta came down, actually in the playing fields. I touched the car of it, which shows what a good view I got of it. Of course it's very small. It only holds three men. It afterwards flew over School Yard as absence was being called and everyone cheered and clapped.

Who, out of all those present on that summer's day of 1913, least of all Arthur himself, could have foreseen that the small boy with the bad stammer who had touched the control car of Beta, would in four short years be one of the most admired and respected pilots in the then infant Royal Flying Corps.

Arthur again finished the half as top of his Division. His Division master wrote:

> He is certainly the best scholar in the Division and well deserves his place. He asserts his superiority, especially in Greek composition, in which he is easily best. His translation, on the other hand, of unseen, is not conspicuous, for he works slowly (a good fault) and his English is immature (also a fault on the right side). In keeping with this I note and admire the childlike simplicity of his ways, as ability is so often spoilt by conceit, of which he shows no trace. Thanks to his tutor his stammering is wonderfully better: latterly he has construed with almost fluency. He is as blameless a boy as I have ever had up to me, but I don't in the least wish to imply that his virtues are negative – he is full of life and merriment and friendly under a little cloak of shyness.

John Crace had been helping a great deal to conquer the stammer, having Arthur read aloud, and he reported great progress. 'If only he could also do a daily ten minutes (reading aloud) for another week or two, I believe he would have broken the back of the difficulty and that would be a real triumph.'

Arthur took the School Certificate Examination in July 1913. He had the highest marks of any boy in the school, beating his nearest rival by fifty-three marks. He was now, in Eton terms, 'a specialist'.

Back at Eton after the summer holidays, Arthur was now installed in a larger room and entitled to eat by himself if he wished. He was now over 5' 4" and obliged to wear tails for the first time. King George V had decided to send his son Prince Henry to Eton and it being the Prince's first half at the school Arthur was eagerly questioned by Vivien in her letters as to whether he had met, seen or talked with the Prince, plus numerous requests for information from other girls at her school and several of the mistresses. Arthur replied with some asperity:

> Prince Henry is now an Etonian. He is just like all the others, nor does anyone know his knicknames, or his knickerbocker names, nor the colour of his tooth-powder, nor the size of his boots, far less his fagmaster. He's just HRH, as the lower boys call him.

Arthur, however, was not completely impervious to the excitement of seeing royalty at close hand. In November he wrote to his mother:

> I saw the King and Queen on Monday, down here paying a visit to their son at Mr Lubbock's. When they drove past me in their motor I was rewarded for lifting my hat by a gracious royal bow from the Queen. The only person who didn't uncover was J.F.C.! His sight, I suppose you know, is not good, and the poor man didn't notice but walked straight past. When duly reprimanded by me he suggested doing a hundred yard sprint down the High Street after them! I also saw the Prince of Wales on Saturday afternoon, walking around the Fives courts with his brother and Mr Hansell, while I was playing fives. He was wearing a green Homburg, light brown spats and a pipe, and he's hardly taller than I am, with a face like a new-born babe!

A football injury kept Arthur in bed for several days during the last days of half before Trials, but he was up and about in good time for the examinations.

> Godfrey is frightfully keen on beating me this half because it's a fight for the captaincy of the school two years hence. He was horribly amazed when I appeared in Trials on Friday. He thought I was staying out and then he would have had a walkover.

That December, for the first time at Eton, Arthur's lower master's report was not glowing with praise: '. . . work not sound enough . . . has not got a firm grip of syntax . . . turns out an insufficient amount in the allotted time.' His Greek prose was still 'most creditable' but '. . . his words are not always well chosen . . . he did not remember the work done over two months ago . . . one of his grammar papers was poor, but all, with that one exception, have been up to a high level.' John Crace, however, wrote in his customary letter:

> Arthur has done capitally all the half and the only fault that I can find with him is that he does not grow more. His work is excellent in many ways – to my mind the lower master's report hardly does justice to his great thoroughness and the keen interest which he takes in what he reads. His diligence is unremitting and there is a danger, I think, of his doing more than is really good for him. The stammer seemed very bad sometimes this half and made me fear

that he was overdoing it. But just lately it has been better again, I think.

Crace also discussed Arthur's future plans at great length. Arthur was still talking of being an engineer and, with that in view, had been taking extra maths, but Crace was proposing to drop them next half:

He is good enough at Classics to make it seem a great pity – a very great pity, to drop them now, when he is good enough at them to be able to read and enjoy the best things – it seems like turning back within sight of the summit. What will he read at university and what university will he go to? He will be good enough, I fancy, to get a classical scholarship when it comes to the time.

After more discussion along these lines, Crace ended his letter:

I only wish he gathered strength physically more than he does and more stature too. He must not do much work in the holidays – let him *play* and *grow*.

But events in the world were moving at an inexorable pace towards a catastrophe which would destroy all plans for Arthur's future. It was to be the last Christmas of peace he would know.

CHAPTER THREE

War

Arthur's first letter home from Eton in 1914 has a portent of things to come. 'I enclose one form to admit me to the senior portion of the Corps, which you must sign. Camp is the first week of the summer holidays.' Caroline, financially conscious as ever, replied:

> I hope the Senior E.C.T.C. don't mean subscribing more than 15/- three times a year – what a swindle that is! But I shall be glad for you to have a taste of camp life. I waylaid the doctor just now on his daily visit to Mr Tysoe opposite and got him to twa three bit scratches with t'pen. He was pleased to hear you are stronger and growing and blowing.

Before Christmas the telephone had been installed at Harboro Grange and was known to the family as 'the domestic convenience'. The domestic convenience had been giving a certain amount of trouble due to the noise made by the wind in the wires. 'It broke out so bad on Monday, wind NW', wrote Caroline, 'that I wrote to headquarters in Manchester and politely stated that we had been politely put off for three months. An intelligent inspector, I said, would have hinted at the possibility of noise, whereupon we would have placed the creature outside the room . . . he came bustling along at once and had the wires outside slackened, saying the pole had shrunk and made the wires overtaut. All is now peaceful.'

Arthur was now happier socially at Eton. The one boy he had disliked had left – 'he had the character of a cockroach and the behaviour of a Whitechapel cur. His going made an enormous difference to me' – and he was now left with only congenial companions. He had not mentioned this problem before, but his mother had guessed the situation:

> It was always depressing, thinking of you being in a chilly atmosphere, which I could only guess at. I'm enormously glad at the present difference. I wish, I wish, I weren't so absurdly fond of you – something's sure to happen to you. I shall have to take

desperate propitiation measures for your safety.

Arthur still liked to tease Nesta in his letters and after one such she replied:

My Dear Boy,
Your letter both shocked and pained me. It is not right to imitate a poor and ignorant girl's idea of writing a letter. It hurt me very much that a boy like you, with average manners, and rather below average commonsense, but with a very pure sense of fairness, should do a thing like that! You, the apple of my eye, and the pear of my pupil. You, who are the dearest creature in my heart. I did not think you would hurt me. Haaaahhhh me! Never mind, you will improve as years go by and you get nearer to manhood stage.

Arthur's letter home on 8 February is full of interest.

On Monday about 600 of the school went up to Windsor Castle East Terrace to see Gustav Hamel loop the loop, including myself. The King was there, of course, and all the royal little ones eg. Prince Henry and Prince John etc, all the nurses, guardians etc. Hamel came flying from Brooklands quite high and made a lovely diving descent onto the East lawn. He had dropped a metal plate of sorts just before landing, without which he couldn't loop, so that had to be found first, which meant a delay of about twenty minutes while he talked to the King etc. The aeroplane, specially designed by himself, was much more short and squat than an ordinary one. The front view, instead of –

 was

on same scale

The elevating planes and the rudder were also very much bigger. The object being obviously to have less weight to carry and more compactness. When the metal plate was found he went up again and after climbing pretty high (involving some wonderfully steep banking) he looped the loop fourteen times. It was not, as I expected a question of

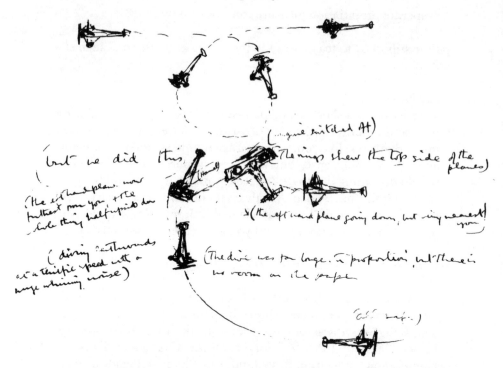

It looked as if the machine had crumpled up at first and then suddenly turned over and dived straight at our heads. Hope you understand these impromptu drawings.

These 'impromptu' drawings show a keen attention to detail and an ability to see just how the manoeuvre was performed, not always easy to do.

Caroline had sent Arthur a complete set of both her own and his father's books and he had placed them on his shelves, to the astonishment of his fellow Etonians:

Binney is very interested, but probably won't read them unless I urge him to, for he is of a dilatory character. However, I'm going to read them and I daresay some other people in College will too. Godfrey came in yesterday and saw them. 'What's all this', he says and opens one of them. 'Good God, no wonder you beat me, with people like that'.

Caroline hastened to reply:

I don't make any claims on your time for reading them. But our work has got this sort of seed-sowing element in it, that it represents a field white with harvest with too few labourers. And we slowly pick up a labourer here and another there. For example, these two days I have corresponded with a professor at Heidelburg, a doctor at Breslau, a civil servant in Burma, a teacher in Ceylon, a parson in Glasgow, a Baptist college in Burma and a parson's daughter in Warwickshire – all working or reading in the field.

Professor Rhys Davids had decided that he wished to retire from his chair at the Victorian University, Manchester, at the end of the 1915 session and this meant that the family would be free from the midsummer of that year, 'and then off to London or thereabouts,' wrote Caroline jubilantly, for she had always thought Manchester a 'drear place'. She was not over-impressed with Eton either:

Darling, what's going to happen about exeats? Only ten weeks and yet exeat. They were perhaps wiser at Summerfields. Or is it so beastly at Eton that things can't be endured much over five weeks at a stretch?

An Easter holiday at Aberdovey was arranged that year, with a programme which included golf and billiards, but Arthur wrote an agonised letter on 15 March, only fifteen days before the end of half:

Mumps has broken out badly in College and there are already 10 cases. So it's quite possible I may have it now, which means it will develop in about a week and I shouldn't be able to go to Aberdovey at all! I hope I shalln't get it at all, though I'm afraid I shall as I was talking in my room for an hour with a boy who developed it badly the next day.'

Caroline hastened to reply:

Dearest. What again that beastly absurdity cropping up? Said something was sure to happen. I send you all the Formamint I've got. They're excellent preventatives for catching things by breath. Put one in your mouth every two hours or so, especially when you're going near other fellows and let it slowly melt. *Just make up your mind you'll not have it*, take the lozenges and run no risk of chills.

But it was too late. Arthur wrote five days later to say that he was in bed. 'Thanks for the Formamint but they weren't no use cos I'd got the mumps when they arrived.'

Caroline immediately sent off a pre-paid telegram, asking for news. Arthur wired back to say that he was all right and that a letter was following. His mother later wrote, disgusted with the telegraph service: 'My Dearlingest, Your wire reached me $3^1/_6$ hours after I had despatched mine from Sale Post Office, which doesn't say much for promptitude in the telegraph service or College.'

Luckily, Arthur's was a mild case and he was just out of the quarantine period in time to go home at the normal time. Golf and billiards were enjoyed at Aberdovey.

The Rhys Davids family seem to have had no inkling of the approach of war. Caroline's letters at this period are full of the golf she is playing and watching – Miss Cecil Leitch had won the English Ladies Championship and it was rumoured that she would turn professional in America – the Welsh holiday she had taken with Nesta and plans for the summer holiday in Ireland – 'the Newcastle Hotel (County Down) wants £4.18.0 per head per week, which is absurd!' Along with the newspaper clippings reporting the golf tournaments, his mother also sent Arthur a clipping illustrating: 'Testing the Wings of a New Aeroplane', which shows sixteen men standing on the wings of a Fokker monoplane. This was a Fokker M 5L and although the newspaper caption makes no mention of it, 'the Dutch constructor Fokker' was supplying aeroplanes to the *Idflieg*, the German Army's Inspectorate of Aviation, for service in the German airforce. The sixteen men standing on the wing were a demonstration – although technically useless – to satisfy the officers of the *Idflieg* as to the structural strength of the Fokker M 5L.

On 21 June, Vivien wrote to say she had seen B.C. Hucks in the air:

> While we were having tea somebody said 'there's Hucks' and we all looked up and heard a noise like three mammoths running along being chased by six traction engines and saw Hucks in his aeroplane sailing over the trees. He was flying in Cardiff for charity in the afternoon. We saw him loop once then twice later. It was simply glorious.

Caroline's brother Charles was now home from India and it was decided that a motoring holiday in Scotland during the summer

would be preferable to Ireland. As he and Arthur were to drive
together to Sale to meet the remainder of the family, Charles wrote to
Arthur from the United University Club in Pall Mall to give him
final instructions:

> We must be off by 9 as it is 180 miles and we shall want all our time
> to do the distance as one must allow for punctures and stoppages.
> Sorry you won't come in your uniform, but mind and scrub your
> boots and have your hair cut. We must get to Ashton that evening.
> Then rest a day for packing and cleaning car and off on Saturday –
> five of us for Scotland!

Caroline wrote to Arthur on 4 August 1914, the day war was
declared, but she made only a passing reference to the fact, 'this
horrid state of affairs', in her opening remarks before taking him to
task for only packing one suit for the Scottish tour and the necessary
arrangements – extremely complicated, as was usual with Caroline –
for procuring him appropriate suits for the holiday. However, she
ended her letter: 'I am too sick at heart at political things to write
more. I simply daren't read the newspapers. Your very doleful
Mother.'

Despite the war the Scottish holiday went as planned, and after
Arthur was back at Eton, Caroline and Professor Rhys Davids
toured the southern counties looking for a suitable house, the most
important factor being that it should have a good golf course nearby.
They called upon a Mr Robinson in these travels, evidently a family
friend, who was Under Secretary to the Board of Trade. 'He is busy,
among other things, cutting off Germany's food supply thro' Dutch
merchants, eg of flour going there thro' England. He was also
concerned to get more leather because of the big demand from
France for English boots for the army.' Arthur's Aunt Mary also
wrote in September, sending him five shillings for his birthday:

> Can't send more! What with appeals for Tommy Atkins, Belgian
> refugees etc. I am getting 'ard up and am trembling less certain
> dividends fail to be paid into your humble servant's bank.

After a little more family news, she carried on:

> Uncle Charles is off tomorrow . . . to Tilbury, where a tender will
> take the passengers out to a Jap steamer in the river. He is rather

nervous about the voyage as these beastly German cruisers are
lurking about and may be nasty. Fancy the Emden shelling
Madras. Awful cheek! I do wish we could get those German
'Oolans and 'Uns out of France. We have a big English Zeppelin
flying over here every day and keeping guard and three
searchlights going all night. Have no news, it is always war-war-
war.

Since he had started at Eton in 1911, Caroline had kept all Arthur's
letters, but after March 1914 – apart from one exception and a few
letters to Vivien and Nesta – none of Arthur's letters to his mother
are among the family papers for the remainder of 1914, the whole of
1915 and part of 1916. This is disappointing for it would have been
interesting to learn how he and his contemporaries at Eton viewed
the first year of the war, and his letters in 1915 would no doubt have
given the first intimation of his reasons and later decision to join the
Royal Flying Corps. But at the end of 1914 this step was still in the
future and his immediate horizon was bound by two goals: sitting for
an Exhibition at Balliol College Oxford, and the Newcastle
Scholarship, which he would take at the end of the next year, 1915.

Back at Eton in October 1914 he threw himself into the necessary
work. He was now in the sixth form and John Crace wrote to
Caroline that he should now have 'the time of his life' at Eton and
'get into a much nicer set.' Caroline was worried that he was now, for
some reason, 'getting no worthy teaching in classics, except for
J.F.C. I hope that deficiency won't militate against your success in
the Newcastle.' She was also horrified at the Eton doctor's bills for
the last half. With her usual no nonsense approach to financial
matters, she wrote:

> I stuck at the doc's second bill and Miss Ward was consulted. She
> wrote politely to tell me of not three doctor's visits, but nine! Five
> before March 25 and four up to April 1. This is probably a lie for
> you were really quite well before the end of March. I'm not paying
> the second bill yet, tho' I suppose I must, so shall be glad if you
> can recall dates in the Sanatorium and whether the doctor really
> did visit you there, since I've got to pay 7/- for every time he
> looked at you! I may have to cross question Miss Ward yet . . . I
> wonder if she gets a commission from him or prerequisites of that
> sort? Of course, I don't want to offend either one of them *in case* you
> got really ill, as Caroe was, and really need their beastly

administrations. For God's sake be prudent and don't risk anything.

The other side of her nature is well illustrated in the remainder of the letter with a homily on Buddhist teaching:

What infernal doom those G-s have brought on their European reputation. Yet France has survived Napoleon's mischief. We had a pleasant Ceylon Buddhist – an ex-surgeon merchant and his wife here this week – Dr de Silva. He considered that Belgium's sufferings might well be the outcome of her Karma (cause bringing action) in both carrying on the atrocities in the Congo rubber trade by the late King and his creatures and in condoning and tacitly approving when horrified England was making protests to his government. A Buddhist, you know, doesn't say that a divine judge is punishing; he says *natural justice*, or that law of nature (the Karma nijămă) causes one sort of action to bring about either analogous happiness or analogous suffering, according as that sort of action was kind, wise etc or cruel etc. We get our notions of Justice, just Providence, from this working of universal law, which we can no more really *explain* than we can *really* explain the law of gravitation or of heredity.

Nesta had now started at the Monmouth High School for Girls, a move not entirely to her liking. She evidently found the discipline rather irksome; their insistence that she conform to what was expected of a little girl of fourteen, rather ridiculous, and she poked fun at the school in her first letter to Arthur. After starting in her usual racy and mature style with: 'Dear Boysie, I haven't got your letter and V refuses to write so I have taken on my shoulders the solemn, grave and difficult undertaking of writing to you,' she suddenly breaks off with: 'Oh, I'm so sorry, I quite forgot', and starts the letter again in a huge schoolgirlish hand, quite unlike her usual mature handwriting. 'My Dearest Brother Arthur. I hope you are very well, as it leaves me at present. I told you, did I not, that we are going for a walk'. She sarcastically continues the remainder of the letter in this stilted language, showing considerable wit and ingenuity in its construction, and her next letter was couched in the same terms, informing Arthur, in the same large, careful hand: 'As perhaps you will observe, my writing has had very serious attention. I hope you like it. I think it is very beautiful. I went to church this morning and behaved well. I put a penny in the collection.' Such stilted letter writing was completely foreign to Nesta's nature and sense of fun, and Arthur thought them 'priceless'.

Vivien was now in her last term at Monmouth before trying for a place at Oxford. 'We – in Va and V1 – are going to give an entertainment for the fund for providing food for the Belgians who are coming to our cottages and we are giving a concert and a play. Nearly every girl has relations at the front, or enlisted.'[1] Refugee work was also in progress in Manchester, and Caroline was scathing in her criticism of the 'entertainment' put on for fifty of the Belgian refugees. They had a 'scruffy Boy Scout escort' at the station and although she had hoped it would be a 'picturesque function' she found it a decidedly 'second rate sort of amateur entertainment'. It was eight o'clock before things began and the Sale Brass Band in the Hall did not make waiting any pleasanter.' After a short lantern slide show the entertainment continued:

> two comic sets and two ragtime-dressed youths dancing and one matinee singer who recited a backwoods story. The songs and tableaux vivants – all in English and explained in English, one Sale citizen making a poor attempt to say the titles in French, after another had gassed at length in English. Thus lots and lots of English talked, sung, recited, to guests who only spoke French or Flemish. Of course, the programme ought to have been entirely cinema and music, needing no speaking. Too stupid!

That October, Caroline visited Arthur at Eton, going on from there to Monmouth to see her two daughters. She arrived at Monmouth in the late evening, went to her rooms, then 'up the hill, five minutes to the school.'

> Fine moonlight. Great Halloween revels were on, in a fearful jubilant din, but Viv came running down expecting a girl-hoax when I sent word that Lady Wyndham wanted to see her. Tableau. I went up to the Hall and received a sort of Scots Greys cavalry charge from Nesta, who looked bigger and rosier than ever.

---

[1] Large numbers of Belgian refugees were arriving in England at this time.

Although she had only been able to see Arthur at Eton for an hour and a half, she continued:

> It was very sweet to me, that 1½ hour with you, and well worth going for. I can now picture you day and night, in your room and college makeup, as I could not before.

England at this time, late 1914, was full of the latest sayings and pronouncements on the war by its popular hero, Kitchener, now the Minister of War. Arthur had evidently been told by the adjutant of the Eton Officers' Corps that Kitchener had said that the war was six months nearer the end than he had calculated it would be. This was good news to Caroline Rhys Davids: as a mother she was no doubt anxious that the war was over before her beloved only son could be dragged into the destruction. But in the train going home from Monmouth she met a woman who related yet another Kitchener saying: that the war would last five years. Caroline commented:

> Which is, all round, but especially for Germany, financially impossible. This makes me very sceptical as to whether Kitchener ever really says anything. I think it far more likely that he makes no prophecies to anybody whatever. But I can't help thinking the German case is in a poor way. If they couldn't break thro' to Calais with all that fury and weight of men and artillery, they'll get thro' nowhere.

Arthur spent his long leave at Guildford with his cousins and evidently reported that everyone there was engaged in 'war cult'. His mother agreed: all at Sale were also absorbed in the war. Local women had enlisted for Red Cross work, taken lessons, and were now working day and night shifts at Altrincham hospital. Wounded were arriving there weekly, at the Linden Lee hospital, and 'the Atkinsons' big empty house near the church is to be fitted up.' Caroline herself admitted that her own share was small 'but unlike most married women here I have my real day's work always claiming me as soon as house and family business is done. With most women here – not all – as soon as that's done, amusement begins.'

With her usual forthright commonsense she later commented:

> I rather wonder at the fuss made over Captain v Muller's (Emden) chivalry and all the rest of his virtues. Because he has

warred against helpless merchantmen (bar only his brief fling at a Russian warship, which he approached dastardly by flying a Jap flag)[1] and did *not* commit the horrible barbarity of sinking crew with vessel, but only sank a lot of the work of men's hands – food for other lands and scientific treasures – poor Professor Geddes – *therefore* he's patted on the back. Let's hope to goodness he won't be made much more of anymore.

She had not heard the rumours of a big naval battle to take place soon and rather doubted it. As for another rumour, that the German army on the Western Front was about to throw in the sponge: 'ugh, the fiends they were in August – have you seen the latest Belgian report? Frightful!'

Vivien was to go up to Oxford to sit for a scholarship on 7 December 1914. She wrote to Arthur:

You can help me by asking – praying – if you want it said outright – tho' these things are beastly hard to say. Will you? One of the girls has just heard of her father's death in the war. Only went out quite a short time ago. What a ghastly thing it is. Wouldn't like to be those German militarists in the next world. Told you two girls have brothers in the London Scottish, didn't I? They've no news – they may be dead for all they know. Miss Payne's brother was near Ypres and as he's only a private they hear nothing – isn't it tearing, this lack of news? Seems to tear and draw all the life out of one – waiting, waiting. Yet Miss Payne's as cheerful and plucky as – oh, she's just splendid. War brings out heroism in women just as well as men. 'Theirs is the harder part'.

Caroline sent off a guinea's worth of Christmas presents to the Cheshire Regiment at the front, in addition to wool helmets, mufflers and mittens, 'also tins of chocolate biscuits and shortbread and baccy. Also a contribution last week to the *Daily News* pudding fund – 'a huge business'. Houses in the home counties were still being looked at, but none was suitable. The war intruded more and more. 'Accini has again rather lost her head about war horrors and fears of invasion and disappointment over the navy, and this and that! Pity she hasn't got a little more British phlegm, or intellectual ballast. She

---

[1] This was a common and accepted practice of the war at sea and was used extensively by the navy in Nelson's time during the Napoleonic wars.

writes as if a German army were ready to pop over here now. I ask her – where is it?'

Like many people of their position in England at the time, the Rhys Davids were worried about the payment of their usual dividends, a vital part of their yearly income. In her last letter before the Christmas holidays, Caroline wrote:

You, of course, know that it is our first 'Lean and Kine' Xmas as to spending on presents and treats. No pinch of course has come yet. Our autumn dividends – Chinese Railways, Jap bonds and General Trade were paid up punctually, the first with bonus. And I have hope that 1st Jan divs will come in – Clerical and Medical, Brit Steamship and Port of London and Empire Transport. But the shipping ones are not certain not to defer payment (Auntie has a Canadian investment that has actually done so!) and of course the Hungarian Bonds – luckily a very small thing – won't pay.

However a bigger income tax will have to be deducted from all these and from father's pension. Then the professors are *invited* to settle a per cent reduction of their salaries – a most mean thing that universities are doing – bleeding men to whom they give, here at least, no pension. So a few pounds will probably go that way. And a bigger income tax is to come. On the other hand *no one is expecting presents or giving any.* I have just sent off an Xmas offering in the name of *you three* to any of the Cheshires now at the Front, thro' the Manchester Guardian's organized despatch. This year we must consider the giving to those splendid fighters, our Tommies, our Xmas fun.

Caroline had no illusions that the British public were being told the whole truth regarding the war. She felt that: 'The naval victory has done public feeling a lot of good and eased the scare feelings,'[1] but she had misgivings over the 'raid fiasco of the submarines at Dover.'

I wonder how they were spotted so well at 4am and 6.30am. It's odd that there is no more in the papers. I only hope nothing more has been hushed up, as the mysterious loss of the Audacious was off Ireland.[2] When shall we hear the truth?

[1] Probably a reference to the Battle of the Falkland Islands on 8 December 1914 when British naval forces sank the *Scharnhorst, Gneisenau, Nürnburg* and *Leipzig.*
[2] HMS *Audacious* was sunk by a mine on 27 October 1914, but the reason for her loss was kept from the British public.

She had again been looking at houses, but had still found nothing suitable, especially with Professor Rhys Davids' health in mind. She wrote, making a rather macabre play on words:

> You see it's *really important* as this is his last *home* and every year he must necessarily be getting less fit to rush about, that we get a place that suits him down (in) to the ground. A wide embrace. 'Yer' Mother.

*

At the beginning of 1915 Arthur's stammer was still giving trouble and Caroline sent him to a speech therapist, a Mr MacMahon of Wimpole Street, who, after talking to Arthur, reported to her: 'The stammer is not, I consider, very deep-seated and when it occurs it is largely due to nervous and severe constriction of all the muscles of the throat, as an endeavour to force the voice through.' MacMahon suggested that Caroline show his letter to her own doctor and then, if she wished, he would take Arthur for lessons. Caroline, with her usual customary cautiousness over money matters, was appalled that 'the beggar charges one guinea a lesson for forty minutes' but considered it would be worth it for 'releasing you from an unsufferable plague.' She was confident that the stammer would ultimately yield to treatment and that Arthur would conquer it, 'as father, Mr Plummer, and I and lots of others have conquered it,' but she was anxious that he not neglect his studies and efforts to win the Balliol Exhibition and the Newcastle Scholarship by concentrating too much effort to eradicating his stammer, and she suggested postponing lessons with MacMahon until the 'comparative slackness of next term'.

In May 1915, Caroline and Professor Rhys Davids decided on a house named Cotterstock at Chipstead, Surrey. The vendor had agreed to put in gas and electric fittings and a price had been agreed. Caroline wrote to Arthur:

> It has only five bedrooms, but 1: three large sitting rooms, one has had a 3/4 size billiard table. 2: 500 feet altitude. 3: adjoining golf course. 4: very pretty country. 5: Station seven minutes, quick to London.

Although Arthur's stammer was still a cause of some anxiety, his general health seems to have improved considerably and he played

cricket, tennis, football – both Rugby and Association – Fives and
the Wall Game throughout the year. In July he played in a scratch
XI against the 2nd Life Guards. He wrote to Nesta, sparing her the
details of the score and match, which he knew would not interest her,
and concentrating on the lighter aspect of the game:

> There was one fellow playing (he made 45 and bowled me for a
> duck, curse him) called Lieutenant Graves who was exactly like
> the German Crown Prince, hence dubbed 'little Willie' by his
> fellow officers. He was a splendid example of the hearty military
> man. Much swearing and frequent exclamations of 'What'
> adorned his conversation. He swore at the band for playing things
> which had no tune (ie things other than musical comedy songs).

In July Arthur wrote to Caroline to say that a small book of verse by
Etonians was being published privately, to which he had made a 'few
contributions.' He had also won the Hervey English Verse Prize,
which brought him £6 worth of books.

That Arthur was now in a robust state of health is shown by his
playing in the school Wall Game. In October 1915 he played for
Lord Kingsborough's side, the Eton Chronicle reporting that he
displayed 'neat kicking' and made some 'splendid kicks'. On St
Andrew's Day he played for the Collegers against Oppidans in the
annual match and threw a goal: 'The first time it's been done in a
first class match or game since 1909. Quite a fuss about it.'[1] Despite
Arthur's goal the Oppidans had their first win since 1901. *The Eton
Chronicle* reported that Arthur was 'clever with his feet, but rather
inclined to cool'. His place was fourth at 9st 10 lbs.

Arthur had attended summer camp with the Training Corps, but
was now in the Battalion Scouts. He wrote to Nesta:

> Thank goodness. They are rather awful people, but the work is so
> much better and more useful (and slacker) than the proper Corps.
> Owing to our train being late on the Field Day I was captured in
> the first ten minutes. Most charming! And then yesterday – ye
> Gods! I enclose the programme. Isn't it beyond your wildest
> dreams? That Schubert is simply adooorable. It's fighting hard
> with the Tannhauser for first place. Next I liked the Hebrides and
> the Tschaichovsky. Of course, Irene Scharrer is a frightfully good

[1] Goals are very seldom scored in the Wall Game.

player. It was she who played the 'Moonlight' last half, resulting
in my effort in 'Sense and Insense'.[1]

On Monday 6 December 1915, Arthur travelled up to Oxford to sit
the first of his scholarships, staying with his old headmaster at
Summerfields, Doctor Williams.

> The dear old man asked me quite early in the half – before he lost
> his son, M.E.E. Williams, in College my first half. Did I tell you
> about him? Killed by a shell in France.

The examination lasted from Tuesday to Friday, with an interview
with the Master of Balliol beforehand.
    Nesta wrote to say how much she detested her school, especially
now that Vivien was up at Oxford. Arthur replied with a surprising
admission which he had never even hinted at in any of his previous
years at Eton.

> I have experienced just the same thing. There was a time when I
> hated this place more than words can say, but now I am dreading
> the time when I have to leave. I am getting so fond of the place
> now – two years too late, and my time will soon be up d... it!

On 12 December 1915 Arthur learnt that he had been successful in
winning a Domus Exhibition to Balliol College Oxford. It now only
remained for him to take the Newcastle to secure his future at
university and crown his achievements at Eton.

*

Back at Eton in 1916, after the Christmas holidays, Arthur wrote to
Nesta that despite a large and painful boil on his face – which he
illustrated with two graphic little drawings – he was 'very happy'. 'I
am going to enjoy this half simply hugely.' He was playing Rugby
and hoping to get his colours, 'by a fluke'. His next letter to Nesta
gave her the news that he had been picked for the XV and was to play
against Wellington in a few days' time. 'I really am having a
frightfully good time, enjoying every minute of it'. He was now
Captain of the School and a member of 'Pop', the Eton debating
society, and, in the hierarchy of Eton, a person of some consequence.

---

[1] A book of poetry by Etonians, published that year.

'At last', he wrote to Nesta. 'There's not a person in the school I'm afraid to go up to and have a chat with'. He had also spoken for the first time at Speeches. He confided to Nesta:

> Now, speaking before the Headmaster, some other masters and 150 boys at the top of the school is a ticklish job for a fellow like me. But it went off without a hitch. I couldn't very well help it with the speech I chose – the one we heard Lewis Waller do, Henry V to his soldiers before the walls of Harfleur. 'Once more into the breach' etc. I do love it – it just carried away me and the audience too'.

The Eton Chronicle commented:

> Rhys Davids is much to be congratulated on his spirited and dramatic rendering of Henry V's famous speech, though perhaps it occasionally lacked the weight and dignity which seem to be inherent in the words of Shakespeare. We were very glad to hear him speak and wish that the Captain of the Oppidans would do so too.

Eton played Wellington at Rugby on Agar's Plough on 19 February with Arthur in the side. He was anxious to justify his inclusion in the XV and played his heart out. *The Eton Chronicle* reported the match, which Eton lost by six points to Wellington's twenty-five: 'The Eton halfs had to do more than their fair share of defence. Rhys Davids particularly got through an immense amount of stopping and tackling and played magnificently.'

Arthur confessed to Nesta:

> It was a fairly easy win for them, but it was a jolly good game and we thoroughly enjoyed it. Of course we had no chance against the best 'back' division among the public schools. Our forwards were alright, but our 3/4s were merely outplayed. There were six KS [King's Scholars] in the XV which is about a record. I was playing stand-off half against their best player, a very nice boy called Whitworth.

Despite his sporting activities, Caroline was still worried about the general state of her son's health and her fears were compounded in the first half of the term by an outbreak of diphtheria at Eton. 'Curse the people who let that boy bring it into college – how ever am I going to get through the next few days thinking of you? I do wish tomorrow were a week later and *that I had you here!*

The diphtheria scare seems to have passed with no undue consequences and Arthur played Rugby against the Royal Fusiliers on 29 February. The School was beaten by fourteen points to four. 'Rhys Davids was exceptionally good as usual', wrote *The Eton Chronicle*; and in 'Characters of the Team' commented: 'Rhys Davids, stand-off half, is always in the right place at the right moment. An exceedingly good tackler and kicks into touch well'. Arthur played his last match in March, playing for the College against the School Second XV. 'Probably the last game of Rugger I shall play here. How awful!'

In addition to his sporting activities Arthur was now working hard for the Newcastle Scholarship, which he was to sit at Easter. The winner of the scholarship in 1915 had been C.J.S. Sprigge KS and he wrote to Arthur from the Base Depot of the Guards Division BEF France.

I hope very much you will bring it off all right and apologize for my scandalous behaviour last year in shaking your self-confidence. I assure you nothing was ever less intended, and I know how galling it must be for a favourite to yield to a rank outsider. I only wish I could have been a real scholar like yourself and not a literary dilettante, but that could never be. I have a sieve-brain and have already forgotten, I expect, most of the little I knew, though a real and valuable result of an early acquaintance with classic masterpieces cannot be lost. May I be heavy fatherly and remind you, in your scholarly fervour, that the mere scholar is a useless person and that technical scholarship must be a means, and must be accompanied by a general appreciation of the whole fabric of things, so that you can correctly model your own part of the 'edifice', as the preacher's metaphor has it? There is an inspiration in scholarship, as in art, music, poetry and religion, and it is possible to have a complete perception of all the paraphernalia without ever acting the part properly – not that I think there is fear of you doing that.

I do hope you will join my regiment – we look almost like having quite a happy little party in France in about two years time and we shall be able to tell Boccaccioian tales under the nose of death, if any of us survive, which will be most dramatic.

Very much luck to you in that (the Newcastle) as in everything.

Forgive my inherent priggishness, and write again, do.

The Times of 7 April 1916 carried an announcement that Arthur had won the Newcastle. Among the many letters of congratulation was another from Sprigge:

> A thousand congratulations! I doubt if they will ever reach you, as I have no idea of your home address, but it pleases me to place on record the pleasure I experienced at 9.12pm on Sunday, April 9 when the news reached me that the illiterate Scotsman had been ignominiously put to flight by the sturdy Welsh-born aviator – or shall I say that the dour spectre of John Knox had fled in confusion from the triumphant image of the Lord Buddha – Prince Siddartha styled on earth. My gallant aviator, even when the military octopus has pressed its outer and gentler claws about your tender soul, before you feel or realize the full horror of war, continue to write and bring much consolation to your humble servant and affectionate friend.

This letter from Sprigge contains the first hint that Arthur was intending to join the Royal Flying Corps. None of the family letters contains any suggestion that this was in his mind and he had probably intimated to Sprigge his intention to do so when answering Sprigge's earlier letter, with its expressed hope that Arthur would join his regiment.

Arthur had found the study for the Newcastle to be a drudge, but despite the distractions he had stuck it with all the will and determination that he always brought to any task, disagreeable or otherwise. In a revealing letter to a family friend, however, he made no secret of his feelings about the work involved in winning the scholarship:

> As a matter of fact I must shatter your ideal in one aspect. I am afraid the connection between the Newcastle and Greek drama is dreadfully thin. The Newcastle is of course the thing to finish up one's classical career at Eton, but as a performance of merit to me at least it ranks a long way below my exhibition at Balliol – that is to say as a test of scholarship, in the real sense. As a matter of fact I was very pleased to get the Newcastle because it (a) as you say, pleases Mother and Father so, and generally it is useful and satisfactory in most ways. (b) because it shows I can still beat

anybody else at classics at Eton (c) because I had other work of a much more attractive kind in Eton which I managed to get through and yet not spoil my chances for the Newcastle. The latter reason may sound strange, but I must tell you the Newcastle consists of nine classical papers and *three divinity papers*, and these divinity papers just murder it as a classical examination. We do every year one paper on the Acts, one on a Gospel (this year St Matthew) and one on General Divinity, which is a mixture of general Biblical learning, Church history and Prayer Book. Now it gives me acute pleasure to read the Acts or St Matthew as a book, almost as a novel, but anyhow as a book to read and think about, but when it comes to *days* reading it from the point of view of answering questions such as 'Give a list of the parables in this Gospel' and such like, it becomes at once a mere drudge of the worst character. You see the senior examiner of the two is always the Cambridge man, and I am afraid the Cambridge ideal of thorough technical knowledge of *one* subject to me is just appalling. It is all so different from Balliol where you can really put down ideas of your own and not be afraid.

Well you see that was the state of mind in which I began working for the Newcastle. As a matter of fact the papers were much nicer than those last year, and the examiners gave us much more scope than I had expected. (they were Montague James, the Provost of Kings, and a man called Genner, a Welsh non-conformist, a tutor of Jesus College Oxford who had been at Balliol). We had a very nice 'Critical' paper with plenty of choice – the only paper not entirely confined to bare facts. There was one question which I actually revelled in. It was 'Is it a true description of Attic tragedy to say that in it there was no sham heroism, no impossible villainy, no maudlin sentiment?' I thank my stars that I was able to get through a good amount of work on the Divinity beforehand, even though I loathed it all the time. And just think, besides the divinity, there were translations from English into Greek and Latin Prose and Verse, and vice versa, making eight papers in all, and the Critical. And the translations from one language into another. I suppose they show your knowledge of the language, but you can't help thinking all the time that you must first please the examiner and then think whether you like the piece or not. The curious thing was I won mostly on my divinity after all. Well, *thank God* all my examination cram is over now! I have been spending most of my time lately, by way of a delightful contrast, in having long philisophical talks with father. I have never quite realized before his attitude towards Christianity and religion in general. He is a pantheist, (I suppose that's the only word). However, more of this if we can meet sometime which I devoutly hope can be arranged. Excuse this lengthly perambulation.

Your small friend,
Arthur.

In May 1916, Arthur started his last half at Eton; a relaxing half with little or no work to do. He played in several cricket matches and took part in the school Speeches on 3 June, playing Fluellen in an extract from *Henry V*; Theseus in *A Midsummer Night's Dream*; Euripides in Aristophanes' *Thesmophoriazusae*; and gave a soliloquy from *Hamlet*. His mother, father and Vivien went down to Eton for Speeches, 'the last opportunity for us'. On arrival they saw Arthur walking down the High Street, arm in arm with two other boys, the centre of the trio. Vivien remembered the moment her whole life. 'Arthur always had a marvellous expression – he was either smiling or looking as if he were about to. As he came towards us I thought. Gosh, how goodlooking he is – like a young god'.

Arthur finally left Eton at the end of the summer half and in August he wrote to his mother from Chinhurst Hill, Wonersh, Guildford, the home of Sir Henry and Lady Babington Smith. He was having a 'great time' helping Sir Henry keep down the rabbits, gardening and playing cricket. He had met Sir Henry at Speeches, Sir Henry's son being his fag at Eton, and Sir Henry having been fag to Arthur's uncle Harry during his days at Eton.[1]

Arthur had already had an interview for a commission in the RFC and he wrote to Vivien on 16 August from Coombe Bank where he, Caroline and Nesta were on holiday:

I went up to RFC Headquarters on Monday, and after waiting two hours discovered that they were taking no particular steps about my commission. The same man as I saw before – Capt The Hon E Charteris – was again too nice for words, and he said he

---

[1] Arthur had also met his old friend Sub Lt R.S.W. Dickinson at Speeches. Dickinson had taken part in the raid on Constantinople on the night of 14/15 April. He had been awarded a DSO and given a month's leave from the Royal Naval Air Service.

would take me at once. He asked when I wanted to start. I said in a week. He said that would not quite do as it took them a week to get the papers out. So I expect to hear from them as to time of going to Oxford about Wednesday next week. I shall then also get my actual commission and back allowance. My pay, when I get my wings, is 24/- a day! Gee, ain't I an almighty swell.

Charteris was as good as his word. On 17 August 1916 Arthur received his orders to report for training as a 2nd Lieutenant on probation in the Royal Flying Corps.

CHAPTER FOUR

Royal Flying Corps

On 28 August 1916 Arthur reported to the No 2 School of Aeronautics Oxford for his initial training and was billeted in Exeter College, sharing a room with two other probationary officers. He wrote home:

> Royal Flying Corps.
> Exeter College
> Oxford.

Dearie Mums,

Gurn, but time is full up! Let me tell you what happened since my last PC. By the way, I have since discovered from a reliable source that all the fairy tales about pay are, as I thought, exaggerated: we get 7/6 a day regular Temp. 2nd Lt's pay, and various allowances which make it up to about 12/-. Then later we get 5/- a day flying pay extra for every day's flying we do, and finally either 20/- or 24/- a day when we get our wings.

The mess bills stand at present at 6/- a day – my only regular expense – which is very high indeed for not *very* good food but there is a general agitation on foot and there are possibilities that it may be reduced. Well I found myself last night put into a completely bare room at this place with a Canadian of a very alert and self-confident type, who had been in the Army 1 year 7 months (after volunteering in Canada) His accent was of the knife cut order, but not unpleasing. The other is a distinctly lower individual from some yeomanry or other who is pleasant but not much else.

Well I had no camp bed or any other outfit, so I went down to a shop after my first parade before the adjutant here, which only lasted a few minutes, and ordered all the outfit, including bed, chair, washstand – all fold up, a fleece bag to sleep in and an air pillow, costing in all about £6.17.0. – not expensive. These, of course, as I discovered today, were sent to Brasenose, so I slept the night – after mess at 7.30 in Exeter Hall – on the floor, with my army allowance of 3 blankets and a sort of mattress thing kindly lent by the Canadian. There seemed to be little washing facilities and I did not sleep over well being on the hard floor with a British Warm as pillow.

So I awoke not in the best of spirits, to get up for breakfast at 8am. Then I discovered there was an excellent bathroom open for short periods morning and evening, and got in a moderate wash, followed by a nice breakfast which altogether altered prospects, and I was fairly happy on parade at 8.45. We then marched up to the Museum, ie all the new squad of officers for the RFC, either new like self or from other regiments, about 2/3 the latter. We are in Christchurch, Brasenose, Exeter and Lincoln and are at least a hundred. We were fallen out there and went up to a lecture theatre, as they call it, and were told there by a smart young captain of about 28 that we were to start our four weeks' course next Monday, and till then we would be 'squads in waiting'. We are in squads of ten officers each, under the senior officer of the ten, usually a full Lt, in three of the twelve squads a Captain.

Our programme is roughly:- up at about 6am(!) parade at 6.30 for half hour physical and other drill, then exercise of any sort till breakfast at eight. Parade 8.45, marched up to Museum for workshops and instruction from NCO instructors – obviously very good men – from 9 till 11.45: lecture 11.45 – 12.30. Lunch 1.00: parade at 2.00 for workshops same as morning till 3.30 with lecture, then free till mess at 7.30 (must attend) then nothing till bed: place locked up at 1.00am. In the workshops we do all sorts of things on rigging (ie structure) Bombs, Artillery Observation or reconnaissance, Photography, a little wireless signalling (Morse) besides engines, doing them in squads with various instructors. This morning we had a very good introductory lecture on rigging and the theory of flight, followed by afternoon of signalling. After the four weeks we have an exam and then go home and wait for wire summoning to flight squadron for actual flying (or repetition of course if failed).

This evening I bought a mackintosh thing for nearly £3 as it had been raining all day and I was pretty wet. I also found out about my lost camp kit and spent 13/- on (1) a cigarette case, 6/6 silver, which I shall take as my birthday present from all of you (2) a cigarette holder – nice one, amber, or sham rather, gold tip, 2/6 (3) a baccy pouch like father's, but smaller, 3/6, some baccy etc. Am shaking down and recovering from first depression. By the way can you send along as soon as you can (1) a pair of shorts – a brown pair if you can find them. (2) a pair of my green stockings.

(3) a small bath towel. Have bought one cheap latter for time

Love to all

Arthur.

Ps. I am allowed to wear top boots (brown) which is excellent. Am having pair made.

It was a cruel stroke of fate that had sent Arthur to Oxford. During the ensuing weeks, walking the streets and colleges of the city, he must have been bitterly disappointed that, but for the war, he would have been there as an undergraduate, a cherished ambition he had worked so long and hard to achieve.

His disappointment must have been compounded by the fact that Vivien was on vacation from Oxford during his period there, but he had a friend living in the neighbourhood, and he was able to spend his free time with the family. 'His mother played some Chopin preludes and Etudes – especially that lovely prelude N.VI – and some Schubert to us after tea', he wrote to Caroline. 'I am going again this afternoon and probably on the river in the afternoon and more music in the evening.' He had also had his rates of pay explained more accurately:

The CO at this place gave out details as to pay the other day. It is 7/6 a day with allowances which make it up to 11/3 per day while we are here. When we go to a flying squadron we get 4/6 a day extra flying pay, which is doubled when we get our wings, and 5/- a day extra when we are in France or on active service. We start our course in earnest tomorrow and then it will be deuce hard work for a month thank goodness, then comes the really pleasant part of the job. I may be able to get stationed at Purley, with luck.

Nesta wrote early in September to say she had seen Leefe Robinson bring down the German airship SL 11. Arthur's reply was typical:

Just like you to go and see that jolly old Zepp come down. Why wasn't I there too? Why the . . . wasn't I upstairs in an hairyplane to light Old Boche's cigar for him?

King George V visited the school on 13 September. Arthur's letter to Caroline relating the event shows a certain amount of irreverence, tinged with sympathy for the King:

Old George Guelph came down to inspect us today on a surprise visit. At least we only knew about it a day or two before, which is not much for a Royal visit. We were all in our classes, and going on (officially) as usual, when he came in with the CO. George RI said 'carry on': we carried on (with signalling Morse) and he vanished. He was covered with decoration ribbons – three layers of them, with red all over him – hat and shoulder tabs, and not without much brass work. Altogether loud turnout, though impressive. Poor little man, he had to do us and all Cadet Corps and hospitals in Oxford in one day!

It was not all work at Oxford. Arthur was playing a great deal of football – 'I must ask you to send along those old football boots of mine. They are (or were) underneath my bed.' – and on 22 September the school held a 'beano regatta', with NCO instructors, cadets and officers rowing in eights against Lincoln, Queens and Christchurch. There were canoe races, tugs of war in punts, pillow fights in canoes and sculling races.

The examination was just over a week away now but Arthur had no qualms about it, although his Canadian roommate was less confident. 'He works fearfully hard and seems to learn nil – result of not having had a classical education.' The probationary officers had been given an offer to sign on as observers, which would have meant getting to France quickly, but Arthur turned it down. He was determined to be a pilot. He was hoping to get leave after the examination, go to a concert in London with his aunt, visit Eton and spend a few days at Cotterstock, but these hopes were dashed. At the successful completion of the course at Oxford he was posted straight to Netheravon to begin his flying instruction, sending a postcard home from there on 6 October:

Instead of going to Upavon as I expected, we were turned off here, which is about two miles further into the wilderness, viz 10 miles from the station. There are quite a lot of people here already and the huts and hangars make an enormous rambling village.

The family were still in touch with their ex-cook at Ashton and she wrote to Arthur while he was at Netheravon, thanking him for his letter describing his new life and hoping that he 'won't be too daring all at once, your people are bound to be rather anxious.' She expected that there was 'a lot to learn about engines, but you were also so good at anything like that, though it only seems like yesterday that you were building Meccano models.'

Caroline was indeed rather anxious for the safety of her son. On his being posted to Netheravon, she wrote:

> My Beloved Son
> Wire, letter and card have all reached us – Friday, Sat and today – and we have been flattened, and then a little comforted in consequence. Comforted because anyway you have been sent to learn of the best at the best, so that my first misery – your coming to grief, as so many do, every week one or two by the papers – during training is less likely to be justified.
>
> I felt when I watched you off in that train, waiting for that waved hand to me that never came somehow – I think Vivien got it all – it was so uncertain when I should see you again. A mightier thing has swallowed you up.

After giving all the news of her work in the garden at Cotterstock and the rearrangement of the rooms, she asked:

> I am given to understand that searchlights are now made as to be able to convey electric shocks in their rays – is this all fluff? I should like to know. Shall you want your bike? I can send it. Or can I advance you something towards a motor bike?'

Arthur wrote to Nesta on 10 October:

> I am posted here for flying. Here I am and perfectly happy. I went up for the first time as a passenger yesterday for twenty minutes, and again this morning for half an hour. Then this afternoon for 25 mins up to 3,000 feet taking part control of the machine. It's absolutely ripping! You just sit still and the earth moves under you, except when you are coming down. We are all right in the middle of Salisbury Plain, with vast open space to land in and heaps of room everywhere. There is no red tape and everything free and easy.

Nesta was predictably excited over Arthur's first venture into the air, Caroline rather less so, but she was extremely interested, as always, in anything he undertook. Arthur had written telling her how safe it was, but she replied:

I was so often wondering when you start your joy and other flights. I felt sure you would call it very safe. But it is good to think you are getting the best training the country can give. Please pour forth more flights letters; they are absorbingly interesting, and above all be content to learn slowly. It's a verra noo craft, after all.

Nesta had dozens of questions:

What's it like . . . do you have a separate hut to yourself . . . are they big huts . . . like a dormitory . . . is the country bare . . . how long do you stay there . . . when do you get leave . . . I suppose Viv sent you that scarf. So glad it's useful. Is it long enough? If you want anything else doing, socks, mittens etc (I don't suppose you wear the last named article.) The Tommies want them a lot and I'm *sick* of knitting 'em. Have done three pairs already, just tell me and I'll do it.

Vivien was more composed. She was now back at Oxford and wrote:

Dearest Arthur,
Don't often begin like that do I? How progresses the world or rather the air with you? S'pose you've been up more times than you can count by now – lucky thing. But I'm so glad to hear you love it so. Seems funny to pass squads of flying corps men going to the Museum from Exeter and the House every day and feel you've been here among them. Wish you were here now.

Nesta, in an orgy of knitting, produced another scarf. Arthur responded:

I hear that a certain woollen scarf was nitted by you, O most bricky sister, you Adam's apple of my eye, or shall we say throat Whereon, many thanks. Its purposes or uses at present are two: 1. It keeps my neck warm for early morning flying – 6.00 to 8.00am. which is apt to be on the frigid side. 2. It serves as an auxiliary pillow at night. Altogether most useful garment. Things are progressing nicely. I have been up some nine or ten times, I forget which, but over four hours in all. Quite soon I shall be going up alone for the first time.

Arthur finished the course at Netheravon on 2 November 1916 with a 'half hour's flit in a fog on Thursday morning', and was given leave until the following Monday. After spending some time at home he went down to Eton, staying overnight with John Crace and playing football against the school the following day. This visit to Eton has an air of a passionate desire to reassure himself that some things in the world – his world – were still normal. He wrote to a friend at this time:

> I seem so depressingly old nowadays and my hitherto vast ambitions for the future have rather faded into contemplation of a golden age in the past! Perhaps that is owing to the fact that I have just been down to Eton and have had all my lovable memories of that never-to-be-forgotten place freshly revived. Anyhow, my life still centres entirely on Eton and Etonians.

Despite his joy in flying, Arthur did not enjoy army life and the – to him – coarse and uneducated company. Many boys from similar sheltered backgrounds must also have found the transition from school to army life equally traumatic. But he was soon to meet a kindred spirit. After returning from leave he was posted to the Central Flying School at Upavon for further training and one of his instructors there was Keith Knox Muspratt. Muspratt was about the same age as Arthur, had been educated at Sherborne College and had taken his Royal Aero Club certificate as a pilot while in his last year at school. He had developed into a brilliant pilot and as soon as he was old enough had enlisted in the RFC. Recognising his ability, the Corps had made him an instructor. So alike in age and temperament, education and outlook, Keith Muspratt and Arthur became firm friends, a friendship which was to last until the end of their brief lives.

Arthur had flown three hours solo at Netheravon and was now to graduate to fly aeroplanes of the type used on active service, as distinct from the 'school machines' at Netheravon. He hoped to get his wings by Christmas, 'but that entails 25 hours' solo flying, night landings, cross country, artillery observation, bomb dropping and photographs, at least it does for my squadron.' At Upavon he was flying BE2cs, Avro 504s and, with Muspratt, a Bristol S 2A., nicknamed the 'Sociable' because pupil and instructor sat side by side – an unusual arrangement in those days.

By December 1916 Arthur no longer flew with an instructor, having flown the required number of hours 'under instruction'. 'I

just go on flying solo and practising regularly until I get my wings.'
He managed to get leave to attend St Andrew's day at Eton, staying
the entire weekend and travelling straight back to Upavon on the
Sunday evening, the pull of Eton being even stronger than that of
mother or home. He wrote to Nesta: 'I have transferred to the scout
squadron' and sent off a long and philosophical letter to Caroline
explaining his dislike of army life:

> CFS.
> Upavon.
> Wilts.

December 10.
Pomme de Oeuil,

Where *did* you get that knack of writing letters? Not lines of ink
on paper, like this, but *letters*, real live and kicking. Sort of thing
that make you wriggle when you read them. My dear Mums, you
are very hard on my sealed look: *I* didn't seal it and you probably
know whether my thoughts run in numbers or not after my telling
you that I am living in a state of complete stupor. I am just
walking up my hills, only there are thick clouds quite low down all
around me and I can hardly enjoy it at all. Some day I may get
through to the top where it will be clean, but it is very possible that
I shall merely lose my way instead and wander round and round
without getting any higher. You can't imagine how I long to
discuss Buddhism and other things with you, but it can't be done
through letters. Then when I start discussing religion or *something*
interesting at mess I find (a) it is against mess rules! (b) it is hard
to find anyone with any ideas on the subject.

My darling Ma, you also can't imagine how much I loathe the
army and how much my thoughts are *always* in Cotterstock or
Eton. I just drift on quite mechanically. Nobody except the little
few I have collected around me understands me in the least: above
all nearly everybody is so *common* and so sordid – especially after
Eton, where one did make *friends*: here one merely makes
acquaintances by the score. I have found one really admirable
person called Wilcox who has just been married: he is really
artistic, but even he is saturated with a veneer of Cockney
commonsense which just mars the perfect friend. Yet I like the
flying and am really having a good time. I am longing to be in
France, where I can really *do* something, but that won't be for two
months at least yet.

Persistence of individuality! I am not hard put to fathom the colossal depths of your epigrams, but I can say that my first view of life is as one vast symphony, and that in symphonies individuality is only lovable because it combines with other individualities. There are so few individuals here: nearly all are animal creatures; some have manners, very few sympathy – which is everything, in fact only another word for love. My thoughts are very wild, and it's so hard to put them into numbers, it's like putting a square peg into a round hole. Someday when I get time I shall shape the peg to fit. Thanks for sending Mrs Philpot the poem. I want her to see it. Strange to say I still believe in God.

Love

A.

Arthur had kept the news of his transfer to scouts from his mother, but she was unwittingly told by Nesta. Arthur wrote to reassure her:

As regards the idea about the most dangerous branch of the Corps etc. you will understand perhaps, dearest Mums, even if it does sound a bit callous, when I say it almost amuses me to read your contention. First of all it is no more dangerous than any other branch of the RFC, if done well; secondly, it's twice as much fun, and thirdly, Mums, you know I simply cannot and will not *shirk* in any way just because I happen to have more brains than some of the people here, in fact that is all the more reason why I should be in a position to use them on the more difficult job. Don't you see that the army is slowly killing me, and I am not going to be killed by the army without a jolly good shot at getting a real good time out of it. Mums, how lovely your letters are! But do remember the gorgeous lines of Henley you quoted 'we can dare and we can conquer', and I wouldn't want to share in 'the rich quiet of the afterglow'[1] unless I had dared. I want to be worthy of my salt and of your name.

Two days before Christmas he wrote to Nesta, thanking her for yet more socks: 'I have them on now over another pair of thick socks and they fit admirably and just do the trick as regards keeping my feet warm.' He also sent her a small present:

[1] 'What is to Come We know Not' – W.E. Henley.

. . . which I humbly offer upon my needless to say imperial knees as a Christmas present. It is made from the aluminium piston (of a 80hp Clerget engine) which bust into bits in the air while I was up in the machine. The rest of the engine held all right and took us down to the ground, where I seized a bit of the piston and tried to make a ring with it. However, not being a skilled enough workman and having no tools I dismally failed and made this absurd little trinket instead. I just send it along as a temporary mascot until I can find out what you would really like. I wouldn't dream of letting it be a reward for your superb pair of heaven-beknitted footgear.

Arthur had no leave over the Christmas period and wrote to Caroline on the last day of 1916. He was again in a contemplative frame of mind:

Dearest,

Thanks ever so much for the letter and enclosure, which I haven't quite thought over yet. But my dear Mums the only epithet I can think of for the Horizons is 'colossal'! It's so huge! I really honestly think it's the best bit of prose I have ever read in my life, and the Credo is not far behind. That too is big – and it makes the ordinary Christianity look so small. I shall be occupied these next few weeks in thinking out a way of expressing my view of the dear Christ and his philosophy which shall be as big as yours, if not bigger. I believe it can be done alright, in fact I am sure it can, because I know in my own heart that it is bigger, if rightly considered, though it may not seem so to you. I should say you have taken Socrates and Gotama, chiefly Gotama, and just eliminated all the bad points, substituting little beautiful bits of yourself. Which is just my idea, only I want to have a large slice of Christ to be the background of it all. Because Christ's idea of love is *the* main theme of the whole symphony. There are one or two points in the Credo I should like to quarrel with, but I must read it many more times first, I can't quarrel with the Horizons – it's too lovely. Now for some good news. Most of my philosophy has been changed by two lines of Shakespeare which I found on the title page of my Henley:

The Summer's flower is to the Summer sweet
Though to itself it only live and die.

Now ain't that good? Just hits off one aspect of my case nicely. No flying for the last three days, which is appalling – high winds and clouds very low, air just like a rough sea. Excellent prospects for me now as some new scouts are coming to the squadron.

> Best love to you, dear dear angel.
> Arthur.

*

By the end of January 1917 Arthur was flying Sopwith Pups almost exclusively. A new batch of these delightful little single-seaters, which were a great favourite with all pilots at that time, had arrived at Upavon; Arthur wrote to Nesta on 28 January to say he had looped one:

> I looped the loop four times, wasn't that rash of me, dear Nesta? It was so funny feeling the whole earth whirl around my head. I didn't know where I wasn't until I straightened out again, and the machine gave a fearful lurch because I had got in my own backwash. Wasn't it funny, dear Nesta!

He had been expecting to be sent to Hythe for a gunnery course, but in January 1917 it had been decided to make Hythe the gunnery school for observers, embryo fighter pilots being sent to Turnberry, Ayrshire, and at the end of January, Arthur wrote to Caroline:

Incredibly Much Beloved,
    A new development has arrived. I am being deliberately left out of the people going to Hythe for the course which starts tomorrow – where I thought I should be going – in order to go on flying scouts – the new single seaters which have arrived. I shall not go out to France until the beginning of March. Which is appalling in a way: yet I don't much mind as it means I shall get firmly established on single seater fighting scouts, and therefore am certain to go out on them, which is superb. They are pouring in now. Three of the type I shall fly (Sopwith Pups, baby Sopwiths, little, v light single seaters) have been fetched from Coventry. I flew one for forty minutes, quite safe on a wretched day – she wanted to climb like s... the whole time and I had to be holding her down all the time, and she came round on turns like greased lightning, right up on one side so – altogether quite lovely. They do about 110 mph full out and level. Then I took off a bit cross wind next time up and had my first smash, ripped the

undercarriage off without leaving the ground and sat down
boomps, breaking a plane, d... silly show. Of course, I wasn't in
the least hurt. Cheerio and don't worry.

Arthur had now graduated as a pilot and had his wings. He wrote to
Caroline:

26/1/17   CFS
                                                      Upavon.
Dearest,
    Inclosed please find notice, one, from *London Gazette* of 2nd inst,
as to the worldly welfare of your progeny. Which notice means
that I am officially the proud possessor of an income of £1 per
diem. I have indulged in a new brown leather and fur flying cap,
chin piece and goggles, all about as good as can be got, for my use
on the scouts, which are a wee bit drafty as one has to be peering
about so much in order to see anything, which cost me the vast
sum of £3.19.0. – well worth it. I am now completely wrapped up
as to face in the air, which is most comfy.

His being posted to Turnberry instead of Hythe upset Caroline and
Arthur's plans, as she and his father had hoped to go down to Hythe
and stay there for the duration of Arthur's course. Arthur next wrote
from Turnberry:

16th Feb. 1917   Station Hotel
                                                   Turnberry.
Dearie Mother
    Here I am in a vast palace of a hotel which makes a most
comfortable mess. . . . I am sharing a room with another fellow of
similar position at CFS – same squadron. The hotel has been
taken over but is still being run as regards food and furniture by
the Company and so is extremely comfy. It is a vast great palace
on a little eminence about 200 ft above the sea and about ¼ mile
back from it, with steps leading down to the golf house and course
in between. The golf house is now our instructional headquarters
as it were; the pro, Fernie junior, still carries on and sells us
notebooks etc for our gunnery notes. Today, after short lecture, we
sat in little wooden huts in 8 squads of about 8 each and learnt
what the gun (Vickers machine gun) was made of etc., all of which
I knew before. After a day or two of that we go and fire daily on the

ranges. We work all day, every day, so there is not much chance for golf, except Saturday afternoons, which we have off. Two of us are borrowing clubs from the pro and are going to play tomorrow. It's not worthwhile sending my clubs along, I think, as I don't expect I shall play more than twice. There are a few machines here, but I am afraid I shalln't get any flying.

Arthur finished the course at Turnberry on 1 March, was given leave and wrote to Nesta from Cotterstock a few days later: 'I finished my course on Thursday night and passed just moderately as I expected to. I mean I didn't do very brilliantly, but just well.'

By 6 March he was back at Upavon, awaiting a posting to a squadron, and on 7 March he sent a jubilant postcard to Nesta:

Just a hurried line to tell you I have got about the best job going. In about a week or more I am going to No.56 Squadron, London Colney, near St. Albans, with 3 others from here, under Captain Foote (sic) a brilliant fighting pilot who is temporary fighting instructor here. He is taking us to this brand new squadron on a brand new type of single seater scout which is fabulously fast and about the latest word in scout machines. The whole squadron is going out about the first week in April or a bit after, so I shall see you again I hope. Capt. Ball is also going to be a Flight Commander (as well as Capt. Foote) so what with some friends from here and a great pal there I met at Turnberry, and a gorgeous type of machine, it should be absolute heaven.[1]

Fifty-six Squadron had been formed at Gosport in June 1916 and had moved to London Colney in Hertfordshire three weeks later. On 1 February 1917, Major Richard Graham Blomfield was given command of the squadron to bring it to a state of readiness to fly to France. Blomfield, 'a prince of organizers', was determined to lead the finest fighter squadron in the RFC and left no avenue unexplored to achieve his aim. His first requirement was to find first class flight commanders and he succeeded in having Captain Albert Ball posted to the squadron. At this time Ball was the most famous fighter pilot

---

[1] That this postcard, giving details of a new squadron, was sent through the mails and shows how far security was from the mind of the average officer at the time. It is ironical that letters home from France, written by other ranks, were censored, even though the average ranker knew very little of consequence – sometimes not even exactly where he was.

in the RFC, with thirty victories to his credit, a DSO with two Bars and an MC and Bar. Although perhaps not having Ball's exceptional talent as a fighter pilot, the other two flight commanders picked by Blomfield were nevertheless also pilots of great ability and experience. Captain Ernest Leslie Foot – nicknamed, not surprisingly, 'Feet' – had served in 60 Squadron with Ball and was a brilliant and aggressive fighter pilot; and Captain Ian Henry David Henderson was also a pilot of some experience, having flown with 19 Squadron throughout the Somme battles of the previous year.[1]

The squadron's equipment was to be the new fighter from the Royal Aircraft Factory at Farnborough: the SE5, and its later variant the SE5a, was to become one of the most successful fighter aeroplanes of the First World War; the mount of many of the highest scoring fighter pilots of the RFC and RAF. Equipped with the SE5, and with Ball, Foot and Henderson on its strength, 56 Squadron was a talking point throughout the RFC and great things were expected of the squadron when it started operations in France in the spring of 1917.

Arthur also wrote to Caroline, giving details of his selection for the new squadron.

7th March 1917.

Dearest Mums,
  Just a line to say I have got the job on the new scouts at London Colney near St Albans, where Captain Gallop and the man Potts are. Isn't it splendid? Muspratt and two others have got it. I was playing billiards with Muspratt this morning (there has been a wild gale and no flying yesterday and today) when Captain Foot came in. He is second only to Ball as a fighting expert, and *both* are to be flight commanders in the new squadron. Well he is temporary fighting instructor here, and he came up to me and said 'Would you like to fly SE5s (ie. Scout Experimental, 5th type) So of course I said I would love to. Then he said we would go along to London Colney as soon as the machines arrived there, and we

[1] Owing to the scarcity of records from this period the sequence of the early flight commanders of 56 Squadron during its days at London Colney has been in some doubt, but the Rhys Davids letters now seem to resolve this point. The original three were Ball, Henderson and Foot. Henderson broke his nose and was replaced by Crowe; Crowe then fell sick and was replaced by Meintjes. Foot had a car accident the evening before the squadron flew to France and was replaced, in France, by a recovered Crowe.

would go out at the end of this month, which means probably the first week in April. Gee! ain't I bucked? Just think Mums: I shall be with my friends Muspratt and Potts; we have for flight commanders the two best fighting pilots in the RFC and, on top of it all, as you know, the best scout machine that has yet been brought out. Oy! I expect to leave here sometime this week for St. Albans. Of course I will let you know when. Also it is so much nicer going out as a squadron than singly. I shall probably fly out, not go by boat.

Best love,
Arthur.

Only four days after this excited letter to Caroline, Arthur received orders posting him to 66 Squadron, then working up to strength at Filton, near Bristol. The squadron was two pilots short through illness:

So the glorious idea of going to 56 is not coming off because Captain Foot had only just 'bagged' me for his flight and it takes time to get the names through officially. I was given to understand that I was certain for 56 and I believe I still have a chance of being transferred if the weather keeps dud for a few days more. However, if 56 is the best job going, 66 is a very good second: Pups are my favourite machines, if I can't get SE5s, and it means France at once, which is a comfort. I really don't mind much, though, of course, I would have preferred the other.

On arrival at Filton, with another pilot, Arthur found that 66 Squadron was also two machines short; they were not wanted immediately and were given leave until 8 am the following morning. Arthur went home to Cotterstock. 'I had a very pleasant evening. For all I knew it might have been my last before I went out.' He caught the 1.00 am train the next morning for Bristol, arriving back at 66 Squadron at 6.45. 'Then at about 9.45, to my huge joy, got my orders to come here (London Colney) one of the sick people having recovered.' He travelled back to London, had his photograph taken at Bassano in Old Bond Street, saw a film at the Scala Theatre of the tanks in action at the battle of the Ancre – 'very good and oh how it makes one itch to be out and doing' – and caught the train to Radlett for London Colney aerodrome. That evening he wrote triumphantly to Caroline:

Here I am in the abode of the Gods! I found one Kay (my other late instructor at CFS with Muspratt and one of the four chosen by Capt Foot for this squadron) just arrived here so we are sharing a room. We had an awfully nice little supper in this jolly little mess, only about eighteen officers here, and the great Ball was there too. He is quite dark and very small and very unassuming and quiet. He has rows of medals thus. [Arthur here made a sketch of Ball's ribbons] Everything is very promising, but of course, I know nothing yet. The first SE5s are being fetched tomorrow, if fine. I hear that being in this squadron is *competitive*, ie some of us will be chucked out. You see it's absolutely the *tip top*, it and they are going to have a good lot, so I shall probably be sent into something else first. Nothing more now.

Love. A.

PS. Thank goodness I have left Filton.

The next evening he wrote to Nesta. After telling her of his adventures at Filton, he carried on:

We are very comfy here; a nice warm mess, excellent food and nice people. A1. CO and Flight Commanders and quite good quarters. I have been flying about, yesterday afternoon and this morning, on new types of machine – I mean machines I have never flown before, and an hour ago (5.30pm) the first two SE5s arrived from Farnborough by air. Captain Ball brought one.[1] A funny little dark fellow: very homely and absolutely no 'side' – with *rows* of medals. The machines look A1.

Arthur's next letter to Caroline told of a flying accident:

As regards Potts and his accident, lor lumme it *wasn't* me, and I'll take jolly good care that it won't be me this side of the water. I think Potts was a bit rash if not actually to blame. He had heaven's own luck in falling into trees. He was up and walking about this afternoon with a bandage round his head, and will probably be flying again in a fortnight. As I matter of fact I had a slight crash or two: I was diving at a target in a lake and firing at it from about 100ft, and when I pulled the machine out of her dive the engine wouldn't pick up, so of course I had to go down, and alighted

---

[1] This was 15 March 1917.

neatly on a hedge, sticking the nose down into the pond and the tail in the air! I was not even shaken. Spend all my time here either looping about in a scout or formation flying in some heavy old stagers we have here as well. Have not been up in an SE5 yet. Very windy most of the week.

He next wrote on 1 April:

There is a rumour going round that the Admiralty can't take our transport over for a fortnight, which I suppose will mean that we shall not fly over for a fortnight, but as usual things are in hopeless jumble as regards dates. General Henderson was down this afternoon to see his son (Capt Henderson, one of our Flight Commanders) who broke his nose in a smash a day or two ago and will not be coming out with us unfortunately. I spoke with the General about the engine in my machine, there being a complication as regards spares (my original engine was dud and had to be changed) owing to the differences between English (Wolseley) and French-made Hispanos – the name of the engine (viz.150 hp Hispano Suiza) on the SE5. I suddenly had the offer of a car ride up to town last night: got into town about 7. Knew it was hopeless to find anybody at that hour, so went to Rendezvous and had a very nice dinner, and then went and saw Romance – a very good show indeed, Doris Keene and Owen Nares acted splendidly, and a nice mixture of comedy and drama – well worth going for. I then caught last train to St Albans – got there at a quarter to one am! and walked about *9 miles* back to my billet in Radlett, getting into bed about 3.15am this morning! Luckily it was a very fine night. I am in a big house called Aldenham Lodge near Radlett station on a hill – sort of a residential club. Excuse great haste and scrawl.

This was Arthur's last letter from England. On Saturday, 7 April 1917, 56 Squadron left for France.

CHAPTER FIVE

The Great Adventure[1]

The long straight road from Doullens to Amiens runs almost due south through the open farmland of northern France. Despite the periodic bursts of noise and activity from the aerodrome, Vert Galant Farm, six miles south of Doullens, was a peaceful, rural spot: a small farmhouse on the west of the road; outbuildings, substantial brick barns on the east; and a quiet apple orchard behind the farm, were almost the only signs of human habitation between the two towns. The farm had been an aerodrome from the earliest days of the RFC in France and in April 1917 was the home of the fighter squadrons of 9th Wing, commanded by Lieutenant Colonel C.L.N. Newall, whose headquarters was at Fienvillers, six or seven miles to the north-west. On the evening of 7 April 1917, when the thirteen SE5s of 56 Squadron slipped in to land in the large field to the east of the road, the other two fighter squadrons of 9th Wing were already in residence: 66 Squadron, equipped with Sopwith Pups, on the smaller field to the west of the road, and 19 Squadron with Spads, the efficient little French fighter, on the east.

Accommodation at Vert Galant was limited and the arrival of 56 Squadron gave rise to a considerable amount of improvisation until the squadron could erect tents and organize its own messing facilities. Several officers – the lucky ones, as the weather was bitterly cold, with frequent snow showers – were billeted in the farmhouse itself, but the remainder were either under canvas at the northern end of the aerodrome or found corners for themselves in the outbuildings of the farm, their companion squadrons welcoming them into their messes until the squadron could set up its own cooking equipment.

The following morning, several practice flights were made to learn the country. Arthur took off at 10.45 with Leach and Lehmann and they flew near enough to the front line to see something of the war. Arthur's first morning in France was destined to be traumatic, almost a personal disaster, as it placed his future with 56 Squadron

[1] Letter from Caroline to Arthur: 'You have left on your great adventure.'

in some jeopardy. On returning from this practice flight he landed badly and overturned his SE5, breaking the fuselage in two and badly spraining his back. He wrote home that evening, detailing the events of the previous day and his own inconspicuous debut in the Great War:

8/4/17   56 Squadron.
                                          Royal Flying Corps
                                                         BEF.

All of you best beloved.

Here we are at last. I am writing this in a homely little French farm about twenty miles behind the lines, sitting in a nice quasi-parlour which is to be the Squadron mess, when at some unknown future date our transport arrives and we get settled. Tell my dear Sis Viv that I have not even had time to read her letter and that I hope she understands. And tell Mother that the letter with the unclassical handwriting was from the junior bursar at Eton containing my first £40 for the Newcastle! Well, perhaps I had better start from the beginning and tell you all about it.

I got back all safe by the 8.55 and got up at 7 am Saturday morning to find a bright promising day with a little ground mist about. I had a fearfully busy time getting my machine ready to go off, and could not get a message through to you at all, especially as I found that my fur cap, chin piece, and my nice goggles had all been blatantly stolen out of the sheds while I was away, which absolutely infuriated me. So I bought a very inferior pair of goggles from a pupil in the Reserve Squadron, and then flew all the way without a fur cap at all, just wrapping my scarf around my head. At first we heard it was misty over the Channel, but we eventually got off about noon, having decided to fly round north and east of London, crossing the Thames at Gravesend and going past Maidstone. Neither did we go in a 'V' formation, except the first five (including self). We crossed the Channel starting at 8000 and finishing up about 4000, as there were clouds on the French side. We saw one airship over the water, and a few warships off Calais, also a seaplane, but not much else. France looks absurdly different to England from the air: it all seems ploughed up in hundreds of patches, there are practically no hedges and the roads are very white and straight, and the railways mostly overgrown with grass.

Well, we all landed in fine style at St. Omer, and eventually got some lunch at 3.30 pm in the town itself: a delightful meal consisting of omelette, cold meat, figs and wine, also coffee. There was a man going back to England as soon as he could, so we all gave him wires to send off when he got back: I hope you got mine. About five we teed off again and came along to the aerodrome, flying nearly due south all the way. We all landed in fine style. There are 2 other squadrons here, both on single seater tractor scouts, one being 66, who seem to have picked up marvellously from their disastrous start, and are doing quite well. I am having meals with them until our mess gets properly started.

Last night I slept in a small, completely bare garret, out of a bed made of a little straw, four blankets and a *Warm*, which wasn't warm at all. Two others pinched a big mattress and made quite a reasonable bed of it, and between the 3 of us and the windows closed (sealed up!) we managed to keep fairly warm, though the walls are of canvas and reach halfway to the roof. This morning 4 of us went on a trial trip round the country, and for the first time I actually saw real war, absolutely *it* going on. There were about five balloons up, my dear Viv, and the h... of a strafe going on down below: we were only 1500 feet up and besides innumerable flashes there was an uncommonly large noise which made me periodically look round to see if my tail was there or not!

After passing over lots of famous battlefields (though what with keeping close to my formation and looking about I was very uncertain of my whereabouts) we came home, and I went and did just *the* last thing I wanted to do, viz. made a bad landing, went clear over upside down, smashed the whole machine and ricked my back rather severely. I hit my head a fairly good crump on the ground when I came over, and was left dangling upside down hanging on my belt which was most undignified! Which made me absolutely sick even unto death – completely fed up in fact: so was the CO. The indirect cause of my crash was that these goggles I bought came uncomfy in the air. I put up a hand to rearrange them and one glass came out, so I flew all the time without goggles, and I presume my eyes must have got watery or something, because I thought up to the last minute that I was making quite a fair landing – ie I thought I was about one foot off the ground when I was six! But that's no excuse for the crash, it was absolutely my fault. Thank goodness I am not the first one to have done it. The CO degraded himself by saying that in the Army if you lose things you have just got to pinch somebody else's!

Never mind, I am in France, and I have *seen the real thing* and been in action – just!

Best love to all – send me some cigarettes can you?

Arthur.

Before he had left England, Arthur had arranged a code with Vivien so that he could let her know his approximate whereabouts in France. If at Cambrai, he would address or refer to her as 'My Dear Sis'; if at St Quentin, as 'My Dear Buzzy'; if between the two as 'My Dear Viv'. If north of Arras he would use 'My Dear V'. His reference in the first letter to his 'dear sister Viv' successfully gave the family his location at the Front.

The crash which sent SE5 A4847 back to Candas for repair was to leave Arthur without an aeroplane for nearly a month, effectively grounding him and preventing him from taking any part in the initial patrols flown by the squadron. Owing to the amount of modifications to bring the first batch of SE5s to combat readiness, 56 Squadron did not fly its first patrol until the morning of 22 April, but Ball, flying a Nieuport 17, opened the squadron's score the following morning, sending an Albatros two-seater down to crash by the side of the Tilloy to Albancourt road.

Before Arthur made his first war flight, an escort in the early afternoon of 3 May, the squadron had flown over thirty offensive patrols and escorts, and had scored twenty victories. Most of the victories, of course, had gone to the experienced flight commanders – Ball, Meintjes and Crowe – but of the new boys, Barlow, Kay, Maxwell, Leach and Knaggs had all opened their accounts. To a boy of Arthur's temperament the situation must have been frustrating. Bearable, perhaps, while his fellow pilots were still testing and readying their aeroplanes, but well nigh intolerable after 22 April when war patrols commenced and he was left standing by as patrol after patrol of his comrades left the ground and returned with stories of the fighting and their first successes. While his strained back was mending he could rationalize his inactivity, but his next few letters home give some hint of his frustrations and his anxiety, hardly to be contemplated, that he might be posted out of the squadron.

14/4/17   56 Squadron.
Dearest Mother,

Just a brief line to say things are going moderately alright. My back is nearly alright, but not quite, and I have had a silly cold these last three days, and having no machine to concern myself with I have been wandering around doing nothing or being assistant Adjutant at the Squadron office, which means helping to sort maps, receive telephone messages, censor letters etc. The men's letters are really quite funny sometimes – very much in the style of Nesta's little orphan in Manchester. They never put in such luxuries as full stops or even commas, and they almost invariably end up with rows of crosses. Ball has got a baby Nieuport of his own – beside his SE5 – which he has now brought up to his own satisfaction – and had his first trip over the lines this morning. He had two scraps with no result: he is going off again tonight – that is all by himself: when he goes in the ordinary way with his Flight of the Squadron in formation he will take his SE5.[1] A baby Nieuport is about our best scout after the SE5, and Ball brought down nearly all his 30 Huns on them: they have a very small lower plane, a fat stumpy body, and are immensely strong: they climb to 10,000 feet in 8 minutes which is good going.

Did you see that poor Garnett was missing? He went down in flames on a Nieuport.[2] Did you get my last letter? All I want now is some baccy – not cigs – John Lofton Mild or Three Nuns. The first mail came today. Transport expected daily. Food very good. Weather fine but windy since yesterday, which is a great comfort: rain depresses one; Makes whole place so muddy. I have quite a cosy little garret to myself now, with a comfy mattress to sleep on.

Four days later he wrote again, making light of his fears of a posting out of the squadron. After thanking Caroline for a parcel and telling her it was not necessary to send tobacco as he had found that he could 'get some stuff nearly as good here' he carried on:

You say at the end of your letter, tell me you are none the worse, the machine mended and your face armour [word unreadable] Well the first and last are in fact alright, my new face apparatus having just arrived from London, but the machine was a complete goner from the start, in fact it went away the same day – almost a complete wreck. As regards the meanness of stealing: my dearest Ma, remember (a) in the Army the great thing is to pinch as much

[1] Ball disliked the SE5 and General Trenchard had allowed him the use of a Nieuport for his solo patrols.
[2] Lt W.P. Garnett, 60 Squadron. Killed 30 March 1917. Nieuport 17 A 273.

as you can for yourself and never mind anybody else. (b) there were others handy – ie another pair of goggles, but they were 'ration' stuff and no good – one must get good private ones if you want to be comfy. (c) no one thinks of providing stuff in case of losses, because first of all our squadron stores were packed up and gone, and secondly, the ordinary Army officer if he loses his own just goes and pinches somebody else's, which is what the CO said in so many words he thought I should have done, so of course a person like me gets ragged – but that can't be helped and I don't mind in the least. God knows, I *do* know that anything that hurts me gives you 'gooseflesh'. It must be so, considering what your blessed self is, but I wish it wasn't. These little things don't matter to me; thank God I have taken away with me so much of my dear Pa; and if they are nothing to me – I wish they would be nothing to you, that's all. And things might be far worse. So if I have worse crashes, you know it's only my husk that's hurt, and that doesn't count.

The luggage arrived two days ago which is very good. I had a fine day in bed yesterday, after a very tiring day running about in a tender or lorry over those vile French roads after various stores for the squadron. The dear old CO very sportingly said I could take a day in bed, which I did, and finished off the little pamphlet on the Poetic View of the World, which is good reading. But then as Blake said in a curious moment 'to generalize is to be an idiot' – almost as bad as the Irishman who said it was very unlucky to be superstitious. I think one can't *distinguish* philosophical religious and poetic world views, though each have their points, but it was absorbing reading and taught me a lot. Then I read some 400 lines of Euripides and wrote 3 or 4 letters, altogether very delightful, though my little garret was a bit dingy. I share it now with the equipment officer of the squadron, a very amiable, extremely businesslike and commonplace young man, very like the others.

Nothing much is happening. Having no machine I am general handyman to the squadron and do all the odd jobs and racketing about, which might be worse. I believe there is a chance that I may be pushed off to another squadron which is in need of a pilot, and as I am not of any immediate and compelling need here. God forbid, but it doesn't really matter. It will probably be a Nieuport squadron if I do go, and a baby Nieuport is a heavenly machine, only it hasn't got the pace of the SE5 and has only one gun. And I shall meet many of my old CFS friends, but I think I shall manage to stay here, and I know the CO wants to keep me. We get all the English papers here the day after issue, or the French papers of the day, but any big news we always hear by message over the phone – hear before you do. The guns are always going at night. We have about 100 German prisoners mending our roads and building our huts for us. All of the same type, sturdy surly looking beggars with one or two intelligent looking faces. The Squadron mess is getting quite swagger now: we have 2 ground floor rooms of the farm, one dining room where the whole 17 (so far) of us feed, and this room, containing piano, gramophone, ½ dozen deck chairs and a stove. I have visions of another poem coming. It started yesterday in bed I think: anyhow it's about you. I haven't settled the metre yet, but things are simmering. Weather still bad, windy with rain and much mud. I have ample clothes, bedding etc. On the whole I might be a great deal worse off. But I want to start work. I find I have the French accent and a few idioms, but I am short of vocabulary and sometimes not sure of grammar. I can always get along though.

Best of love. Give N a kiss.

Arthur.

On 22 April he wrote again, still trying to alleviate his mother's fears for his safety and well-being.

Two letters of yours received, the first of which took over a week in coming, and I presume mine must have taken a long time in getting to you. Candidly dearest, your first letter almost annoyed me. For heaven's sake remember, if you don't hear as soon as you think you should, it is alright. *Silence* means I am alright and have no time to write: if anything goes wrong I shall write at once, as I did about that smash. Anyhow this is my 4th letter in a fortnight, apart from one to Viv I sent a few days ago. Thank God the fine weather has come at last, though the high winds are a great nuisance. I go for a walk every evening between 7.30 and 8.15 all by myself, and the sunset quite cheers me up. I have had some splendid letters already from my old pals, they are quite invaluable. I have not yet got a machine but my back is quite alright. I am getting quite restless not having been in the air for a fortnight – and seeing these other people buzz off every day.

We started work proper today; result – 2 Huns both brought down by Ball, who was away on his own. The second time he tackled 5 Hun scouts single handed, brought down one and the other 4, after making a nasty mess of his machine, cleared off. I really am getting along jolly well, *but* (a) it is sickening being 'odd man out' with no machine. I don't count the five new people who have just been shoved on to us, and are in the same position as me: they hardly seem part of the squadron yet. And I am longing to be flying again and after Huns. (b) there are only one or two people in the squadron I have the faintest hope of making a real pal of, and it is next to impossible that I can do even that. They are all just the 'ordinary good fellows' with nothing remarkable about them; none of them have any real intellectual ambitions. *But* I AM IN FRANCE AND DOING THE REAL THING AT LAST!!!

Arthur's reference to 'ordinary good fellows' shows more than just a touch of intellectual snobbery in his make-up, plus an almost arrogant assumption of his own superiority. His earlier remark, that he found the squadron equipment officer, H.N. Charles, 'a commonplace young man', despite the rather condescending acknowledgement that he was 'amiable and businesslike', shows a lack of understanding and sympathy for the worth of others. In his own field, engineering, Charles was certainly the equal of Arthur in his. Charles was a brilliant engineer, with an honours degree in engineering before he was twenty, and the success of the SE5 and the SE5a was, in no small measure, due to his expert modifications to its engine and carburettor.

Perhaps Arthur's attitude is understandable in a boy only a few months out of the rather rarified atmosphere enjoyed by a classical scholar at Eton. His shocked reaction to Major Blomfield's suggestion that he should have 'pinched' somebody's goggles to replace his own which had been stolen, and his reference to the ragging he came in for over his attitude to this advice, illustrates how difficult it must have been for the young men of his generation, many of whom had led extremely sheltered lives – even by the standards of the day – to adjust to the hurly-burly of army life.

Arthur's next letter to his mother, written on 28 April, holds out hope for an aeroplane of his own and gives news of Ball's continued success:

Absolutely nothing has happened – just the same: weather fine but with a cold wind: tonight it is dull but warmer. I believe I am getting a new machine in a few days time. Meanwhile Ball brought down two more Huns yesterday, making a total of 7 in three days. This time he was alone against about 15 Huns and fired away every cartridge he had on board. He deserves the VC 3 times over.

On 29 April Arthur collected SE5 A4867 from No 2 Aeroplane Depot at Candas, flying it back to Vert Galant. A4867 was the penultimate SE5 of the first production batch. The following day he ferried SE5 A4868, the last machine of the initial production series, from St Omer to Vert Galant, landing at 2.00 pm. Two hours later he left for Candas to collect yet another SE5: A8902, the fourth SE5 of the second production series. This latest SE5, which had modified wingtips, improving the aileron control, was allocated to Gerald Maxwell, but Arthur was given A4868. He at last had an aeroplane of his own and his delight is evident in his letter home detailing his ferrying activities.

May 1st.   56 Squadron.
Dearest Mums,
    Today is the 1st of May – gorgeous weather, which now, thank the good God, is keeping up. It makes an enormous difference to me. Anyhow, things are moving at last. On Sunday I went to our 'base' or aircraft depot for a new machine: while waiting for it to be finished I had a 'joyride' in an artillery machine which was being tested – that was the first time I had been up for three weeks. Then I took this new machine across country to the aerodrome and managed to get down without smashing anything this time – though the landing was by no means perfect! She bounced once but I gave her a little engine and somehow I felt the wheels running along the floor, so I just shut off the engine and slowed down – don't know how I managed it. This was after making one attempt and going round again as it didn't shape well. I mean the last hundred feet of the glide. Then yesterday I had another joyride in an artillery machine – an old BE2c (Nesta might know what that is – she saw lots at Colney) up to the depot in the north where we originally landed in France – about 60 miles away, for another new bus. On arriving there I ran into that quaint Canadian who used to be in my room at Oxford. He was very effusive and kind: gave me a wash and brush up in his billet before I went back.
    Just before I left I heard he was posted to No.40 Squadron on

Nieuports – the CO is an Old Etonian named Tilney who used to command 'D' Squadron (Pusher) at CFS whose bowling I have often played at the old place. Well I brought this second new bus from the depot down alright, nearly lost my way once, but found it again at once, and this time I made a better landing about 2 pm. At 4 I was rushed off again to that other depot – which is only about 7 miles away, and at 8.30 pm I brought yet a third new machine over here – it has different shaped wings which make it much less sloppy on the ailerons ie the lateral control (for explanation apply to N and tell her the ailerons are on the edges of the planes and are moved by waggling the stick from side to side – and she will remember me showing her how things worked in the Bristol Scout at Colney). And the 2nd machine I brought – the one from the northern depot – is to be *mine*, what ho! and I should be busy attending to it now and not writing this letter. It's having various alterations done as usual, and should be quite a good one by the time it is ready, which should be tomorrow morning.

So at last I have started aviating again, and having made quite a 1st class landing the third time I don't think I need worry about that anymore – it's merely getting used to landing the particular machine. By the way, as regards the cap and goggles. I got these sent out years ago from a shop in town where I bought the first set; so that's alright too.

Well, having been at work for a week we have accounted for 14 Huns, ma chère, which is a jolly good start. Yesterday I'm afraid we had our first casualty. Poor old Kay, who with Muspratt taught me to fly at CFS, is missing.[1] Three SE5s were tackled by 8 Huns, we got two and perhaps a third, but poor Kay just vanished. So he is over in Hunland somewhere, whether dead or alive we don't know.

Well I shall be busy in earnest for the next day or two getting my machine in order. Well, best love to all and I hope you understand re photos how flat this place is.

After a brief test on the evening of 2 May, A4868 and Arthur were ready for the war, and next morning Arthur made his first war flight: an escort to the Martinsydes of 27 Squadron on a bombing raid to Don. Taking off after lunch, Arthur, Leach and Barlow met the

[1] 2nd Lt Maurice Alfred Kay, killed in action 30 April 1917. 56 Squadron's first casualty.

bombers over Fienvillers and escorted them to and from their target. Arthur later wrote to Vivien:

3/5/17   56 Squadron.
Dearest V,
    Just a brief line, can't write much now as I have so many others to write. However, I enclose a piece of my joystick as promised and as well a small piece of wood which once formed a vital part of Capt Ball's machine which was fractured by a direct hit from 'Archie'. He has got 8 Huns in our first week's work, making a total of 37 altogether! The squadron has got 17 altogether in 8 days – some going. . . Today I had my first trip over the lines, escorting a bomb raid. Not a Hun to be seen in the sky, but we had a little Archie – rather amusing than otherwise. Fine weather is lovely and I have been very busy these last two or three days and have had no time to write, but now my machine is OK and I have settled down and have some time. Yesterday night I had a game of badminton on an improvised court; we are also making a tennis lawn. By the way, heaps of thanks for that delightful letter, I haven't had time to think about it yet. About you sending on letters to Mum – so nice of you to ask – if there is anything in them you think Mums would particularly like to know, well, send it on, but as a rule I should say don't send them on, because I'm not afraid of making you anxious, but will not depress Mother. Well, I'm quite cheery but I always have that quaint feeling of complete isolation: but there are one or two people in the squadron I might make a good pal of – just one or two.

Arthur next flew on 5 May: the 'early show', leaving the ground at 5 am. With Captain Crowe leading, the five SEs – Crowe, Barlow, Chaworth-Musters, Hoidge and Arthur – patrolled from Cambrai to Estrées. Between Estrées and Courcelette, flying at 10,000 feet, they sighted what appeared to be a formation of friendly Nieuports, five hundred feet above them. As the SEs passed under them, however, the 'Nieuports' dived to attack the British patrol, making off after a brief skirmish. These 'Nieuports' were Siemens Schuckert D1s, a German copy of the Nieuport and in general configuration enough like the little French fighter to mislead the experienced Crowe. The SEs then attacked an enemy two-seater over Noyelles, but all overshot it in their eagerness and it dived away towards Douai. The bright sun and a ground mist now made visibility extremely bad and the patrol returned to Vert Galant.

Arthur had no more patrols for the remainder of the day and the following day he wrote to Nesta, telling her how he had occupied his time. He adored his younger sister and in many ways they were closer to each other than the other members of the family. With Nesta there was no need to live up to his reputation as a scholar and thinker, no need of pretence, no need for any philosophical reflections or literary aspirations; Arthur could be completely the boy he still was, for all his academic brilliance. He knew exactly the style of letter Nesta would enjoy:

6/5/17 56 Squadron.
Dearest Kiddie,

Just a 'urried page to thank you ever so much for your delightful if illiterate letter, and also for the photos therein, which I think are jolly good. In the one of us all 3, don't you think it looks as though I had arms like a gorilla – right round Father and Viv; and Viv doesn't seem too cheerful, perhaps owing to my Sam Browne sticking into her or a fly on her nose or some other national calamity. Bar that, good picture. The one of me and Father also v good. Father looks as if he's lost the top of his head somewhere and was trying to remember where he had left it.

This gorgeous sun is glorious for you, but it's everything out here. Today there is a bright sun, but the deuce of a wind blowing from the east which is apt to unfrigerate the atmosphere, rather more than is compatible with one's internal felicity. Yesterday, having been over the lines on the early show – 5 am off the ground – I had nothing else to do for the rest of the day, after a few little things to be seen to with regards to my machine, and in the afternoon I went about two miles from the aerodrome and lay down in a little copse of young trees on top of a rise in the ground, and felt very happy.

A little yellow bird came and perched about 2 yards from me and looked around as if he knew there was *something* queer about, but he didn't quite know what. He took about five minutes making up his great mind, and then – no, he didn't lay an egg, nor did he have a bath, but he just moved up one twig and began washing his face ie. polishing his beak! I offered to lend him my handkerchief (silk, one, officers and birds for the use of) but he said he had one, only he didn't know which pocket it was in for the moment. On the way back I found a poor little bird with a crumpled right plane, so I pursued him and having captured him skeefully in my hat I was

proceeding to see if his crossbracing wires were alright when he
suddenly endeavoured to detach a lump of flesh from my
forefinger with extreme asperity. So I desposited him gently on the
ground and told him to go and bathe it and I would send the bill in
later. He hopped off and seemed quite bucked with life, so I left
him in peace. Must stop, have told Mum all the news and you will
no doubt get it forwarded. Enclosed please find one little knife as
keepsake.

He also wrote to his Mother, more disenchanted in tone; his attitude
to the war was already hardening a little:

I have now been over the lines twice; once escorting a bomb raid
and the next morning at 5 am five of us started off for a patrol. It
was rather misty and mysterious: anyhow, my machine was not
going quite right, but we did not see any Huns. Very good fun on
the whole. That was yesterday. The day before I fetched another
new machine from the northern depot, after a 70 mile ride in a car
to get there. We fairly buzzed along all through the brown and
barren country. A few woods breaking out, a few little slopes up to
600 and the rest a great patchwork of brown fields and poplar
lined roads. My God, how this weather makes me hate the whole
damned business: I would give anything for a friend worth calling
one – and some hills, and above all some freedom. And I have just
got a letter from Wilcox who is now back in a London hospital,
after a month's service, with appendicitis. I enclose a little trinket
I picked up in . . . as a present for Father. If he doesn't want it will
you keep it your dear self. Have bought a Victor Hugo (selection)
but have not started reading it yet. Best love to the dear Pa, am
writing to N but am telling her to expect this letter. And this is a
bit of 'La Belle' France! My hat!

The next patrol in which Arthur took part was to have a disastrous
outcome for 56 Squadron. The weather conditions on 7 May had
deteriorated during the day and by the afternoon storm clouds began
to gather. The general opinion was that there would be no more
flying that day, but while the squadron was at tea orders came
through from Wing HQ to fly the scheduled evening patrol in the
Cambrai – Douai area. People in the squadron at this time, recalling
the events of the evening, have said that a challenge had been
dropped to von Richthofen's Jasta II to meet this patrol, but no one

(Left) Caroline Augusta Foley in 1893, just before her marriage. (Right) Professor Thomas William Rhys Davids and Caroline Rhys Davids in 1894.

Arthur, Vivien, Nesta 1907–1908.

(Left) Arthur in 'Snowdon Country', summer 1904. *(Right)* Professor Rhys Davids with Vivien, Nesta and Arthur, 1905.

(Left) Arthur on Scafell, August 1906. 'The tallest man in England'. *(Right)* Brynhilda, 1902.

The Gymnasium Eight, Summerfields School, summer term 1910.
(Back row L to R) French, Arthur, Peto, Jacques.
(Front row L to R) Kemm, Udny, Sergeant Morley, Champernowne, Fenwick.

(Left) The new King's Scholar. Entry to Eton 1911. (Right) Captain of School. Leaving Eton 1916.

(Left) Arthur as a newly commissioned Second Lieutenant in the Royal Flying Corps.
(Right) 'It looks as if I had arms like a gorilla – right round Father and Viv.' Arthur with his father and Vivien.

Newly commissioned: Arthur, left, with Lieutenants Clarke and Pierce. Exeter College Oxford, Summer 1916.

Arthur and Keith Knox Muspratt in a Bristol S 2A 'Sociable'. Central Flying School, Upavon, 1916.

The Sopwith Pup. 'She came round on turns like greased lightning, right up on one side, altogether quite lovely'.

(Right) Captain Albert Ball at London Colney, March 1917. 'He is quite dark and very small and very unassuming and quiet'.

(Below) London Colney. 56 Squadron leaving for France on the morning of 7 April 1917. Albert Ball's aeroplane just in front of the others.

Arthur Percival Foley Rhys Davids. March 1917.

(Left) B Flight Commander: Captain Cyril Marconi 'Billy' Crowe. 'Our excellent leader'.
(Right) Leutnant Kurt Wolff: '. . . the tiresome young man in the red bus'.

At Estrée Blanche. Lt Taylor, Lt Reason, Lt Johnston, Arthur.

Thais Marson and Arthur. . . .
'a perfectly delightful girl of
eight, who has stepped
straight out of a Greek vase'.

Lt Cecil Lewis, Capt Geoffrey
Hilton 'Beery' Bowman, Capt
Ian Henderson, Lt V. P.
Cronyn, Thais Marson, Arthur.

Picnic lunch at Bekesbourne:
Ruth Eadon, Arthur, Nasra
Eadon, Mrs Maybery, Richard
Maybery.

(Left) Major Richard Graham Blomfield. Commanding Officer 56 Squadron from February to October 1917. The door of his office in the background has the famous sign, 'Enter without Knocking'. (Right) On Leave in August 1917. Arthur in a confident mood, wearing his MC and Bar.

'The Children'. Keith Muspratt, Arthur, Maxwell Coote. Only Coote survived the war.

The SE5a. Alongside its contemporary, the Sopwith Camel, the SE5a was the most successful fighter aeroplane of the RFC/RAF during the 1914–1918 war. B4897, shown here, is typical of the SE5a's used by 56 Squadron during the summer and autumn of 1917.

'The Office'. The cockpit of an SE5a. A view familiar to Arthur.

(Left) Leutnant Karl Schaefer, Staffel Führer Jasta 28. 'I wanted to go up close and watch his flying instead of scrapping'.

(Below) '. . . the type of thing I see in the air everyday'. The Albatros scouts of von Richthofen's Jasta 11 lined up on the aerodrome at Roucourt, near Douai. The second machine is von Richthofen's red Albatros D.III.

(Right) Lieutenant M. A. Kay (at back), 56 Squadron's first casualty, was killed in action on 30 April 1917. *(Front)* Lieutenant Keith Knox Muspratt MC.

(Below) The DFW CV 799/17 of Flt Abt 7 crewed by Leutnant Mann and Uffz Hahnel shot down by Arthur and Keith Muspratt on 12 July 1917.

Leutnant Werner Voss. Voss was flying this Fokker Triplane in his last fight. McCudden wrote . . . 'his flying was wonderful, his courage magnificent . . . the bravest German airman whom it has been my privilege to see fight.'

(Top left) Lieutenant Leonard Monteagle Barlow MC and 2 Bars. *(Right)* Captain Richard Aveline Maybery MC and Bar. . . . 'a damn fine scrapper and a "pukka" gentleman'. *(Bottom left)* Leutnant Karl Gallwitz, Jasta Boelcke. Arthur Rhys Davids was his fourth victory.

Arthur Percival Foley Rhys Davids.
The Orpen portrait.

remembers seeing this actually taken or dropped and it seems unlikely that such a challenge was issued.

Officers serving with anti-aircraft batteries in the Arras area had told Major Blomfield that each evening a large number of enemy aeroplanes were in the habit of congregating in the area, keeping just to their own side of the front line, and it was understood that these were aeroplanes of the Richthofen Jasta. Blomfield had obtained permission from Wing to attack this enemy formation at the first opportunity, and this no doubt was the origin of the 'challenge' rumour. The fact remains, however, that the squadron did mount an unusually large patrol that evening. Eleven SE5s – the order from Wing had only specified six – left the ground at 5.30 and made for the patrol area.

The weather was very bad: thick layers of cumulus cloud ranged from 2,000 to 10,000 feet, with gaps of various sizes between them. Ball, leading A Flight, crossed the lines south of the Cambrai–Bapaume road. Flying at 7,000 feet, and whenever possible keeping just below the clouds as a precaution against attack, they flew a course to take them to the north of Cambrai. The rest of the formation climbed to 9,000 feet. C Flight – Meintjes leading Hoidge, Lewis and Melville – went north-east towards Cambrai; B Flight – Crowe leading Leach, Chaworth-Musters and Arthur – passing over them at 10,000 feet and flying a course to take them south of Cambrai.

Over the Bois-de-Bourlon area, B Flight ran into a thick bank of cloud which took them some time to get through. Chaworth-Musters had left the formation just before it entered the cloud and had gone in pursuit of an aeroplane. Arthur saw him enter the cloud some five hundred yards behind and slightly lower than the other SEs. He was not seen again.[1] Crowe, Leach and Arthur came out of the cloud over the Arras to Cambrai road, just above the railway station of Sauchy-Lestrée. Crowe and Leach then attacked an enemy scout, an Albatros, flying at 8,000 feet just to the south of Vitry, and in his second attack Leach sent the enemy down to crash to the east of the town.

Arthur had been about to join in the attacks on this Albatros when he was attacked by another, coming from the direction of Douai. This Albatros, coloured red, with a green band round the fuselage behind the pilot's cockpit, was flown by Leutnant Kurt Wolff, a

---

[1] Shot down and killed by Ltn Werner Voss of Jagdstaffel Boelcke.

leading member of von Richthofen's Jasta II, with, at this time, over
twenty victories to his credit. Arthur was unaware that he was under
attack until he saw Wolff's tracers. He admitted this in his combat
report, adding that the enemy scout's guns were 'very silent'. He
evaded Wolff's initial pass and a duel for position followed. Arthur
had jams in both his Vickers and Lewis guns, but he managed to get
up to Wolff's height and take evading action. But in his first pass
Wolff had hit the SE5 in the engine, undercarriage and wings and
Arthur was in an extremely hazardous position.

While he was considering how best to extricate himself from the
combat, Wolff, for some unknown reason, broke off the fight and
dived away towards Douai. Arthur, his engine streaming water,
turned west and made for the safety of the British lines. Two miles
west of Arras his engine finally seized up. He attempted to glide to
Belle Vue, the advanced landing ground, but he had insufficient
height and made a forced landing in a field near La Herlière.

At Vert Galant, as the endurance time of the SE5s came and then
passed, anxious groups searched the eastern sky. Only two SEs had
returned, Maxwell and Melville, but there was still no sign of the
others. Then, on the last dregs of their petrol, Knaggs, Lewis and
Hoidge appeared and came down over the edge of the aerodrome. All
three were eagerly questioned, but only Knaggs had any good news
to report: he had seen Arthur's SE down in a field, apparently
undamaged. There was no sign of the others. Of the eleven SEs
which had left Vert Galant, only six were accounted for. Arthur was
believed safe, but what of the others: Ball, Crowe, Meintjes – all
three flight commanders – plus Leach and Chaworth-Musters.
Blomfield and Marson, the adjutant, began telephoning along the
front for news.

Slowly it began to come in. Crowe had landed safely at Naval 8's
aerodrome and Leach, wounded in the leg, was in No 4 Canadian
Hospital, but by midnight it was only too evident that the remainder
– Ball, Meintjes and Chaworth-Musters – were either dead or
prisoners of war. Next morning brought the welcome news that
Meintjes had force-landed near Gouy with a fractured forearm, but
there was still no news of Ball or Chaworth-Musters.

The reason for Kurt Wolff breaking off the combat with Arthur
will never be known – his own guns may have jammed or he may
have been low on fuel or ammunition – but there can be no doubt
that Arthur had flown extremely well against a vastly more
experienced opponent. He had remained cool and kept turning,

denying Wolff an easy shot, and attempting to gain precious height despite the pressure he was under. It was an indication of his future worth as an airfighter. The next day Arthur wrote to Vivien, describing the fight:

Just a hurried line to enclose one trinket, sisters for the use of, which I picked up in the neighbouring city of Blank of which you have no doubt heard. I have already sent N a similar one, and Father a gold one for a birthday present. I hope you got my previous consignment of curious goods: I sent it off about a week ago, or rather less. By the way, before I forget, your little writing pad was so extraordinarily useful, or rather still is, that I should very much like to have another if you can remember where you got it. It is called the 'Allies' writing pad, if that is any use. I have about umpteen, in other words, two other pads, but I always carry the little one in my pocket, and it will not be very long before it is finished, and I shall want another pocket one.

I still have had no time to have a think over your great letter, but you see with the weather so fine one is either flying or seeing to one's machine or guns and ammunition most of the day, and the rest I spend in reading papers, writing letters, or in affable if pointless conversation – a great deal too much really. My little garret is getting quite attractive now. Now I am alone I have half a dozen photos of my pals up on the canvas wall, six in uniform, and six old Eton photos and one of Father and you, I wish I had one of Mums and Nesta. I thought I had, but can't find any.

As regards this tedious war, the expected thing has happened. I had my first 'pukka' scrap last night, and was shot down. No, don't get alarmed, I'm not writing this from Hunland, and I was not officially shot down, because for some curious reason my machine is intact, but the fact remains that I was hopelessly beaten and shot down. We had a big show on, starting at 5.30 pm, with a large number of our machines out, and eventually 3 of us, my flight commander, Leach (an old CFS instructor and one of the stoutest fellows I have ever met) and myself got separated from the others in the clouds and after cruising around a bit we saw a Hun, a bright red beggar below us; this was about 5-10 miles over the lines. Down went the flight commander and down went I after him, but thank goodness that somehow I managed to remember to look behind me first, and saw another bright red and green beggar coming down on to my tail. So I came up again and we began turning round and round, he diving and firing at me, and then climbing up again, while I had all my work cut out to get out of the light and to climb up to him gradually.

Meanwhile I had heard one bullet go into my undercarriage with the deuce of a whonk, one or two others were making themselves unpleasant by spoiling the appearance of my immaculate planes, and the tiresome young man in the red bus finally was unkind enough to plonk one into my engine, which we found out afterwards made a hole six inches square in the water jacket. Then for some curious reason he completely sheered off, or in other words, cleared off towards Hunland ie. the east. And I knowing very well my engine was wounded, proceeded to turn west, and after about five minutes, during which time I must have covered about ten to twelve miles (aided by a strong E wind) the engine stopped altogether. So after gliding as far as I could – from 7,000 feet – I perched neatly in a field not far from another aerodrome where I got help and stayed the night. Today we took the machine to pieces and brought it back here on a lorry, and I hope to put it together again tomorrow.

Anyhow, I'm jolly lucky to have got off so light, the man up against me was obviously a far better pilot and fighter than I was – one of the few Hun pros I expect. I can't think why he left me when he had me stony as if I had had to go on turning much longer I should not have been able to get so far over the lines with my glide, which would have meant alighting in a dugout or minecrater or some other disused patch of earth, in which case the bus would have displayed an alarming tendency to lay on its back and kick its dearie legs in the air. Why it didn't anyhow, in the field, I can't think. Old Hun, of course, didn't know he had plugged my engine. Never mind, I got a jolly good feed at noon at the cookhouse of a neighbouring RE Dump before we started packing the machine up and that fortunately lasted me till dinner at 8 tonight.

And now having umpteen letters to compose and having not much more to say in addition to the news you will get some time in my last letter to Mother the day before yesterday, I will conclude by wishing you a very good night. Please send this on to Mums as soon as may be because I strike at writing it all out again for the family. Ah, this terrible war. My bus looks so silly in the lorry – like a dog down a rabbit hole.

Love A.

PS. The result of our show was that we got four certain, perhaps more, and have lost two plus 2 other pilots including Leach wounded. I am terribly afraid the wonderful little man is one of the missing – you know who. All the best Huns were up against us.

Arthur missed writing on one side of a sheet in this letter and he used it to send a further postscript:

(I have omitted to use this space, can't think why. Anyhow let it represent my frame of mind when I was waltzing around with that Hun. My mind was 'a perfect blank ruled over by a few hard and fast lines' which I followed for some reason. Bless that Hun: he was a beautiful flyer and he was jolly decent to buzz off just when he was winning hard: curious fellow – doesn't approve of too much war, same as me.)

Vivien sent this letter to her Mother, who in turn sent it to Nesta:

My Sweetheart,

I pass on from Vivien a letter – it was very nearly being no letter but a War Office telegram reporting Arthur as 'missing' – the sort of telegram, or worse, that I look for daily now. How the squadron is thinning off! Kay and Ball missing, Leach and another wounded! It is a very very modest account; not a word of any shots of his fired at the Hun, and no sign of any idea of turning tail when he first found he had to play up singlehanded against an expert. The Hun may have sheered off 1. because he had no ammunition left, 2. because he himself was hit 3. saw others approaching 4. was that rara avis, a sporting Hun and judged he was fighting a babe. The last is very improbable, but not impossible.

The next patrol flown by Arthur was on the morning of 12 May. Led by Gerald Maxwell, six SEs took off at 8 am and crossed the lines over Arras, flying north towards La Bassée. East of Lens, the flight sighted a patrol of ten Albatros scouts, a thousand feet below them, and Maxwell led the SEs down to attack. The enemy scouts scattered quickly and only one was engaged at worthwhile range. Maxwell, Broadberry and Lloyd attacked this Albatros from a hundred yards but it dived steeply away into the clouds. The remainder of the patrol was uneventful and the SEs returned to Vert Galant. Arthur wrote to Caroline, a hurriedly scribbled letter, at 6.00 pm, half an hour before he was due to leave on the evening patrol:

I sent Viv a line about 3 days ago about my first scrap and the sequel, which you have probably got from her by now. Since then nothing much has happened except that I have changed my quarters from the top floor – my little garret in the farm which contains our two mess rooms – to one portion of what is known as a 'Nissen Hut'. We have four of them side by side, and they are made of wood with circular corrugated iron roofs.

Each is divided into compartments, usually one half from the other and across the middle and one half bisected again by a partition up the centre. All the partitions are a kind of brown canvas, floors just boards, but I have bought a straw mat and also a 'descent delit' in other words a 'get-out-of-bed' alias a very nice quite ordinary little flooring of carpetlet.

My little den is about four or five yards long and three across at the bottom, and I have got the sunny side of the hut looking out on the aerodrome, with a quaint little suburban garden in front consisting of a circular bed with some bedraggled daisies and violets in and 2 outer beds with nothing in them at all except Mother Earth and some choice weeds. The man next door did it before I came in – appalling effort. I have got all my photos up round the room and a row of books on an excellent fold-up wood and wicker table I have bought in the town where I first landed in France ie. on the aerodrome near where I first landed – we bar landing in market squares. Beyond the garden is a badminton court and beyond that a new cinder tennis court which we have just made with the assistance of Hun prisoners – a healthy looking lot who work very well and seem quite happy if sullen.

By the way, would you send along my white flannels and that pair of tennis boots I believe I have got somewhere at home. I was on the first show this morning at 8, my 4th time over, and I am going again at 6.30 pm – in half an hour's time. Wherefore I must stop pro tem and see that everything is OK. Beyond the tennis court is the aerodrome – my hut faces due south and has a window 4 feet square, which is immense. Have just been reading Henley again: do you remember 'The Song of the Sword'. Is it true? I don't think so at present. But I love 'What is to Come' – thoroughly agree. Love to all. A.

Crowe led the evening patrol, a strong force of eight SEs. The

German anti-aircraft fire – popularly known as 'Archie' – was intense and Lieutenant Jessop's aeroplane received a direct hit, spun for a few hundred feet, then broke to pieces in mid-air. The remaining patrol members, badly shaken by this sickening sight, returned to Vert Galant.

Gerald Maxwell led Arthur and four other SEs in the first patrol of the morning of 13 May. The weather was bad at take-off and after a short time the visibility became so poor that Maxwell decided it was pointless to carry on and fired the washout signal. Arthur's SE developed engine trouble on the way back and he was forced to land in a field near Doullens. Barlow landed to asertain the cause of the trouble and took off again to fetch help. It was hot in the field and Arthur took off his flying clothes and sat in the shade of a nearby haystack to await the arrival of the squadron tender and mechanics. While there he wrote to Nesta:

13/5/17   France.
                                           Under a haystack in a field.
                                              10 miles from nowhere.

Dearest N.

Your delightful if brief letter announcing purchase of wool received yesterday. May it soon coagulate into a pair of foot preservers, but please don't hurry as I have plenty in stock. The reason one is always wanting new ones is that it is so hard to get them at all decently darned in these furrin parts.

Glad you approve of St Pauls but sickening about Brit. Mus. hibernating like that. Did you get my last letter with small present enclosed? I have since sent Viv a similar one.

Now as to why I am at this strange address. I was on two shows yesterday: 8 am and 6.30 pm and with a test flight for guns in the middle I did 5 hours flying in the day and so I had done well. On both patrols I saw one or two Huns in the distance, and in the evening one 2 of them – big two seaters – came round behind me when we had just turned round after going some way back over their lines. I was last man in the formation. I nearly went back and tackled them but one is supposed to stick to the formation, so I thought discretion the better part of valour, and beetled off again *quam celerrime*. Then I was on the early show this morning. I got up at 5.30 am. We didn't go off until 6.30 as the weather conditions were doubtful, but eventually we pushed off. However, when we had been out about ¾ hour the leader apparently thought it was no good and came home. We came along in a series of dives right down from 10,000 feet to about 1500, and at that height we waddled along over the country towards the aerodrome.

At this thrilling juncture of the game my engine suddenly had a fit and declined to rotate, in other words struck work, or as it is popularly known in the RFC, 'conked'. So I hastily looked about for a field, and by great good luck happened to find a nice long narrow strip, where I accordingly perched with great éclat, and as on my previous forced landing (after that scrap which you will know all about by the time you get this) to my huge amazement the machine stuck the right way up and showed no tendency to lie on its back and kick its dearie legs in the air. Then one of the other chaps came and landed by me, saw what was wrong, and buzzed off again to send my men along and get things right. Also two cooks from a neighbouring labour camp turned up and lent a hand – one from Liverpool, the other from Oldham! Now they have gone away to direct my tender when it turns up and not a soul has been near since.

So here I am all alone with a gorgeous May sun and a little finicky breeze making things so nice, with a lark or two above simply bursting with the joy of life. I can just hear the guns going but bar that the war seems very far away, thank God. It seems such blasphemy to wage war in weather like this. It's quite lovely tootling back from a patrol in the evening knowing your day's work is done, with the West aflame and the East dimly mysterious. Anyhow, I am having an incredibly good time. I do so hope you have a good time with your bike and the hills and the river. O you lucky angel! there isn't a hill or a drop of running water for miles around the aerodrome. Only a few stagnant pools that we fire at from the air to test our guns. Never mind, I have about a dozen photos I love, and about eight books which make all the difference in the world, and I am always looking for most scrummy letters. I am afraid I hate the whole business like poison: I wish it would show some signs of ending this year.

Meanwhile it is 11 o'clock and I had a cup of tea and a bit of bread and butter at 5.15 am and nothing since. I call it a shame. Are you one of the Kernit tennis players in the School nowadays? And are you prefect, priest, potato peeler or any other high official? Or just unofficial 'great man': so much the best.

Best love and please send to Mum.

A.

Caroline commented on this letter to Nesta. 'It is interesting and poignantly so to see how the clean sweet message of Spring makes him call out against the whole hideous business and his own mental loneliness.'

For the next four days the weather conditions were too bad for any war flying and Arthur, in common with many other pilots, went into Amiens to shop for a few comforts and see the sights. On 18 May he wrote to Caroline, continuing the story of the forced landing and bringing her up to date on the latest news.

18/5/17   56 Squadron.
Dearest Mother,

Just some pages to say nothing has happened, the weather being dud. I forget when I wrote last, but anyhow about the 13th I went on my 5th patrol which was quite a tiny one, and coming back low over the country my engine conked ie. stopped and I had to land about 10 miles from the aerodrome – I forget if I told you or not – anyhow by great good luck I found a convenient field underneath me, stubble baked hard by the sun, where I perched with great éclat. Another fellow in the patrol landed by me, and went off to tell them what was wrong – this was about 8.30 am and then I waited by the machine till my mechanics turned up which was 12.30. Meanwhile I sat down under the lee of a stupid looking haystack which was dozing in the sun near by (by the way, does one 'dose' or 'doze') and composed a letter to the dear Nesta, with full details which she has probably sent on to you. Eventually at 12.15 I wearied of waiting, and went down and got some lunch at the mess of a Labour Battalion with some officers of the Cheshire Regiment – one old gasbag who had been in the Army for thirteen years and had joined the RFC and been kicked out: but he was most hospitable and gave me an excellent lunch. There was a vast crowd of Tommies round the machine when I got back to it, and I got off alright, thoroughly frightened most of them, and then beetled off home.

Since then I have been having further alterations and amendments done to my machine, and the last three days have been quite unfit for flying – overcast with some rain, so we have been doing no shows. I have twice been into the neighbouring town of Blank, which you have often heard of, to shop. Horrible job, at least the second time. Once quite enough. Today I went over to the southern depot and spent the afternoon with Muspratt

– my late co-instructor with poor Kay – who is now out in France
and may be coming here. I have had a delightful letter from
Auntie, a quaintly formal one from my fag, ending up 'yours
truely H.G. Babinton-Smith'! which is a bit hard on me, I think
. . . have just heard I am on the early show so must go to bed,
although I think it will be dud tomorrow.

Best Love. A.

SE5 A4868 seems to have been plagued with engine trouble. Arthur
was forced to abort from the patrol with a faulty engine on the early
patrol on 18 May and again force-landed, this time near Bois-de-
Onze, between Wanquetin and Simencourt, returning to Vert
Galant by lunchtime.

Arthur flew his next patrol on 20 May, Crowe taking out the flight
after lunch. After a brief skirmish with a group of five enemy scouts
over Waziers the SE5s reformed. The German scouts also reformed
and a long range, rather scattered fight took place, the enemy finally
breaking off the action and making off towards Cambrai. The SEs
then met a formation of DH4s on a bombing raid to Douai and
escorted the bombers to their target, saving them from attack by
enemy fighters, which sheered off on sighting the British scouts.

Having seen the DH4s safely back to the lines, the SEs patrolled to
Carvin, returning south when the area proved devoid of any activity.
Crowe had been having trouble with his guns and landed in an
attempt to rectify the faults. Lloyd landed at Bertangles for more
petrol and Captain Broadberry returned to Vert Galant. This left
Arthur and Leonard Barlow and they flew back towards Carvin,
where they attacked a two seater. Barlow fired at close range until
both his guns jammed. Arthur then attacked, but the trigger bar of
his Vickers gun broke at the crucial moment. The two seater dived
steeply away and escaped to the east. After landing from this patrol
Arthur wrote to his mother, describing the action:

Dearest Mother,
    I have got your last letters, one enclosing Father's and the one
after. Honestly I nearly cried when I read Father's: the only
serious letter I have ever got from him, and it just made me thank
my God that I was the son of one who could write a letter like that.
It just made me and all my surroundings feel so awful small, and I
just love it. I am enclosing a reply to it, but I cannot write it now –
this is 6 pm and I have just been on my seventh patrol from 12.30

onwards, and I am now hoping to go on the evening show, which is best of all, to avenge my foolishness this morning. I must go now and see if the show is on (I don't think so as it is raining) and then I will continue.

One hour later. Rain stopped but the weather looks dull and threatening so we are going on the early show tomorrow instead. By 'we' I mean our Flight, B Flight – officially consisting of six machines but now only comprising four as the squadron is not yet up to full strength in machines. Thank goodness we have a perfectly ideal Flight Commander: no, it is not Foot. I think I told you he hurt his head in a car accident the day before we came out and so has left the squadron altogether.

My Flight Commander's name is Capt Crowe and he is one of the most senior Flight Commanders in the Corps, but as he has not been pushful to get his squadron (ie. his majority) he has been passed over by many others who were his juniors. Naturally his great experience is very valuable: he has been out flying in France 3 times before this, and he is not afraid of anything and goes after old Huns like a rocket and yet he is extraordinary prudent. I mean he is not like Ball who used to rush at fifteen Huns with himself and two others. Crowe's father owns a big iron and steel works in Durham, now making shells, and he is very fond of the lakes and hill country. So that except for the fact that he is engaged and rather loose about wine and whisky we have much in common. Anyhow, I couldn't have a better man to follow over the lines. This morning his guns wouldn't work and he had to come back and land, two of us, self and deputy leader, went back over the lines after seeing him safely to an aerodrome, and we got after an old Hun 2 seater, but both the other fellow's guns jammed, one of mine did and like a fool I forgot or anyhow didn't think quick enough of the other gun and I didn't go in and finish him, so he escaped. Whereat I am wrath. However, I haven't finished with brother Hun yet.

Not much other news. I hope to get my first leave in about 3 weeks or a month: we get a fortnight which is very good. I want some ordinary bootlaces which for some reason are very hard to get here. Have had 2 delightful letters from Viv and one from Crace, thanking me for the letter and photo, but quite brief as he had no time. I love that man. If everybody were like J.F.C. the world would be almost worth living in. No, that's pessimistic – but he's a great man.

Now as regards questions in your letter. First of all why did I call the unknown Hun a 'pro'. Because my dear Ma, he drove with extreme vigour and his putting (of bullets into me) was quite good until he lost his ball at the tenth tee, where he was four up, and that just made him go to pieces. Neither did the old Hun 'feel that he was up against a relative tyro.' There are many worse pilots than me in the RFC. I flatter myself so far, and I think I displayed extreme agility in removing myself when he shouted 'fore'. I'm afraid that I didn't shoot at him at all, as both my guns were out of action – one badly and the other temporarily. And one is not reported missing until at least 2 days afterwards. And cut out those 'horrid telegrams'. I have already got through the dangerous time, which is one's first month. And no praise for 'pluck' please: it smites my conscience and anybody else would have done 4 times as well. Raining again now.

Best love, wonder of Heaven. Arthur.

From the volume of the correspondence between Arthur, his mother and sisters, both at Eton and during his service life, the impression given of Professor Rhys Davids is of a somewhat shadowy figure, rather in the background. He was, of course, a very busy man, travelling and lecturing a great deal, and it was perhaps inevitable that the family life should have revolved around Caroline Rhys Davids. There can be no doubt, however, that Arthur was extremely close to his father and, as with his mother, was very conscious of his father's example and of his hopes for his only son. On 20 May Arthur received several letters from Caroline and one from his father, prompted by the small present he had sent for his birthday. That night, sitting alone in his hut, lit only by a small candle, he replied to his father.

Dearest Father,

If you have to thank me for a little present to be bought with a little money, I have to thank you a hundred times for a letter of gold, quite beyond value to me. I don't know if you realize that it is the first and only serious letter you have sent me by your own hand, all the others have gone through the beloved mother, but anyhow it is letters like yours which make all my surroundings so incalculably small – lost in a great wilderness of swamps below, while I wander dreamily amid billowy uplands with a breath of love from you that blows all the discontent out of me. I have often wondered whether I would sooner be in your position or mine: in yours with the comforting knowledge of noble work done, or in mine with the ambition to do as much and thanks to you and mother with the best promise and hope that I could wish.

It is jolly late; I am writing by the light of a solitary candle in my little den and everyone else is asleep, and somehow the right words won't come tonight, but you will see through a few pencilled lines a tangled skein of thoughts, I know.

How curious it is that people seem to consider themselves exempted from interest in religion because they are under the bar of war. And everyone persists in regarding the war as such a big thing – so it is in its ultimate end, but not as regards the part it plays in each soldier's life, and besides they don't think of it as a time of total exemption from work or worry. There are two things I try to remember. (1) 'There shall be wars or rumours of wars, but take ye not heed of these things, they are the beginnings of troubles'. (2) – this is always so cruelly true. 'For many be called, but few chosen'. And people still go on talking about 'the Church and the War' and the fulfilment of the Old Testament prophecies. I must go to bed as I am on the early show. Goodnight my beloved master.

Your small son. Arthur.

On the morning of 21 May, Crowe took Barlow, Lloyd and Arthur across the lines at Croisilles, but it began to rain heavily and the flight turned back for Vert Galant. Crowe landed at Belle Vue and Lloyd, following him down, lost control near the ground and crashed badly, completely wrecking his SE5 – happily with no damage to himself. Continued bad weather effectively stopped all war flying for the remainder of the day and Arthur took the opportunity to write to Vivien. His comments regarding 'Billy' Crowe, his flight commander, are well justified. After the disastrous events of the evening of 7 May, morale in the squadron had slumped badly. The pilots, remembering Ball's earlier condemnation of the SE5 and its qualities as a fighter, restated the old arguments: it was too stable, not agile enough, heavier to fly than the highly manoeuvrable Sopwith Pup or Nieuport.

Crowe spoke out against these views. He believed the SE5 was an ideal fighter aeroplane. It was strong, fast and a remarkably steady gun platform, he argued, plus the fact that its armament, if not ideal, was superior to that of the Pup or Nieuport. What was needed, he insisted, was a different approach to airfighting; new tactics were now called for. He advocated more diving attacks, followed by a zoom, away from trouble and to regain the all important advantage of height. It was largely Crowe's example in the first few weeks after the losses of 7 May that held 56 Squadron together, restoring its morale and fighting spirit.

21/5/17   56 Squadron.
Dearest V,

Not much of a one this time, but just a line to thank you ever so much for your two delightful letters and for the packets, which will do excellent. It is such a relief to have writing materials always at hand. If you can find a handy and cheap edition of Wordsworth I should love it. But don't please worry about it or spend too much monies. I have had two or three more shows since I last wrote, only one exciting, in which I should have got a Hun but didn't. Mother has full account and will no doubt forward. I'm afraid I didn't give that first Hun anything in exchange as both my guns were jammed.

Nothing certain about Ball yet. One of the other Flight Commanders – C Flight – was wounded in the wrist in the same fight, but the third, which is Capt Crowe, B Flight Commander, is still going strong, and is a perfectly admirable Flight Commander, thank goodness I am in his Flight.

So glad you are getting on in the tennis line. Also that you like A.L. Smith. I should love you to have a talk with him.

That great old pusher you hear over you is probably a 'Voisin' an antique French machine which however is still used a little I believe. You can recognize it by its 4 wheels on the undercarriage.

I'm not sure that I'm glad about Nesta being confirmed. I wonder if she has thought enough about it: I wish I was certain myself about many things of primary importance, but one merely does not get the time to think them out.

Muspratt, my co-instructor with Kay at CFS and my much more intimate pal than Kay, has turned up here. He was testing at Ipswich while I was at London Colney and out here, and is now some pilot I assure you. And he is in our Flight too, which is very good. Nothing else has happened to speak of: we did a dud show this morning: went out about 7 am and found the clouds very thick and so came back.

Read Henley's 'Song of the Sword' and tell me what you think

of it: do you agree? I love that man more and more every day.
Best love, you angel. Arthur.

Arthur was delighted at Keith Muspratt's posting to 56 Squadron.
Very much alike in outlook and temperament they had formed a
close bond of friendship while at CFS together and wrote regularly to
each other when Arthur was posted to 56 Squadron. Muspratt had
written to Arthur on 14 April from Martlesham Heath:

My Dear RD.
    I had been meaning to write to congratulate you on your
successful arrival in France when I got your lengthy and
exceedingly interesting letter and it has forced my laggard pen to
turn intentions into actions.
    I was awfully sorry to hear of your sad mishap, but I hope all
will soon be well. We all expect to see 56 do wonders and I am sure
the travelling circus will soon cease wandering. Last Sunday I was
at London Colney and wept to hear you had gone. I was returning
from delivering a Bristol Monoplane (with the Admiralty rotary)
to Farnborough and I did the journey from Radlett to
Farnborough in seven minutes!

Muspratt was also overjoyed at his posting, writing home the next
day:

22/5/17   56 Squadron RFC.
My Dear Father and Auntie,
    I moved here and have met many old friends. This is the
squadron I was to have gone to originally and which was at
London Colney.
    The mess here is simply magnificent and I pity you all at home.
When I got here I borrowed a machine from Rhys Davids (whom
I taught at the CFS) and flew about an hour: I had flown a very
similar machine at Martlesham but the type as used on service is
very much better.
    I shalln't go on a job for a bit but when I do remember the
machine is far better than any Hun.
    The country is ripping here and we are miles from the war. . .
Could you send out tennis shoes as we have a tennis court and
more than enough rackets.
    We do ourselves extraordinarily well and have every luxury

except books: could you send a Hardy (Thomas) and a Stanley
Weyman; I believe they should be good. . . If possible could you
send my 'Phantasmogoria', in my room I believe.

On 23 May, despite the appalling weather, the squadron flew three
patrols during the day. After an uneventful morning patrol, curtailed
by the adverse weather conditions, 'C' Flight went up again in the
early afternoon and Cecil Lewis shot a two seater down out of control
over Beaumont. Arthur took part in the last patrol of the day, led by
Captain Phillip Prothero – Ball's replacement, who had arrived on
14 May – with Crowe holding a watching brief. The flight saw a great
deal of action, resulting in Arthur's first aerial victory.

Crossing the lines at Arras – where Muspratt and Turnbull turned
back, being new pilots – the remainder of the flight, Prothero and
Broadberry with Arthur (Crowe had landed at Belle Vue with gun
trouble) flew towards Vitry. Over the town they saw three Albatros
scouts, green in colour and flying at 11,500 feet. Prothero led the SEs
round until the evening sun was behind them and they attacked out
of its glare over Aubigny. A short, sharp fight followed. Both
Prothero and Edric Broadberry, who had tackled the same Albatros,
were initially forced to break away with gun stoppages, but Prothero
cleared his and sent the enemy scout down out of control.

Arthur picked his own opponent, closed to within fifty yards and
fired a long continuous burst of Vickers and Lewis into the green
scout, following it down to 7,000 feet. Prothero then fired a green
light, the signal to reform, and Arthur left the Albatros, still going
down, and rejoined his companions. The cowling of Prothero's SE
was 'badly ripped' and he signalled that he was returning to Vert
Galant. Broadberry and Arthur escorted him as far as Arras and
then climbed back to 12,000 feet and flew northeastwards. Over
Henin-Liétard they attacked three enemy two-seaters. Broadberry
was forced to break off his attack and return to base with a burst
water jacket, but Arthur stayed to fight the remaining pair. These
were extremely well-handled and co-operated well. Although Arthur
attacked out of the sun, firing short bursts at each of them, they
finally eluded him and dived steeply away into the cloud cover.

Arthur, now alone, climbed back to 10,500 feet and flew towards
Arras. Before he reached the town he met three Albatros scouts,
flying east from Lens and five hundred feet below him. Without the
slightest hesitation he attacked the rearmost of the three, closing to
within forty yards and firing both guns. The Albatros spun steeply

down to 8,000 feet, 'completely out of control'. Arthur followed the stricken scout down and came under attack from its two companions, but he rounded on these with such determination that they broke off their attacks and dived away to the safety of their own lines.

Arthur, feeling extremely confident now, returned to Arras, hoping to find Crowe, but there was no sign of his flight commander at the rendezvous and it was not until he had patrolled alone, north of Douai and then south to Bugnicourt and Marquion, then back to the Arras area, that he finally found Crowe over Drocourt. The two SEs attacked a two-seater over Moeuvres, but this dived away under the cover of its own anti-aircraft batteries and they lost sight of it in the poor visibility. After patrolling towards Lens and then back to Douai, they finally returned to Vert Galant, well satisfied with the evening's work, which had seen a scout credited to Arthur as out of control, a two-seater out of control to Crowe and another scout out of control to Prothero and Broadberry.

The following day Arthur was again in action. Taking off in the evening, B Flight – Crowe leading Arthur, Turnbull, Hoidge and Muspratt – crossed the lines at 10,000 feet and patrolled ten miles east of a line Bailleul to Croisilles. South of Douai they sighted a formation of five enemy scouts at 10,000 feet and Crowe closed in at once to attack it. A very sharp fight followed, with all the SEs being engaged, fighting the hostile scouts down to 6,000 feet. One of the Albatri went down in a slow spiral, which developed into a spin and nose-dive, and this was credited as out of control to the flight as a whole. Another of the enemy scouts went down in a more controlled fashion and the remainder broke off the fight and cleared east.

Crowe, mindful of the fact that the flight was now a long way east of the lines, and very low, reformed the SEs, regained their height and patrolled towards Cambrai, honour well satisfied. There was no activity in the Cambrai area and the SEs turned towards Douai. Halfway to the town they sighted an enemy two-seater escorted by five Albatros D.IIIs flying two thousand feet above. Hoidge and Arthur dived to attack the two-seater while their companions stayed up to protect them from its escort. The two SEs drove the hapless two-seater down to 4,000 feet, firing from very short range, until it finally burst into flames over Gouy-sous-Bellone.

Reforming, the flight then caught another two-seater at 8,000 feet over Sains. Arthur tackled this one alone, closing from one hundred and fifty to fifty yards, firing both guns. His fire killed the observer, effectively silencing the rear gun, and the enemy aeroplane fell away, out of control and smoking profusely. As he pulled away from this encounter, Arthur was attacked by an Albatros with a red fuselage and tail, which had come down behind him. But Hoidge had seen this manoeuvre, rapidly closed to within twenty five yards of the Albatros and shot it off Arthur's tail. The red scout turned sharply away and, followed by Hoidge, dived to 5,000 feet, where it went into a series of spins, the usual evasive tactic employed by the German fighter pilots.

These two days of exciting and successful combats had lifted Arthur's spirits and he was full of confidence. After dinner that night he wrote jubilantly to Caroline.

24/5/17.
Dearest Mums,

I believe I last wrote on the 20th telling you about my 2nd scrap – 2 of us against the two seater. Nothing much happened on the Monday, Tuesday it rained and I went into the big town nearby to shop. viz. to buy some nutcrackers for the mess! and one or two other things. It was an appalling day. How I loathe shopping for other people, especially in a town where the shops are moderate and the prices exorbitant. But yesterday and today I have had a simply gorgeous time – twice running I have been out on the evening show and both times I have had 3 scraps in each. Yesterday first of all 3 of us tackled 3 Hun scouts quite far over the lines. They were quite good but we had them beat every time: we think we got one. After that the leader's guns went dud and we two carried on and tackled three two seaters. Immediately after the start the other fellow's engine had a burst pipe so he had to give up and come home. I sort of fooled about alone with these 3 Huns and eventually they all beetled east without much damage being done. Then I tackled 3 Hun scouts and put many bullets and the fear of God into one of them: I discover today that the Wing HQ think it good enough to claim, so he's my first Hun. A gorgeous evening. Gee, it's great fun – absolutely superb game.

Then today I was lucky enough to be on the evening show with my great pal Muspratt, over for his first trip. First of all we attacked five Hun scouts and I think I got one: anyhow we drove them down from 11,000 feet to 5,000 and thoroughly frightened them. Then I went after a two seater who came lumbering past us: and him I also drove down from 10,000 (approx) to 4,000, where I left him going steeply east with clouds of smoke coming out – and my Flight Commander Crowe saw him go down as far as about 2,500 feet in the same way. Then I climbed up again and soon I spied another 2 seater and went after him, and after my first dive I did not get fired at at all from the back seat as one usually is in dealing with a 2 seater, which has pilot in front and gunner behind, so I think I killed the old gunner, and he was seen later going down in flames by some other machines of ours. I then found that one of the newest type Hun scouts was in turn coming down after me, while five more were hovering up above. However, 3 of our people stayed up above, and the five others did not come down to attack, while the fifth who had come down after me dealt with the Hun scout after me – he was a red one and therefore probably one of the better Huns – and possibly got him down. Anyhow, we didn't have time to see and we beetled off home very happy. Two splendid nights running! Yah! So I think I have 2 Huns so far with 2 other possibilities.

By the way I picked up in this town where I was shopping a book by Esther Carpenter called 'The Historical Jesus and the Theological Christ' which sounds jolly good. I have only read the first 30 pages so far which are a sort of introductory chapter but are extremely good reading.

Altogether, with the arrival of Keith Muspratt, two glorious scrapping evenings and good books to read, and the return of the sunshine, I am living on as well as in the air. I hope this goes on for quite a long time. I cannot give you my details of place, but we are going from here in a week. The squadron to date has got about 41 Huns in a month's work with the loss of five missing and 2 wounded – complete record. Must stop now – will give you further details of scrapping later. Best love to Father. Arthur.

The following evening Arthur had more good news to report. Crowe had led Arthur, Muspratt, Bowman, Lewis and Hoidge off the ground at 5.30 that morning. The sun was blinding, straight into the eyes of the British pilots as they flew east. They saw nothing for over an hour. Then, over Beaumont, they sighted a pair of two-seaters on an early morning reconnaissance. Crowe tackled one, leaving the other to the rest of the flight. Muspratt, flying in his first action, attacked from broadside on, firing good bursts as the enemy aeroplane flashed by, a mere ninety feet away. Arthur was also attacking, from underneath. Pupil and teacher fighting together, neither yet twenty years old.

The two-seater dived away with Arthur on its tail, his fire either killing or wounding the observer. The enemy pilot suddenly steepened his dive, then flattened out. Arthur saw his chance. He dived to within twenty yards and fired a long burst from both guns. The two-seater, pouring smoke, crashed by the side of the Lens to Douai road. Arthur came under heavy AA fire and he hedge-hopped west to recross the front lines:

> This morning early we had another splendid show. We were off at 5.30 am but no Huns appeared until about 6.15. Then we (five of us) saw 2 two seaters below us and rushed down at them. We got there at about 9,000 and I chased my man down to 3,000: after my first rush the observer stopped firing which means I probably got him first. Then I just closed in and it was mere bullying: he had no chance. Down he went and hit the earth with a boomps about seven miles over the Hun side of the lines. I then began getting Archie badly – of course I was an easy target at that height – naturally I had started off home at once. I buzzed along going west all out, crossed the trenches at 1500 feet – great fun that – and climbed up again on our side of the lines and rejoined the others. Then the sky got simply *lousy* with Hun scouts: about four or five little bunches of six or eight lying about at various altitudes. But they didn't dare attack, though we were the only British machines as far over as all that. All they did was lay traps by keeping some down below as bait and waiting for us to go down in order that they might all collect and come down after us. But our excellent leader (Crowe) wasn't having any, thank you. By the way, I was credited with two machines yesterday out of the three possibilities I told you of, and a share in a third. So my total is now 4 Huns and a bit, which is comforting for 3 days work. The squadron now has 45 in a month.

Arthur had previously asked for his tennis shoes to be sent out, but he now wrote:

> I don't suppose I shall use them much. As a matter of fact we are moving soon and leaving our tennis court behind. I don't suppose I shall want them for a while. Boots (cricket pairs, one, nailed, officers for the use of) blazer and bags will be very useful.

How Caroline reacted to these tales of fights in the air can only be imagined. It was only one short year ago or less that telegrams were sent to Eton at the slightest sign of ill health; that her beloved only son was now in constant danger of his life and, in addition, killing people himself, must have been well-nigh unbearable to her.

B Flight flew the evening patrol on 26 May, taking off at 6.30. Crowe and Muspratt were forced to return early with gun and engine troubles, but Arthur, Broadberry, Prothero and Toogood carried on and sighted a formation of four two-seaters and two scouts at 9,000 feet over Gouy-sous-Bellone. Ignoring a large formation of twelve enemy scouts a little to the east, Prothero, Toogood and Broadberry dived to attack the two-seaters, leaving Arthur to tackle the two scouts. The first turned sharply away from his attack and dived; Arthur turned his attentions to its companion, firing from twenty yards range and watching his tracers pushing into the cockpit of the enemy scout. The Albatros went down: first in a vertical nose-dive for a thousand feet, then side slipping towards the ground. Arthur was then attacked by one of the two-seaters, but he turned towards it and the enemy pilot, thinking discretion the better part of valour, sheered off.

Arthur was again in action the following morning. In company with Barlow he first attacked four two-seaters over Plouvain. Barlow despatched his first opponent in great style, shooting the wings off the unlucky two-seater, the fuselage falling 'like an arrow'. He then attacked another, shooting this one down to crash within half a mile of the first.

Arthur, after an indecisive fight with one of the two-seaters, attacked an 'ordinary' Albatros (probably a DII) which had been in action with a formation of Sopwith Pups from 66 Squadron. Assisted by a Pup, he forced this Albatros to land, evidently hit in the engine, in a field to the east of Brebières. Arthur had suffered from gun stoppages during this engagement and came under heavy and very intense ground fire. He turned west and climbed back to 8,000 feet, rejoining his comrades over Arras. Crowe then led the SEs towards a fight taking place over Corbehem between the Sopwith Pups of 66 Squadron, Nieuports and enemy scouts. Arthur left the formation before it entered the fight and attacked a pair of two-seaters east of Lens.

Seeing the SE5 diving towards them the enemy pilots dived away east, but Arthur chased after the nearest, which was flying red and black streamers, and secured a good firing position. To his annoyance his Vickers gun jammed, but he managed to empty a full drum of Lewis into the two-seater before breaking off the combat. His fire had hit either the engine of the enemy aeroplane or the pilot had switched off, for the two-seater began to glide down with its engine stopped.

Meanwhile Arthur, now very low over enemy territory, opened up his engine to full throttle. He took many hits from machine gun fire from the ground and over Lens his engine stopped. He managed to pump up enough pressure in his emergency tank to restart his engine, but under his furious pumping the handle of the pump broke and his engine cut out again. After gliding a short way he force-landed in a field a mile east of Bully-Grenay. The SE hit a shell hole, turned over and was completely wrecked. Later examination showed it to have numerous bullet holes through petrol tanks and radiator. Arthur was unhurt but he had been extraordinarily lucky, a fact he acknowledged to Caroline in a letter written two days later:

We had our period of rain about the same time as you, then about the 23rd we started scrapping again, as you know. By the way, if I have any more references to pluck etc I stop writing altogether. I mean if Mr Naftel tells that it is a 'tribute to my pluck' or other delightful rot, well bless him it's very nice of him indeed, but *I* don't want to hear anything about it.

A new pilot just come to the squadron is playing Beethoven's Pathétique and now Chopin, after wading through some ragtime. After the Nocturne in E^b he is now playing the little prelude in A. It is a dull and cloudy day and everyone has scattered: the CO and adjutant and 2 Flight Commanders to examine our new aerodrome and four of the pilots to visit the neighbouring big town and only a few of us are left, which is very nice, with nothing to do except read and write. Very bon!

Now for a little history and confession. I have come to the conclusion that I might as well let you have it all, so I am going to frighten you thoroughly (perhaps) and I think it's not going to worry you more than if I didn't tell you. At least it shouldn't – if you do worry, well, my old Mums, I guess you are no true Buddhist (he has just played the old minuet in A by Borchenni! – now it's the Chants sans Parlés)

First of all I forgot to tell you that on Wednesday when I got my first Hun, one of the 3 two seaters I was tackling put a bullet through my machine a foot behind my head – mind you the whole object of this letter is to show that (now the Spring Song) I have an angel over me all the while I am flying with the great golden wings of LUCK spread over my head. The confession I referred to is that I have been an unholy dangerous fool, that I have taken 4 times the risk I ought to have done, and that by sheer *luck* I have come through with a whole skin, a great joy in life and five and a bit Huns brought down to my credit. In fact, I have been going on Ball's lines. But I think I have had enough of that for a time. I started off being ultra cautious, to say the least of it and that riled me; then I began being a mad dog in so much that one evening after a show – the one where I tackled the 3 two seaters – the CO said 'you put up a d..... good show and I'm proud of you' and after my last and silliest effort, my Flight Commander asked me not to do it again, and the dear old adjutant gave me a fatherly piece of advice and beseeched me not to take undue risks, said it didn't pay, which I knew before was true, and which advice I intend to follow if I can.

But, O my old Ma, one can't lay down rules while on mere earth for people on fighting patrol in the air. You are a different man – at least you aren't a man at all, that is I am not – you are a devil incarnate filled with the dazzling thrill of playing the best game God ever created, mad after Huns and just forget everything else but showing the old Hun that there's only one man fit to be in the air and not two. And the only way you are sobered down is when you see fifteen red beggars coming for three of you, on which occasion you beetle off for dear life. And I can say that if I have been a fool, I have been a cunning fool, and I have given the Old Hun jolly little chance of shooting straight.

Now for a little narrative. I believe I told you all up to Saturday the 26th: that evening four of us tackled 6 Huns and claimed 2 – I claimed one: unfortunately one of our four was missing. The Huns didn't even put up a decent show: they all ran like hell. I found a delightful letter from Accini waiting for me when I got back.

Sunday was the great day. Curiously Whit Sunday and Easter Sunday were my two days of crashery in France. However, to start at the beginning. I was on the early show and at about 10,000 we saw five HA (hostile aircraft) at about 6,000. Down we went. I pursued two of them down to 3,000 where I found one miserable looking Hun scout – the other five were two seaters – whom I chased down like a dangerous lunatic to 600 ft!! – this six or seven miles over in Hunland. O but it was fun! My hat, he was frightened – he just couldn't go down any further to get away so he had to stay and fight and then my d..... gun wouldn't go. So I left him hedge-hopping in a huge hurry and beetled west. Up again to 7,000 where I saw 2 more 2 seaters at about 4,000, away down about five miles over. So once again like a dangerous lunatic I rushed off after them and followed them down to 500 ft!! – and again my gun wouldn't work. So I left them also hedge-hopping east and rushed back west, going about 120 mph over the houses – it was the mining district and every house was full of machine guns and I got peppered proper. However, I didn't mind, they only put about a dozen bullets in the planes, but unfortunately one lucky shot got both petrol tanks. First of all it let all the pressure out of the main tank and the petrol was forced into the engine and so she stopped – Lord! where am I?, seas of trenches and shell holes below me, put her on the other tank. Ah! starts up again. On again looking for a landing ground. Stopped again. Help. Am I over Hunland? Glided a bit, turned round and landed into wind all OK.: then saw I was running along at about 30 mph over the field, down went one wheel into a shell hole: the machine did 2 loops and one roll on the ground and eventually stopped right side up. I leapt out and looked around for approaching Huns. No signs, then – huge relief, though I knew pretty well all the time – 2 Tommies appeared and I found I was about two miles behind the front line trenches.

So I phoned through from a neighbouring Engineers Observation Post to my CO (it was then 8am.) and went down into a little shell bespattered village near by and got some breakfast with 3 officers of the Lincolns who were very agreeable: then on my way back to the machine I ran into a company of gunners just going on church parade and the captain in command was to my utter amazement a person who was in Oppidan VI Form about my second or third year at Eton, and whom I had much admired in a distant sort of way – one R.G. Lyttelton, a cousin or nephew of the old Brown Man. He was so nice, and hauled me in to have a drink and later gave me lunch and tea, in the intervals of which I went back to my machine. For some extraordinary reason the Boche didn't shell it, though everybody thought they would, and they were shelling about parallel with us north and south. I went up and watched two of our anti-aircraft guns firing and had a chat with them, then I eventually pushed off with the machine in a lorry – we had an awful time taking it about 300 yds across shell holes and a deep trench to the nearest road –

about 9 and got back here about 1 am next morning.

Next day I did very little, except that my new machine arrived, quite a good one and it may be even better than my dear old bus – 4868 was the number of my old one, and 8901 is my new one. But the old one was a wonder and she did some jolly stout work. When I was pursuing that wretched little 'banana' man (as we call them, because of the yellow body and green wings, which look something like an unripe banana with the peel rolled back and stretched out) I found the old machine was doing 200 mph and stood it like a rock. Well, after all, life is very bon. By the way, tell Mr Naftel that the Daily Mail is so loathsomely untrue that it makes one sick. For instance, the article about the triplanes beating back the 'foe airmen' – once a week they do go over and do some very good work, but most of the time they just sit and funk at 15,000 behind our own lines: they are like the Huns – with exceptions. With a fine machine like a triplane a stout man could do wonders – but the Naval people are so fearfully unreliable, like some army people. However, don't you worry about me: I have finished being mad dog.

Best Love. Arthur.

This is a long and interesting letter giving many insights into Arthur's state of mind; the fact that he had evidently felt the need to prove his worth, to the concern of Blomfield, Marson and Crowe over his recklessness, and, on the lighter side, a delightful evocation of the squadron mess with the newly arrived pilot playing the piano. His recent successes seem also to have changed his mood of introspection and boredom with the war. Airfighting was now 'the best game God ever created'. The last passage, concerning the activities of the Naval squadrons flying Sopwith Triplanes, is hardly borne out by the facts, but shows the strength of feeling prevalent in the RFC towards the RNAS, a feeling reciprocated by the RNAS and in both cases completely mistaken and unjustified.

On the last day of May, 56 Squadron moved north as part of the build-up of British forces for the coming battle of Messines. In company with Nos 19 and 66 Squadrons, 56 Squadron moved to the large aerodrome south of St Omer, officially designated Liettres, but known throughout the RFC as Estrée Blanche, the slightly larger of the two villages, at the foot of the hill from the aerodrome on the road to Brauy-en-Artois and Arras.

With its departure from Vert Galant the squadron had completed its first seven weeks in France. In five weeks of active fighting, for the loss of ten of its own pilots, it had claimed a total of 57 enemy aeroplanes; 23 of which had been destroyed and 34 driven down out of control. Fifty-Six Squadron was now to enter into perhaps its most successful period; a period which was to see its renown spread throughout the messes of the Royal Flying Corps and even to 'the other side of the hill', into the messes of the German Air Force. Arthur Rhys Davids was to play no small part in that renown.

CHAPTER SIX

Estrée Blanche

The atmosphere at Estrée Blanche was very different from that of the almost rural Vert Galant. Here was a large service aerodrome: nine large hangars; dozens of huts and tents; tarmaced areas; a lorry park and unceasing bustle and activity, with constant traffic to, from and past the aerodrome. Somehow the war seemed more deadly, more intense here. It was a subtle change of mood, difficult to explain. The war had been no less deadly at Vert Galant; men – comrades – had been lost: killed or wounded. Yet the change was there and more than one pilot felt and commented on it.

Soon after the squadron had settled into its new quarters, the General Officer Commanding the RFC, General Trenchard – popularly nicknamed 'Boom' – visited the pilots to explain the object of the coming battle. Taking a small group of pilots to the centre of the aerodrome, where they were in no danger of being overheard, Trenchard expounded the strategy of the battle. The main objective was the capture of the Messines-Wytschaete Ridge. The ridge overlooked the British positions and from it the Germans could observe all preparations for the proposed offensive in Flanders; an offensive aimed at clearing the Belgian coast of enemy forces and turning their flank. The group of pilots listened intently as Trenchard told them of the vast tunnelling operations under the ridge: operations which had been in progress for two years. Preparations were now almost complete. Nineteen mines, more than a hundred feet deep, had been dug and filled with almost a million pounds of high explosive. The plan was to explode them simultaneously and literally blow the German forces off the ridge.

'When will that be?' asked one of the group.

'Within three or four days,' replied Trenchard. 'But, of course, I can't tell you the exact day.'

After more conversation on the subject of the coming battle, Arthur, one of the group, piped up, tongue in cheek:

'What day did you say the battle was to begin, Sir?'

Trenchard, caught off guard, replied: 'The seventh.' Then, realizing by the laughter that he had been neatly tricked, hastily added: 'Or the sixth, or the eighth.'

As one pilot who was present later commented: 'Poor old Boom, he was no match for young RD – sharp as a razor blade.'

Flying his new SE5a, A8901, Arthur made his first offensive patrol from the new aerodrome on the morning of 4 June. The Flight made two unsuccessful attacks on Albatros scouts and the second of these engagements split up the SE formation. Arthur patrolled alone to Lille, chasing an Aviatik over the town until forced to leave it by a formation of six hostile scouts above him. He gained more height and flew towards Ypres in the hope of seeing the rest of the SEs. Over the town he was joined by one of the patrol, Lieutenant T.M. Dickinson, and two Sopwith Pups from 46 Squadron. Seeing a formation of Albatros fighters some distance to the east and flying at 15,000 feet, Arthur took his little formation parallel to the front lines, climbing hard to close the height advantage held by the enemy scouts.

Before he could reach them, however, they were attacked by a flight of Sopwith Triplanes from No 1 Naval Squadron, led by Flight Commander Gerrard, and three Nieuports of No 1 Squadron, flown by Lieutenants Fullard, Hazel and Sharpe. The fray had started just west of Moorslede and Arthur led his force into the action, firing bursts at a number of Albatros 'V' Strutters. The fighting gradually drifted east over the Roulers to Menin road. Arthur found it impossible to press home any of his attacks, being heavily outnumbered by the enemy scouts, who co-operated well, climbing and attacking from under the tails of the British aeroplanes. In a brief respite from being under attack he saw a red Albatros, its propeller stationary, dive away from the fight, and looking round he saw Lieutenant Dickinson's SE going down in a slow steep spiral – almost a spin – with two of the Albatri on its tail.

Arthur then came under a concerted attack from nearly eleven of the enemy fighters and he put the SE's nose down and dived for the British lines, pursued by the enemy. No Albatros could catch an SE5 in a dive and Arthur eluded his pursuers and reached the British lines. Here he regained his height, turned north, and attacked five of his recent adversaries who were now attacking British artillery observation machines. Arthur annoyed these enemy scouts for three-quarters of an hour, constantly frustrating their attacks on the British two-seaters.

After one of these attacks he was joined by Leonard Barlow and a Sopwith Triplane, and together they attacked a trio of the enemy scouts. While they were fighting these, the British pilots were attacked by the first five. Arthur noticed that all the enemy pilots avoided the Sopwith Triplane and seemed afraid to get at close quarters with it. All five of the enemy scouts were very well flown, the leader's Albatros having a red fuselage, with grey and black wings. Arthur got close enough to the leader of the enemy formation to be able to see that he was wearing a grey fur flying helmet. At 8.35 Barlow fired a white light, the wash-out signal, and he and Arthur turned for home. On the way they attempted to attack a pair of two-seaters, but these were at 22,000 feet and the SEs failed to reach their height.

Arthur recounted the latest news and the story of this patrol in his next letter home, which he wrote that night. In her last letter his mother had enclosed a letter she had received from a friend, May Smith, who had evidently been informed of Arthur's exploits and had commented rather fulsomely in her letter to Caroline. Arthur's reaction to her praise shows an amused but not totally displeased tolerance. His comment on her feeling that 'nothing can stop him' shows a wry realization that in the dangerous, vicious world of fighting in the air nothing could be easier:

Dearest Mums,
    Perhaps owing to our change of locality I got no letters for three or four days, and then I got six all in one heap, including two from you. Before I forget, I may say that I shall not want tennis shoes now, so you need not worry about them any longer as we left our tennis court behind at the aerodrome.
    We transferred here on the 31st and took 2 days to settle down. We had 2 trial trips to see the country and in one we got up as far as the sea, into which I pooped off a few rounds, just to show there was no hard feelings. Coming back I believe I was 'Archied' by Belgians, at least we were 2 or 3 miles this side of the lines, or rather of the floods which represent the lines, and I don't think it was Hun Archie. Huge joke.
    Today being the fourth of June I had my most exciting patrol yet. Five of us left the ground at 6.30 am and over the lines we chased two solitary Hun scouts down, and after the second one we got a bit scattered. I saw one or two other HA and chased them down and mooned about a bit, scouting round six Hun scouts above me, picking up on the way two other British machines (2 Pups to be accurate and another SE) Then I saw about fifteen Hun scouts coming along, and about 9 of our machines above them going to attack. So we had the (hell) of a show: this was at

16,000 about six miles over; the Huns were mostly coloured red and averaged quite good flying, one or two were quite brilliant pilots. The people up above got 3 Huns, and I rushed about wildly firing a few shots at various Huns, but taking jolly good care that no one put in any accurate shooting at me. I'm afraid the other SE was 'done in' – anyhow he went down with two Huns on his tail, and it was his first scrap. (I'm sure he didn't look round enough, poor chap.) He was an excellent fellow too, one Dickinson in the Indian Cavalry, late of Wellington and Sandhurst, and a cousin of my great pal at Eton.[1]

Well, I suddenly found myself in the middle of about eleven of them; the others had started on top and very prudently stayed there: so I beat it west like stink; in fact I was chased out of the sky by these people. They were pooping all the time but they made jolly bad shooting and they never got too close. Then they left me about a mile or two this side of the lines and I climbed up again. Then for about ¾ hour I played 'tic' with five of them, led by an extremely good pilot in a red, pink and grey machine. I wanted to go up close and watch his flying instead of scrapping. They would dive on a British machine; down I would go on top, and up they would come again and chase me away. Huge fun. Eventually on the third occasion like this, when they dived on another SE who had turned up, I got so close to the leader that I could see he was wearing a grey fur flying cap. He passed about 15 yards in front of my nose, and I was pooping away like blazes. I bet he came down in an unholy mess. I had only one tiny bullet hole through one of my undercarriage wheels when I landed. After a time the five of them buzzed off and we turned to go home. Then we saw our Archie going hard, and perceived a wretched Hun somewhere about 22,000 and miles away. So up we climb and climb and climb – up as far as 17,600 – the highest I have been yet. Higher than you ever got – O angel of plodding footsteps! Then we gave him up when he turned east and I landed after having been up for nearly three hours. Bong!

The aerodrome here is on top of a hill, the fields are smaller and there are more trees about than the other place: it is less barren and more inhabited. Two gigantic slag heaps mark coal mines quite near. There are a lot of quaint Portuguese soldiers here in grey uniforms: nasty looking little peelers, but with fine looking

[1] R.S.W. Dickinson, RNAS.

officers. O by the way, when I got back I didn't claim having slain any Huns, but apparently some of the other machines of other squadrons seem to think I got one, and our Archie saw him crash, so that makes six and a share in a seventh. Also he seems to have been a sort of notoriety known as the 'Pink Lady' owing to the colour of his machine and his (presumably) bong qualities as a scrapper. Quite fluky that I got him; must have made some lucky shooting. I don't think he was the chap in the grey fur hat, but another – but I am finding out for certain tomorrow. Oh, it's a bong game. If you can get hold of a copy of Rupert Brooke (1908-1911) read the 'Song of the Pilgrims'. I'm sure he wrote it after listening to Tannhäuser Overture. . . Ball didn't throw away chances by rashness: he was no fool. But he was a great deal more daring than anybody else and sometimes his policy was undoubtedly risky. Except for one's first half dozen scraps its largely a question of luck – stray bullets.

What a delightful letter from May Smith, but just fancy those two females looking at my face and babbling about courage etc. O mon Chapeau! Kissed it! Zeus! 'Fresh radiant'! Holy Handkerchief! 'Fine and broadshouldered' – Molock's moth-eaten mule! 'Nothing can stop him'. God – that's just the trouble. Bless 'er heart.

I'm afraid the idea of leave is off for a bit. Today is 4th June and an old Etonian has arrived at the squadron – an Oppidan who left in 1913.[1] Seems alright. Love to Father.

The 'chap in the grey hat' was Leutnant Karl Schaefer, the Staffel Führer of Jasta 28 and Arthur's doubts at having shot him down were perfectly justified. Although he was later credited with Schaefer's death – the Pink Lady, as Schaefer's Albatros was known to the RFC – the German ace was actually shot down by the FE2ds of 20 Squadron on the afternoon of 5 June. Arthur was awarded an Albatros from these combats on 4 June, on the evidence of confirmation by the pilots of No 1 Squadron.

Fullard's combat report, however, throws a different light on the events. Fullard stated that while engaged in a bout of tail chasing with a red Albatros an SE5 appeared and shot the Albatros off his tail. The enemy scout, by Fullard's account, then went down in a series of somersaults, followed by the SE. Such a distinctive incident

---

[1] Lt Maxwell Henry Coote.

would surely have been commented on by Arthur, if he had been the pilot of the SE concerned, and it seems more likely that the SE5 was flown by Dickinson, who shot down this Albatros before he was himself shot down by Vizefeldwebel Wittekind of Jasta 28.

B Flight flew the evening patrol on 5 June but although it saw no action Arthur had exciting news to tell and he wrote to Caroline that night!

5/6/17.   56 Squadron.
Dearest Mother
    After my colossal effort of last night it seems a bit superfluous to send this trivial sheet, but I suppose I might as well tell you at once that for some absurdly inadequate reason they have deemed fit to give me the Military Cross. Crowe and another flying officer and self got it altogether this morning: if we deserve the MC Crowe certainly deserves the DSO; or more reasonable would be that Crowe should have teed off his MC and we two should have waited until we had done some work. Why, I have only been scrapping a month, and Crowe has been out France 3 separate times for a few months each time. Of course I am very bucked, but it seems an awful shame. Nothing else has happened to me this morning, except that 3 of us with 3 others of another squadron also here got away in one of our tenders for a bathe this afternoon in a river about 2 miles away – quite delightful. Memories of Eton.

This letter has a note in his mother's handwriting: 'the Scarpe? the Douvre?' and it seems certain from the various forms in which Arthur addressed his letters to her that he had an arrangement with Caroline similar to that which he had set out for Vivien. A letter he wrote to his aunt Seda at this time gives further insight into his attitude to his work.

    I expect mother tells you most of my news about the war so I will not go into details, except to say that I brought down my sixth German machine yesterday. Altogether, considering that I am in the army I am having a really splendid time, and my luck has been near quite phenomenal, first of all in getting into this splendid squadron at all, and secondly in my actual fighting. I love what you say about the Great Presence always helping me, but I am quite happy to think that if I am going to do any good in this place the good God will see me through, and if not, well I do not mind going to rest at once.

Anyhow, there is no game like fighting in the air; it beats football and cricket into a cocked hat. And one can use a little brains. The weather is glorious here, and the sunsets quite amazing; the red and green mosaic in the West lasts till almost half past ten or eleven every night. Thanking you once more for your letter.

Your affectionate nephew.
Arthur Rhys Davids.

Arthur received a letter from Lieutenant-Colonel C.L.N. Newall, commanding 9th Wing, congratulating him on the award of his MC.

Dear Rhys Davids

Many congratulations on your being awarded the Military Cross. I hope you will down unlimited Huns and win many more honours.

Yours sincerely
C.L.N. Newall.

*

The battle of Messines opened at dawn on 7 June. At 3.20 the mines were exploded under the ridge, shaking the ground over twelve miles away. No sooner had the roar died away than the bombardment began, the continuous rapid throbbing of thousands of heavy guns. On the first day of the battle, 56 Squadron had orders to patrol the area: Houthulst Forest, Roulers, Menin, Quesnoy, and after an extremely gallant solo special mission at dawn by Leonard Barlow, Arthur led the first squadron patrol of the day, taking off an hour after Barlow.

Crossing the lines at 10,000 feet over Ypres the SEs swept in a wide curve through Menin and Wervicq at 13,000 feet. The engine of A8901 was not going well and Arthur was forced to fire a green light and head west. His engine picked up again, however, and began to run better and he led the flight back to Ypres. Circling to the east of the town to gain a favourable position, the SEs dived and attacked three enemy scouts at 10,000 feet over Westroosebeke. The British force drove these enemy aeroplanes down to 5,000 feet, Arthur nearly colliding with one in his eagerness: 'nearly collided with one HA after firing from fifty to ten yards with Vickers and Lewis: He turned over and passed a few feet from my wingtip, and went down in a spin, developing into a steep spiral and becoming completely out of control'. While attacking this Albatros – possibly Fritz Kuhn of 1st Marine Jasta – Arthur had been about to come under attack from another, but Harry Rogerson shot this Albatros down before it could close with his leader. Arthur regained his height. Now separated from the other SEs he patrolled back to Ypres. After an unsuccessful, rather long-range attack on a two-seater over Menin, he saw two Nieuports fighting with an Albatros scout just to the south of Passchendaele. Diving to help the Nieuports, Arthur was disconcerted when the Albatros pilot 'hung on his propeller and fired up at me as I dived at him.' In the event Arthur's Vickers gun refused to fire and he pulled out of his dive and returned to the Ypres area.

This patrol does not even merit a mention in his next letter to Vivien, written on 8 June. That only a short month previously such a patrol, full of incident, would have been fully described, is some indication of Arthur's acceptance of the almost daily airfighting in which he was now engaged. Vivien, at Oxford, had evidently asked him to identify some of the training aeroplanes she saw daily in the vicinity of the town. From her description Arthur identified them as Sopwith Camels:

> As regards the new scouts you have with you, with wide planes and short bodies, is the top plane flat and the lower one turned up? If so it must be one of our new machines which should do wonders – an improved 'Pup'. The Nieuport has the shorter and narrower bottom plane, and the same thing as above – top flat, bottom turned up. Many Huns have them so.
>
> Foot never came out with the squadron, surely I told you that he hurt his head in a car accident the day before we flew out and couldn't come out. I'm afraid Ball is dead, anyhow there is no truth in the prisoner rumour as yet. I am so very glad he got his VC (and a French honour) which he so thoroughly deserved.[1] I have heard from Mrs Garnett that poor old Pat Garnett was almost certainly killed on a Nieuport.

Arthur flew no patrols for the next few days. Blomfield gave him a rest from flying on 8 June and bad weather kept the squadron grounded for several days. On 10 June A Flight stood by all day in case the weather conditions improved, but the other flights went up to the trenches 'to see the war'. Arthur later wrote to Nesta, who had

[1] Ball's Victoria Cross was gazetted on 8 June 1917.

recently been confirmed, describing the visit and offering a little Christian advice:

12/6/17   56 Squadron.
Dearest N,

So many thanks for your perfectly immense letter which I wish I could reward by a similar, but somehow I just can't. I have not waged war for four days now: first day I was given a rest having had two different shows the day before, second and third days were cloudy (yesterday it rained) and today is fine again, but as yet no orders have come through. The day before yesterday a lot of us went off, had lunch in the middle of a great big wood about 10 miles from the aerodrome and then we went on and saw the war from the ground; we took our tender up to about 3 miles behind present front line, opposite a place where there has recently been a 'shove', so you can probably guess where. Then we left the tender and went on foot: it was hot and very dusty, but it was most enthrallingly interesting. We first of all passed two big guns, which were firing steadily at intervals, the sergeant in charge had such a dear little black pup, that didn't seem to mind the firing at all. Then we went nearer, along a little light railway over interminable shell holes and rubbish, past several batteries of smaller guns, until we came to the old front line. The curious thing was that our old trenches had been knocked about almost as much as the Boche, and the only strip of green was what had been 'No Man's Land'. Bar that, the whole countryside was just a great brown desert, nothing but shell holes and old dugouts beaten about. There were souvenirs to be had, but I only took a few little bits of wood from a German trench, which I will carve into something later on. We went right up onto a ridge of some fame – which four days back had been in Hunland. There I barked my shins crawling into a derelict tank: it had been hit on the top by a shell and of course completely knocked out of action. Then we turned back and at that moment a few odd shells began coming over, one of which fell well under a hundred yards away. You should have seen a dozen intrepid aviators leap into shell holes or flop on their faces when we heard the shells coming. Then when they went off nowhere near, we all jumped up again laughing. Comic sight. Altogether a most amusing day.

Yesterday three of us went for a long walk out to a wood over four miles from the aerodrome and back. Except that it was very wet in the wood it was splendid. The war was miles away and I can't help feeling what a horrible waste of a gorgeous June it is, though I am having such a good time. I know I am next on the roll for leave but I haven't the vaguest notion when it's coming off. Not for at least a fortnight, I should think, if not more.

About your confirmation. I am so glad you like the man, but for God's sake, my beloved, remember that it does not mean just the extra benefit of Holy Communion at 8 am. After all it is so easy to go and be religious in church: the great thing is to 'do this in remembrance of me' every day. You will find (at least I do) that you can walk with God much easier in a pine wood than in a church: the one great thing is to think as though you were walking arm in arm with God the whole day. Because he is *always* there, not only at HC, and HC should not be just a reminder every fortnight of that fact, as it is with so many people. Best love and please don't be an ordinary Christian.

Arthur.

PS. I still have fumsup[1] alright.

Caroline had written to John Crace, telling him of his former pupil's successes in the air. He replied:

Eton. June 10th 1917.
Dear Mrs Rhys Davids,

I read your news with very great delight and please let me congratulate you most heartily on Arthur's MC – your letter was all the more welcome because there had been a rumour here a few days ago (tho' only very uncertainly) that he had been reported missing – what the source of it was I do not know.

His contemporary Dick Lyttleton (our former Headmaster's nephew) now here on leave from France, brings us first hand testimony of Arthur's doings and speaks in very high terms of the reputation he has been winning for himself, and reports him as something of a genius in the line that he has devoted himself to. I hope indeed that you will continue to get none but the very best news of him. Is there any chance of his having any leave home before our summer term comes to an end?

Crowe took B Flight out on the morning of 14 June, Arthur's first

---

[1] Fumsup was a mascot sent to Arthur by Nesta when he first went to France.

patrol since the morning of the opening of the battle of Messines on 7 June. The SEs saw nothing for almost two hours and when they finally sighted a formation of 'old type' Albatros scouts they had to be content with chasing them east of the Menin-Roulers road as petrol was running low. There were rumours, however, that enemy activity in the air was about to be stepped up and Arthur mentions this in a letter to his aunt the next day:

> The wonderful weather continues after a short interval of cloud and rain and I expect there will be a big war on again soon, The old Hun is waking up again in the air, and I shall be having some lively times soon. Meanwhile there is not very much doing. I tested a new type engine in our machines this morning and got up to 19,000; it would have gone higher but I was cold and miserable so I descended in various contortions – I mean the machine not me. That was before breakfast, and then before lunch a few of us went to a small river near by which we discovered some time ago and had a delicious bathe. This afternoon I have been lying by a little brook reading Rupert Brooke, and on the spur of the moment I patched up this curious little fragment which I send along. I don't claim any metre for it except 'Brook' metre – not Brooke, whom I think a greater man each time I read him. I wonder if you would send the fragment on to Viv or Mother: it might possibly be of interest. This evening I am going to the war again. Thank goodness we are 20 odd miles from the war when we are not actually playing the great game. But it is only a great game and all games are a waste of time, especially in the summer. However, one must waste some time I suppose. I should like to hear your stories of the bomb raid: I hope no damage was done to you or yours.

Arthur's reference to the new type engine refers to the first of the 200 hp SE5a's now coming into squadron service. The squadron had received its second example of the new type on 11 June, Cecil Lewis ferrying SE5a A4563 to Estrée Blanche in the afternoon. This SE5a was the third prototype SE5 now re-engined with a 200 hp geared Hispano-Suiza engine driving a four-bladed propeller running at 1170 rpm, and these SE5a's were known to Charles, the squadron's engineering officer, as 'the 1170s'. Charles did an enormous amount of work and modifications on the carburettors of the 1170s, redesigning the metering and altitude control systems, and modifying the air intake drains. The first 200 hp SE5a received by 56

Squadron was A8923. The exact delivery date is not known, but probably on 7 June in the early afternoon. A8923 was tested by Keith Muspratt on the morning of 8 June when he took off alone to look for an enemy aeroplane reported to be over St Omer.

It is evident from this letter to his aunt, and others at the time to his mother and sisters, that leave was the main item of concern at this period. Arthur had obviously been put back on the leave roster because of his inactivity during his first weeks in France, but he had since been engaged in a great deal of fighting. The initial month of action was always the period of greatest strain on the nerves of First World War fighter pilots – as Arthur himself had written – and Arthur no doubt now felt in need of a rest. It is also evident, from his mention of the poems of Rupert Brooke, that he had not yet lost – if he ever did – that idealisation of the war so evident in the poems of Brooke. This idealism had already been lost by the young infantry officers of Arthur's generation who were serving in the trenches, and they were already writing the cynical, angry and disillusioned poetry exemplified by Sassoon, Rosenberg and later, by Wilfred Owen. From Arthur's next letter it is evident that Blomfield was conscious of his highly strung nerves and was resting him as much as possible before his leave:

15/6/17   56 Squadron.
Dearest Mother of Mine.

First a wee brief line to enclose a cutting from the Mirror: the Colonel told me yesterday that GHQ had apparently credited me with bringing down this personage 'the Pink Lady' that I mentioned in my last letter but one (I think). Which is quite bong. I have not waged any war for the last two days as the CO has very kindly said he thought I ought to have a rest, which is very, very nice of him, but really all rot. Today is misty and I believe we are going up to see the war from the ground. I know I am next on the roll for leave, and I am daily expecting to hear that I can go, but naturally at this stage of the 'military situation' they are doubtful about leave.

Have found a really excellent little book for Father to read at night, among those of my friend Muspratt. It is called 'The Private Papers of Henry Ryecroft' by George Gissing. Of course, I don't agree with it all, but some of it is very good. . .

It was ironical that when Arthur finally left on leave, on 16 June, he was to be followed to England only five days later by the entire squadron. On 13 June 1917 a strong formation of Gotha bombers had bombed London in daylight for the first time. There were many civilian casualties – Arthur's letter from his aunt had told him of this raid, hence his reference to 'your story of the bomb raid' – and the raid had 'stirred the country'. There was a great public outcry for a more effective defence against air attacks on the capital and the War Cabinet met on the afternoon of 14 June to discuss what action should be taken.

The long-term plan was to expand both the RFC and RNAS, but the short-term solution was to transfer from France 'a crack fighter squadron to give the next raiders one or two sharp lessons.' Haig was reluctant to spare any of his forces from the all important work in France, but on 17 June the War Cabinet instructed him to initiate a system of fighter patrols on each side of the Straits of Dover. Much against his will, Haig transferred 66 Squadron to Calais and 56 Squadron to Bekesbourne in Kent.

The pilots of 56 Squadron knew nothing of these controversies in high places. They only knew – and cared – that they were to go home to England. As Cecil Lewis put it. 'God bless the good old Gotha! Good old Jerry! Good old Lloyd George!'[1]

On his arrival in London, Arthur sent a postcard to Vivien at St Hugh's College, Oxford.

6pm. 17/6/17.
Just a line to say I am home on leave till July 1st: you are going to be at Oxford I take it, so I will come over for a day or two about the 25th – depends on Eton fixtures and your convenience, exactly when. I only heard yesterday I was coming: slept that night at Boulogne, perfect crossing this morning: London by 4, delicious bathe here: home 7.0 from Charing X tonight. Let's hear your fixtures and possibilities. A.

[1] *Sagittarius Rising*, Cecil Lewis. Peter Davies 1936.

CHAPTER SEVEN

Home Defence

The squadron's arrival at Bekesbourne cut short Arthur's leave and he was instructed to report back to the squadron. His fellow pilots were elated to be back in England, and the possibility of getting amongst the Gothas, if and when they returned, was looked upon with some eagerness, a welcome change from the weeks of gruelling offensive patrols in France. But to Arthur the whole thing seemed a waste of time. He wrote to Caroline on 26 June, soon after rejoining the squadron at Bekesbourne:

> We are leading a curious existence – almost peacetime. We do absolutely *nothing* the whole day and very little flying even. We spend the whole day playing cards or ragging about and some of us go out every evening on the bust. Last night, after dinner, I went off with one Coote – an old Etonian in the squadron – and Muspratt to visit some cousins of Coote, viz a Mr and Mrs Plumtree who live in a country house on the way to Sandwich. He is the exact image of King Edward and a regular old country gentleman, and his grounds and garden are just perfect, with plenty of old wall overgrown with peaches and creepers, and beds ablaze with Larkspur and Sweet William. Not without luscious strawberry beds. . . Nothing doing. Fairly pleasant life. We have to be near the aerodrome all day till 7.30. I am hoping to get one space of 48 hours' leave or the rest of my fortnight again. Expect we shall be here at least a month.

A letter to Vivien, written the following day, shows an awareness of the success of the German strategy in denuding the Western Front of one of the RFC's top fighter squadrons.

> Of course, I am perfectly wild about missing my sojourn with you, especially as I am doing absolutely *nothing* here and might just as well be on leave. It is a very pleasant life I suppose, as we have completely no work, but it's annoying to feel the Hun has succeeded in his object as regards raids, which was largely to

disconcert RFC attention from France. I would sooner be out any day.

Must go out to tea with the Adjutant's family who live in a farm a few hundred yards from the aerodrome – his wife and a perfectly delightful girl aged 8 who has stepped straight out of a Greek vase – a great mop of gold hair and eyes of watery blue, like a summer sky with wisps of strawy cloud asleep in it. She said to me this morning, when leave was mentioned – clutching at my hands. 'Don't go – I want you.' One of the few females who has ever touched me.

Am going to get with luck 48 hours leave some time soon, followed by all the rest of my fortnight later. I shall go down to Eton on the 48 hours.

The Squadron's Recording Officer – the adjutant – was T.B. Marson and he had taken rooms in a farmhouse nearby. His young daughter Thais – Arthur's delightful girl – was a great favourite with the pilots and features in many of the photographs taken of the squadron at Bekesbourne, illustrating the almost family atmosphere of the posting.[1] Richard Maybery's mother arrived from Brecon and together with Arthur they visited Maybery's cousins, Nasra and Ruth Eadon, two extremely pretty girls who lived at Court Lodge, a 'rambling old farmhouse' in the village of Bishopsbourne, some three miles from the aerodrome. Court Lodge, with its friendly atmosphere and tennis courts, soon became open house for the 56 Squadron pilots and in the heady atmosphere of wartime England a romance quickly blossomed between Arthur and Nasra, the younger of Maybery's cousins. In 1977 Nasra recalled:

> I was a serious-minded young woman for my age, more interested in horses and horseriding than boyfriends – whom I mostly spurned – but Arthur, I realized, was different and I fell deeply in love with him. Richard, my cousin, brought him along to see us soon after 56 Squadron arrived at Bekesbourne on their all too brief stay.

It was decided that the squadron would hold a dinner and dance. A

[1] Soon after arriving back in France, Arthur received a postcard from Thais Marson: 'My Dear Reice Davids, I got home safely and found the pony very fat. I here you have been fighting a lot John sends you his love as so does his mother. I long to come over the fields to the aeroplane. With love from Thais.'

large marquee was erected. Blomfield, with his usual flair, obtained some planking and very soon 'there was a regular Savoy dancing floor'. China and silver were brought from Canterbury and the marquee gaily decorated and lit with candles. Before dinner, in the soft summer evening, Ian Henderson and Cecil Lewis gave an exhibition of 'stunt' flying, then dinner was served. The squadron's cooks had excelled themselves and there was plenty of champagne. After dinner there was a small cabaret, in which one or two of the pilots sang and another played the violin. Then the tables were cleared and the squadron's famous band played for dancing.

Nasra remembered: 'I wore a sea green taffeta dress and satin shoes to match – specially dyed – but unfortunately the dyeing had made them too small and I was in agony the whole evening.'

About this time Arthur wrote to Nesta: a brotherly letter, full of advice and amused explanation of the squadron's work. Nesta, with all the perception and forthrightness of her seventeen years, had evidently questioned the worth of the tactics employed by the RFC in France, commenting that they seemed to 'merely hang around till the Boche showed up.'

> Dearest Little Angel,
>   An awfully belated answer to your adorable letter of June 16th. I didn't answer at first because I was expecting to see you at Oxford, and when all that was washed out by my leave being stopped – well I just haven't had the energy to write much, though I have oceans of spare time. It's always the way when things are slack, I'm so busy enjoying life that I forget all about letters for a while. First of all the usual happy returns on your sweet seventeen. Anything you want perticler? Because it doesn't matter if it's a bit late, does it? Secondly, bless you for saying 'gratters on MC' and stopping there without any of the long ovations uttered by dear fools who talk about wonderful pluck and all the other rot. I do so agree about the rabble – and in connection with that and reading poetry, have a try at Wordsworth's 'I wandered lonely as a cloud' – one of his shorter ones which you will find under 'Poems of the Imagination', and think over the lines about the inward eye and the bliss of solitude.
>   You are quite right about us merely hanging around until the Boche appears: our job is to see that the Boche does not get a chance to do any work in the air at all – I mean useful work like

bombing and observation. What advantage do we gain? We just gain the supremacy of the air, bless you, that's all: we 'ave a notice board put up to the effect.

AERIAL PARK.

PRIVATE.

HUN TRESPASSERS WILL BE PROSECUTED.

And we keep our own machines safe.

Now about reading. As regards prose I know almost less than you do. Is there a book called 'The Private Papers of Henry Ryecroft' by George Gissing in your library? That you would like, and also A.E.W. Mason's books, I think. As regards poetry, the great thing is to dabble in it at first: read the short ones or bits only of the long poems and read fast and often. Read as much Rupert Brooke as you can, also try W.E. Henley. In Shelley try first the 'Ode to a Skylark' and 'The Cloud', 'Ponte al Mare, Pisa' and the 'Witch of Atlas' – in bits. Also 'Night' and any fragments. In Keats try 'Ode on a Grecian Urn' and 'Ode to a Nightingale' and excerpts from 'Endymion.' I will try and send you a volume of selections which is always a good thing to start with. Also have you any of John Masefield's poems in the library? Don't read 'The Everlasting Mercy' yet if it is there.

I have been having a jolly time. I have started dancing – been to two dances, one here and another one away and I am getting on slowly. Anyhow, it is amusing.

Best love. We all went to church this morning. Arthur.

PS. You must get hold of Brooke's Grantchester.

On Wednesday 4 July, the Gothas bombed the naval base at Harwich and the Royal Naval Air Station at Felixstowe. The enemy bombers barely crossed the coast, and although a small armada of eighty-three British aeroplanes took off to intercept them, including fourteen SE5s from Bekesbourne, not one of the British pilots caught so much as a glimpse of the raiders. When he was back in France, Arthur told Caroline of the events and of his last days at Bekesbourne:

Wednesday morning we went up twice after the Huns that bombed Harwich but they would not tell us whereabouts they were and we were miles too late. It was very cloudy and I got up to 12,000 just off the north coast of Kent, but saw nothing and landed again – we got the alarm at 7.30 and were up 10 minutes later and down again after an hour.[1] At 9.09 we got another alarm and up we went, but the clouds were very thick and the people on the ground gave us no information so we came down again.[2]

In the evening we had a great dance at a place called Wye not far away and danced from 9.15 till 3.45 solid. I went home with a friend of mine and his 2 cousins who live near – 2 Miss Eadons, one to be engaged and the other 17½ and great fun – incidentally she taught me to dance. Into bed very weary at 5.30 am, and up again about 9 and packed up to go over. The clouds were fairly low and we did not start till 3.30 pm, after a delightful picnic lunch with the Eadons at the aerodrome. We had a very nice journey over: it took us an hour (not counting circling around at each end) and we went back to our old aerodrome. We had an excellent dinner in a small town near by in the evening and got to bed very sleepy about 11.30 for a good long sleep.

Two photographs of the happy lunch party with the Eadons and Lucy Maybery survive from the squadron's last afternoon at Bekesbourne. Nearly sixty years later Nasra wrote:

Dear Arthur . . . it is all so clear in my mind in spite of the many years that have passed, and for me Arthur's memory will never fade. He was indeed one of the greats – a lovely person.[3]

The squadron landed back at Estrée Blanche at 5 pm on the afternoon of 5 July. It had been recalled by direct order of General Haig, stating that it was urgently needed to be back in France by that

---

[1] Caroline expressed her disgust in a letter to Nesta, written five days after the raid. Current rumour had it that four of the Gothas had been shot down: 'Would not No. 56 have downed a lot more than 4 of the 20 raiders meeting them right in the face as they flew back over N Kent? It's all a most inglorious business, reflecting shame on the fools who look after (?) the protection of a great crowded vulnerable spot like the City and East End.'

[2] This was before the age of ground to air communications, but a crude – and ineffective – system of signals by strips on the ground and anti-aircraft fire had been devised.

[3] After 56 had left Bekesbourne and as soon as she was old enough, Nasra joined the WRAF, becoming a driver. During the Second World War she joined the FANY as a dispatch rider and while in Kenya rented out her cottage in the Cotswolds. Her tenants eventually departed with all her furniture and treasures, including her cherished letters from Arthur, who had written every day from France.

day. While in England the squadron had been under the orders of 6th Brigade Horseguards and when the Gothas again attacked the capital on 6 July the brigade ordered the squadron to intercept, only to find that it was no longer in England.

Back in France, the squadron quickly resumed its normal offensive patrols. Arthur wrote:

> Yesterday I was very busy all day putting up maps in the morning and filling rounds in the afternoon. Then I had a very nice little fly in the evening: and after dinner I meant to write some letters but I was very tired. And this morning I was called at 3 and told I was to go on patrol at 4. I got up at 3.30 but we did not start till a quarter to five. We had a fairly good show with a lot of scrapping but my guns were not very good. It is the first time over in the new machine with the bigger engine (200hp) I did not get any Huns. It is now 9am and I must wash. Best love. I expect to be back on leave again not very long hence.

The patrol referred to in this letter was led by Crowe, who took the SEs across the lines and patrolled from ten miles east of Ypres to the coast. A formation of silver Albatros D.IIIs was seen over Staden and Arthur, flying the 200 hp SE5a A4563, outdistanced his companions and flew under the enemy scouts, luring them down to attack him. The other SEs went down after the Albatri and a furious but indecisive fight took place. Arthur was forced to break off the action with a broken pipe in the Constantinesco Gear, which rendered his Vickers gun useless. He nevertheless flew to the arranged rendezvous at Ypres and there joined up with Crowe, attacking a group of four two-seater Aviatiks over Houthem. Both British pilots suffered gun stoppages and Arthur broke off the action and made for the British lines.

On his way he managed to clear his Lewis gun and attacked an Albatros scout, driving it down to 4,000 feet and leaving it diving steeply east. He regained his height but was attacked by another Albatros. Arthur evaded its first attack and although he had only half a drum of Lewis gun ammunition left – his sole working armament – he turned back to engage it. But his Lewis gun jammed again and he returned to Estrée Blanche.

On landing he found that the propeller of A4563 was badly shot through and that the rear and main spar of the right hand top plane were shattered, the result of the flight having been heavily and accurately Archied all the time it was over the German lines. It gives some indication of the skill and devotion of the 56 Squadron groundcrews that A4563 was repaired and ready to be tested by the morning of 10 July. Arthur made no mention of the damage to his machine in his next letter home.

As a prelude to the Battle of Ypres, due to commence on 25 July, the air offensive was to have begun on 8 July, but weather conditions were bad and it was not until 11 July, a fine warm day, that the RFC was able to begin work. Fifty-Six Squadron flew four offensive patrols during the day, but although A Flight saw a great deal of action, claiming two enemy scouts and a pair of two-seaters, B Flight, including Arthur, saw no action at all. Arthur wrote to Caroline, echoing the mood of the previous three days and giving good news of Dickinson, lost on 4 June during the fight with Jasta 28:

> The last three days until today have been cloudy, resulting in plenty of chess and bridge, largely with one R.A. Maybery, a new pilot in the squadron – he joined just before we came home: he was in the 21st Lancers in India and played Rugger for Wellington against Eton about 1911-1912. He is a first class tennis, squash, chess and bridge player and a damn fine scrapper and a 'pukka' gentleman. By the way did I tell you that the last Indian Cavalry man we had – Dickinson (my friend at Eton's cousin) whom I thought was certainly killed is down the other side badly wounded in both legs but alright. Comforts me immensely, as I was so sure he was a goner when he went down. We had a show last night but did not do much. The Hun is waking up in the sky a bit and we are going to have our work cut out to keep control, but we undoubtedly will.

Arthur's observation in the last sentence of this letter was fully borne out the next day, 12 July. It was a fine day, if a little cloudy, and the airfighting on the Ypres front was intense. Barlow led B Flight off the ground at 1.30 with orders to patrol the Menin, Courtrai, Roulers area. The flight was soon in action, attacking a pair of two-seaters working in the vicinity of Roulers. Arthur, Muspratt and Coote attacked a black and white two-seater but it evaded their attempts to shoot it down and the SEs cleared. Arthur then attacked a single-seater scout, 'many colours, slight extensions. No dihedral on bottom plane.' This was probably a Fokker DV. The enemy scout spun away from his attack over the Menin-Roulers road and was then engaged by Muspratt.

Arthur then saw five enemy scouts of the same type ('new type scouts . . . climb not very remarkable, but speed fairly good. Very small black crosses, square ended top plane') flying at 11,000 feet and heading west from Menin. He waited until these were over the front lines before attacking them. Manoeuvring for position, he got to within thirty yards of one scout, which was painted green. The enemy pilot was unaware of Arthur's presence and a burst of fire from both guns sent it down out of control. Captain Henderson had also attacked three scouts and, unknown to Arthur, had saved him from attack. After leaving the stricken scout, which went down over Roncq, Arthur then attacked a two-seater. This was a DFW CV, No 799/17 from Flieger Abteilung 7, crewed by Leutnant Eugen Mann and Unteroffizier Albert Hahnel. It carried a white arrow marking on the sides and top of its fuselage and the numeral 7 underneath the observer's cockpit.

The DFW dived steeply for 7,000 feet under Arthur's first attack and flattened out over Ploegsteert Wood. As Arthur followed it down an enemy scout dived onto his tail. Henderson, again seeing Arthur's danger, hurtled down after the enemy scout and shot at it from a hundred and fifty yards' range in an attempt to distract it from Arthur. 'The EA turned upside down and went down out of control over Zandvoorde.'

Arthur, unaware of his narrow escape, again engaged the DFW, which was now down to 1,500 feet. He was finally forced to leave it as his engine began continually to cut out and he turned for home. The DFW turned and flew south west over Ploegsteert. It turned east three times, only to be headed off each time by Muspratt, who had now appeared on the scene. Mann fired a few shots at Muspratt, but Hahnel, badly wounded by Arthur's fire, finally attempted to put the DFW down just north of Armentières; it bounced and crashed into a pond. Mann and Hahnel were taken prisoner.

Although Muspratt had prevented this DFW from returning to its own side of the lines, and it had obviously force-landed to escape his attentions, the victory was awarded to Arthur in the squadron lists and combat reports. Muspratt made no claim, nor makes any mention of it in a letter home written the next day.

Arthur, Keith Muspratt and Maxwell Coote were firm friends, kept together a great deal of the time when not flying and were collectively known in the squadron as 'The Children'. During their periods off duty, when the rather more worldly members of the squadron visited the nearest town with its clubs and estaminets, full, as McCudden put it, 'of the fair maids of France', 'The Children' preferred the quieter pursuits of walking and talking. Coote, the only one of the trio to survive the war, recalled: 'We weren't prigs or wet blankets or anything like that. We just preferred to go for walks and talk about every subject under the sun. Rhys Davids and I had been to Eton, Muspratt to Sherborne, and we had many schoolfriends in other squadrons, whom we visited whenever possible.'

July 12, 1917, was a day of heavy and intense airfighting along the entire front, particularly in the 5th Army area. Enemy formations were becoming larger and these, attracting a number of smaller British formations, sparked off large scale 'dogfights', especially during the long and generally fine summer evenings. That losses, on both sides, were relatively small to the number of aeroplanes involved in these actions, is indicative of how evenly matched were the fighter pilots of both sides. When equal numbers of fighters were in combat the results were, as often as not, indecisive.

Captain Ian Henry David Henderson was now leading B Flight, having rejoined the squadron while it was at Bekesbourne. Crowe had been suffering from ill-health for some time and was finally struck off strength on 13 July. It was a sad loss for the squadron and B Flight in particular, but he was to rejoin the squadron in 1918. Arthur wrote home:

> I am sorry to say that poor old Crowe has rather broken down in health: he was not very well when we left and he has now gone to hospital at the base with on-and-off flu and general rundown. He will probably go home and get a squadron (at home) when he has recovered. Our new Flight Commander is Capt Henderson who was to have come out with us originally and was posted to us again while we were at Bekesbourne. Splendid person.

July 13 was another fine day and there was no let-up in the airfighting, the evening again being the time of the heaviest fighting. C Flight flew an escort and an offensive patrol during the day, but saw no action. It was a vastly different situation for B Flight, flying the last patrol of the day at 7.00 pm.

Henderson, taking the flight across the lines at 12,500 feet, could see twenty enemy aeroplanes in various groups, stretching from 'the sea to Lille'. He and Arthur were flying the higher performance SEs with the 200 hp engine and they climbed to 14,500 feet 'well above the 150 hp SEs.' Henderson attacked a hostile scout, sending it down in a cloud of smoke, then attacked another, forcing it down to 2,000 feet. He was then attacked by another five Albatros scouts and he dived away, losing them by virtue of his superior speed and climbing again to recross the front lines. Here he found Arthur, who was singlehandedly fighting eight Albatri.[1] Arthur had been fighting these scouts for an hour and a quarter – 'on and off' – attacking stragglers from the enemy formation whenever an opportunity presented itself. At one time, four of the Albatri had driven him back to the British lines, but he had returned and persisted in his attacks. In one such he had engaged an Albatros from fifty yards, closing the range to within ten yards, firing both guns as he narrowed the distance. The enemy aeroplane turned over and, with engine full on, went down out of control in a steep dive. Henderson now joined him and they drove the rest of the Albatri east of Roulers, leaving them to engage another eleven they had sighted over Iseghem.

Henderson, attacked at very close range by two of these new opponents, was forced to spin away, and when he came out of his spin he found one of the Albatri still on his tail. Henderson zoomed and Immelmann-turned, but the German pilot matched his manoeuvres, sticking to him like a leech, firing all the time. Things looked bad for Henderson. Only the disparity between the enemy pilot's flying skill and his marksmanship had saved him from being shot down. It seemed merely a question of time before the German pilot made one burst tell. But Arthur then arrived and shot the Albatros off his flight commander's tail. The enemy pilot, sideslipping away from Arthur's fire, nearly collided with Henderson's SE, so close were the antagonists. Henderson and Arthur then turned for home, having been in almost continuous action for an hour and a half. Henderson and Arthur were each credited with an Albatros out of control and Barlow with another.

Bad weather stopped all flying by the squadron for the next two days. On 15 July Arthur wrote home:

If you want to see a really interesting photograph get the Sphere of July 14th with a picture of Richthofen's 'Travelling Circus' ie. his crew of fighting machines drawn up ready to start. You will see the type of thing I see every day in the sky. Also in the papers of that

---

[1] Arthur had insisted that the plural of Albatros was correctly 'Albatri'. Bowman, the C Flight Commander, recalled 'We much preferred it to the verbal atrocity of Albatrosses.' The term was later widely used in the RFC.

day you will find in Haig's communique accounts of great airfighting. Our squadron got 9 alone that day – a wonderful day's work. I got two – one I brought down this side of the lines: it was a 2 seater doing artillery work of sorts or infantry co-operation: I caught him at 10,000 feet about, just over the lines and wounded the pilot (NCO) who got very frightened and dived straight for the nearest field, eventually landing about 2 miles behind our lines, where he stood on his nose in a ditch. The observer, an officer, was unhurt and the machine is practically intact. The other was a scout over the other side. The next day we had a most interesting evening's fighting, and I got another scout, bringing my total up to ten and a share in an eleventh. Today my machine is having a thorough overhaul, and I went off to the base – you know where – and saw old Straker again, in fact I brought him along here for tea. What a dear old man he is – he sends his love to you both.

A 4563 was still being overhauled on 16 July and Arthur missed flying in the evening patrol. He wrote to Vivien:

16/7/17   56 Squadron.
Dearest V,
    I am afraid this will not reach you in time for your birthday; I suddenly remembered it this morning, having with typical forgetfulness let it slide completely out of my head. Anyhow, many happy returns of the day before ...yesterday. I hope you will get in a few days a small book I am having sent to you which you may not have seen before, anyhow I have a copy out here and it contains a lot of very fine reading, notably, to my taste, Katharine Tynan, R.L. Stevenson, Drinkwater, Laurence Binyon, and of course the immortal Rupert Brooke.
    You will no doubt have heard from Mother about my movements: how we left England and came back to the old aerodrome. We have been having quite an easy time since ie. we have not been working very much – only one show a day usually, and sometimes none at all if the weather is unsettled, but when we do go on a show nearly every time it has been a very strenuous one – ie. a great deal of scrapping and flying about. I have brought down two more machines the other side and one brand new 2 seater doing artillery or observation work of sorts. I caught him about over the lines and made him land this side, where he was captured almost intact. The pilot had six bullets in him and made

a bad landing, finally sticking up on his nose in a ditch. The observer, who had the Iron Cross, was unwounded, whereas the pilot is now in hospital in a serious but not desperate condition.[1] That makes ten altogether for me, and tonight B Flight were on a show, and we had a scrap with about 25 machines either side – whole air thick with them. Our guns were going badly all round and we only got one of them, which makes a total of 95 for the squadron in 2½ months scrapping. There is going to be some bust up when we get our 100th Hun.

Life is very pleasant now indeed, but I hope I get leave before the end of the month because I want to snatch a visit to Eton before they break up on July 31st. However, I am afraid that is not likely – if I get leave at all it will probably be in about three to four weeks' time from now.

I have sent N as a belated birthday present, a kind of superior anthology of prose and verse called 'The Open Road' by E.V. Lucas – a particularly good selection of the best things. I am glad to hear you sent her a Rupert Brooke 1914.

Am very sleepy – writing in the office at 1.40 am it being my turn to sleep in the office and take phone messages during the night.

Goodnight beloved. yr. Arthur.

The weather was cloudy the following day but improved again in the evening. Henderson took the flight across the lines and saw 70 Squadron, flying their newly issued Sopwith Camels, attack an enemy formation over the Roulers-Menin road. The Camels were in turn attacked by another enemy force until the six Camels were fighting twenty-five enemy scouts. Henderson led the SEs into the fray, followed by some FE2ds of 20 Squadron, a formation of DH5s from 32 Squadron and two formations of Sopwith Triplanes from Naval 1 and 10 Squadrons. The fighting was intense and fiercely contested, the antagonists flying in and out of the numerous banks of cloud. All the SE5s had gun trouble of one kind or another but one sent an enemy scout down out of control. This victory could not be credited to any one SE as the fighting was now so rapid, and the general mêlée so confused, that it was impossible to see who had fired the damaging burst. The SEs all returned safely, Arthur commenting: 'EA strategy was good, but shooting bad.'

[1] Hahnel later died of his wounds.

To the great relief of the hard-pressed pilots the weather was again bad the next day, and although conditions were a little better on 19 July, enabling Henderson to take the flight out in the evening, they saw no action of any kind. That night, Maurice Baring, Trenchard's aide, dined with the squadron. Baring was a great favourite with 56 Squadron, as he was throughout the entire RFC, and he noted in his diary:

> I dined with 56 Squadron. Ian Henderson, Blomfield, Maybery, Bowman, Maxwell, Coote, Marson and Rhys Davids were there. The Squadron band played during dinner. The sergeant who conducted was before the war an important factor in the Palace Orchestra. They played Mendelssohn's 'Spring Song'. One of the pilots said it was being played too slowly; and the conductor thought he said it was not being played slowly enough, and said: 'Mendelssohn was played sprightly.'[1]

B Flight saw no action during a morning patrol on 20 July, the enemy aeroplanes seen not allowing them to come within range. But the patrol was not without incident. While over Ste Marie Cappelle the propeller shaft of Henderson's SE snapped and the propeller flew off. Henderson made a forced landing with no injury to himself, but SE5a 4855 was wrecked. The rest of the squadron had a successful day, with Bowman and Hoidge of C Flight each claiming an Albatros out of control and Maxwell of A Flight shooting down two others; but two pilots were lost during the day's fighting: Lieutenants Jardine and Messervy.

On 21 July no patrols were flown until the evening, but the first held a hint of things to come: Captain James Thomas Byford McCudden flew his first patrol in a 56 Squadron SE5. McCudden was attached to 66 Squadron on a month's refresher course, flying Sopwith Pups, and when Major Blomfield asked him if he would like to fly an evening patrol with the squadron, McCudden needed no persuasion. He had visited the squadron while it was at Bekesbourne and there is no doubt that he had set his heart on joining 56 Squadron as a flight commander when his refresher course was ended.

So it was that Captain Prothero led McCudden, Arthur and Gerald Maxwell across the lines on the evening of 21 July. The SEs, a

---

[1] *Flying Corps Headquarters 1914-1918*, Maurice Baring. Blackwood 1968.

formidable quartet of airfighters, flew first to Nieuport, but finding no activity there they made south to the area of Houthulst Forest. Here Prothero spotted a formation of Albatri and went down after them. McCudden, unused to the tremendous build-up of speed of an SE5 in a dive, was left far behind and only arrived later, in time to 'put the draught up some "V" Strutters', but Prothero and Maxwell had attacked three of the lower Albatri, leaving Arthur to tackle two others flying slightly higher.

Concentrating on these, Arthur failed to see another seven Albatri arrive on the scene. These attacked him. Arthur summed up his reaction in two words: 'I fled.' Even Arthur baulked at tackling nine 'V' Strutters singlehanded. He flew to the Ypres area and here he joined up with Barlow and Cronyn, who had taken off twenty minutes later. There were many formations of enemy aeroplanes in the vicinity, but they made no move to attack the three SEs – which were quickly reinforced by Maxwell and Prothero – until Cronyn attacked one of their number: a large, green-coloured two-seater.

This sparked off a general dogfight. Arthur attacked a black and white Albatros, firing thirty rounds into it, sending it down in a slow spiral with occasional sideslips. His Lewis gun had stopped with a double feed and his Vickers had two stoppages and this kept him busy for a while, but having cleared his Vickers he saw an Albatros above him and he stalled, firing up as he did so. Coming out of the stall he dived to 8,000 feet and attacked a lower Albatros, but while engaged in this he came under attack from another. McCudden, who had just arrived at the scene of the action, saw this Albatros in time, passed over Arthur's SE and opened fire on his attacker from a hundred yards. The silvery grey Albatros turned away east and 'wobbled laterally'. McCudden watched it finally fall into a slow spiral before he was forced to turn away, coming under attack from one of its companions.

Arthur had broken off his pursuit of the Albatros to chase a two-seater over Polygon wood. He fired a good burst of Vickers at this – his Lewis gun had stopped with a broken extractor – but his shots had no effect. After forcing another two-seater to clear east, Arthur went home 'having been out 2¼ hours.'

McCudden did not claim the silver grey Albatros, but Prothero was credited with a black and white Albatros, Arthur with another, and the large two-seater shot down by Cronyn was the squadron's hundredth victory.

A celebration dinner was held that night: not only for the

hundredth victory, but for the award of a Bar to Arthur's Military Cross. His next letter home, jointly addressed to Caroline and Vivien, is strangely muted in tone. After a few lines regarding sent and received letters, he carried on:

> About announcing leave. I cannot send wires from France, but I will send them, one to each when I land at Folkestone. Nothing much happening here. For some totally obscure reason they have just given me a bar to my MC. Will Nesta be home when this arrives I wonder, and has her book reached her?

Such a short letter, barely a page long, was perhaps a sign of weariness and tired nerves.

Arthur flew in the evening patrol of 22 July. The SEs tackled thirteen enemy scouts which had attacked three Nieuports, scattering the Albatri and driving them back over their own lines. During the remainder of the patrol a great deal of skirmishing took place with various groups of enemy aeroplanes but no decisive results were obtained.

The next patrol in which Arthur flew was on the evening of 24 July. Two flights left Estrée Blanche at 7 pm but were both forced to return because of the extremely bad visibility. Arthur flew no more patrols for four days, but his comrades were involved in a great deal of fighting. On the evening of 26 July A Flight took part in the largest single airfight of the war to date. The flight attacked fourteen Albatros scouts over Gheluvelt and within minutes large numbers of machines were attracted to the scene of the fight. At the lower levels, 5,000 feet, enemy two-seaters were attempting to work, being protected by an escort of thirty Albatri, 3,000 feet above, who were fighting to prevent the DH5s of 32 Squadron from getting among their charges. Between 12,000 and 14,000 feet another ten Albatri were fighting the SE5s of 56 Squadron, the Spads of 19 Squadron and 70 Squadron's Sopwith Camels. Higher still, at 17,000 feet, another formation of enemy scouts was fighting with the Sopwith Triplanes of the Naval Squadrons. The SEs finally landed back at Estrée Blanche at 9 pm. Barlow had shot down an Albatros out of control and Maxwell had driven down a two-seater; but against these victories was set the loss of Phillip Prothero, the ebullient Scotsman, and leader of A Flight. His SE had been seen going down at 14,000 feet with both its starboard wings shot off.

July 27 saw a great deal of action, with Bowman claiming two victories and Maybery and Hoidge one each. The amount of victories, however, bears no relation to the extent of the fighting. Both C and A Flights were out in the evening – A Flight being led by Henderson – and were involved in heavy fighting, losing Lieutenant White, who fortunately survived to be taken prisoner of war. Bowman had a particularly hard fight with several Albatri, only managing to finally escape by dropping down to ground level and flying along the rides of Houthulst Forest, one of the pursuing enemy pilots flying into a tree in his eagerness to close the distance between himself and Bowman's SE5. Bowman finally recrossed the British lines at fifty feet and later recorded in his logbook: 'Never been so frightened in my life.'

It was a successful evening's fighting for the RFC: 56 Squadron claimed four victories; 66 Squadron an Albatros destroyed; 70 Squadron claimed two driven down by Captain Collett, and Lieutenant Kellog of 19 Squadron was credited with another out of control. The FE2ds of 20 Squadron, an outdated aeroplane, often dismissed as being 'easy meat' for the German fighter pilots, were the most successful of any squadron engaged in the evening's fighting, claiming no less than six enemy aeroplanes: two in flames, one seen to break up in the air, and the remaining three seen to crash. The total British casualties were four: Lieutenants Burkett and Stuart Lewis of 20 Squadron, who nevertheless managed to safely land their damaged FE; Flight Sub-Lieutenant Roach of Naval 10 and Lieutenant White of 56 Squadron.

The following day, 28 July, was to have seen the opening of the offensive, already postponed, but it was again put back because of bad visibility and the difficulty the French were having in bringing up their artillery. But the heavy ground mist, which so effectively cancelled operations on the ground, had no effect on the war in the air. The day was cloudy, with clear intervals and Henderson took out his flight at 8 am, crossing the lines at 12,000 feet. Arthur's engine was going badly and he was forced to leave the formation and land at Bailleul, and he took no part in an action in which Henderson shot an enemy scout down out of control. Henderson also had engine trouble on returning from this patrol and joined Arthur in a forced landing at Bailleul.

Arthur wrote to Caroline on 30 July, alluding to the opening of the Third Battle of Ypres due to begin the next day:

30/7/17   56 Squadron.

Dearest Mother.

Just time for a short one before I turn in to get some sleep before the great day tomorrow. . . . By the way, I am afraid one sentence in your letter is quite beyond me, viz 'I would copy out Crowe's *epitaph*' You add afterwards, 'I mean inscription.' But what on earth put it into your head that the description of his wondrous work should be an epitaph? Of course I cannot get back now in time to go down to Eton for my leave; I expect to come in between a week and a fortnight's time, and I will wire you and V immediately on arriving in England – which is the best I can do.

Tell me – do you think Buddha himself *really* believed in the Karma doctrine of rebirth? Because it *must* involve animism of a kind and who or what is the judge of one's life work and consequent rebirth in a higher or lower stage? Going to be a war tomorrow. Must sleep.

The reference to Crowe's 'wondrous work' is probably in connection with Caroline having read of his exploits in the *London Gazette* and there is an unusual touch of asperity in her son's comments – unusual enough to be perhaps another sign of fraying nerves.

By a strange reversal of the conditions of 28 July, the weather on 31 July was good for ground fighting but impossible for any air operations, with low cloud and mist all day. Despite this Richard Maybery flew a lone mission at dawn, bombing the German airfield at Heule, the base of Flieger Abteilung No 6, Flieger Abteilung No (A) 250, and Jagdstaffel 10. Leaving Heule, Maybery flew the short distance to another enemy aerodrome at Cuerne, the base of Jagdstaffel 4. On leaving Cuerne, Maybery attacked two German officers out riding and then, turning west, a train on the Courtrai to Menin line. Not content with this, he next attacked a column of two hundred infantry marching along the Menin road, scattering the troops and inflicting many casualties. Zooming for height, he spotted a two-seater and tackled it with such determination that it crashed by the side of the railway. After strafing the people who had run to the scene of the crash, Maybery turned his attentions to another train, but his ammunition was now exhausted and he reluctantly returned to Estrée Blanche. He had flown no higher than five hundred feet during the whole of the actions. This was one of the epic flights of the RFC and the first time an SE5 of 56 Squadron had carried and dropped bombs.

The bad weather of the last three days of July deteriorated still further during the first three days of August. The pilots of 56 Squadron relaxed in their various and individual ways: Maybery and Arthur in one of their innumerable games of chess; others played ping-pong, a great favourite with the squadron, or a ball game called 'Bumble Puppy'. Those not reading, writing letters or playing the gramophone, played bridge and other card games. It was a welcome rest after the hectic airfighting of the past weeks.

The weather cleared a little on 5 August and Arthur flew a patrol in the evening in which Leonard Barlow shot down an enemy scout – possibly a Roland D.II. These enemy scouts were painted blue and green or blue and yellow. One, which Arthur thought manoeuvred 'very well', sported a blue and yellow striped fuselage. This was the last patrol Arthur was to fly before he went on leave. The next two days were foggy and on the 8th the longed for day finally arrived and Arthur left Estrée Blanche for England on fourteen days' leave.

*

Arthur returned to Estrée Blanche on 22 August. Keith Muspratt was glad to see him back; he had written home: 'RD is on leave so I am all alone, but bearing up.' As always, Arthur's first thought was of his mother and he wrote to tell her of his journey back to France and to bring her up to date with the squadron news:

22/8/17   56 Squadron.
Dearest Mother
   I hope you got my PC from London. I travelled down to Folkestone very comfortably and after a short wait the boat started at 10.50. About ten minutes out of Folkestone we saw a raid going on in the distance over Dover, just a lot of anti-aircraft fire which looked not at all bad, aimed at a bunch of black specks in the sky, which vanished somehow, except for one which suddenly realized it was time for lunch and beetled off home as hard as he could. At BLANK we found a car waiting for us and soon arrived here. I found myself back among the old crew again, including Potts who has turned up here much to my delight. I had my first flip tonight but the machine proved unsatisfactory and I expect I shall not go to the war tomorrow. We got eight Huns ourselves today-being the first day for a long time without a strong wind which has been causing all the trouble.
                        Must go to bed now. Very sleepy. A.

Arthur's bald statement that he had been up but that the machine had proved 'unsatisfactory', is a classic piece of understatement. The test flight, in SE5a B507, very nearly cost him his life. He had taken off at 6 pm for a routine test, climbing to 14,000 feet. After making a slow right-hand turn he dived back towards the aerodrome. After 2,000 feet he suddenly felt a violent wrench and a severe jar. He immediately let go of the controls. 'The tail wheel being neutral she came out at once, slowed up and dropped the right wing. I then saw that one pair of flying wires had snapped and other wires were much strained.'

He came down, turning on rudder alone, as he had no aileron control, and managed to land safely. On examination of the SE it was found that all the lift and drift wire fittings had been drawn into the wood, one main lift wire attachment being broken at the bolt. The rudder fin was badly buckled, the tailplane loose, and the whole machine was described as being in a 'loose condition'. Unrepairable in the squadron workshops, B507 was returned to No 1 Aeroplane Depot. This was a narrow escape from disaster, averted only by Arthur's cool and expert handling of an extremely nasty situation.

The weather now set in and the squadron flew no patrols for the following two days. Only one patrol was flown on the 25 and 26 August before conditions deteriorated still further, washing out all war flying for the next four days. The rest was not unwelcome. While Arthur had been on leave the squadron had done a great deal of fighting. Although it had claimed twenty victories during the fortnight he had been in England, it had lost eight pilots killed, wounded or prisoner of war. Arthur wrote to Caroline on 25 August, following it three days later with a letter to Vivien:

25/8/17   56 Squadron.
Dearest M,
    Nothing happening at all. Thursday and Friday both very windy with some clouds so we did not go up. I have got a new machine as I expected, which is slowly getting into fighting condition. I find ping-pong is going strong now, I also have great hopes for the Rugger XV. Maybery and Muspratt are both going strong, former having now got 8½ and latter 4 Huns. The squadron now has 144 Huns, of which B Flight has just reached its 50.
    I went over and had lunch at the Wing yesterday and saw my friend Prout and staff captain, bless him. This is all for the present.
            Best love to all three. Arthur.

To Vivien:

> Nothing doing here; a furious gale with a lot of rain, making tents of doubtful comfort. Three days ago – before the windy weather set in – I developed a sore throat, got some pills for it, and it vanished at once, or rather changed to the next floor down, and the last 2 days I have been feeling absolutely rotten with a curious feeling of congestion just where my lower ribs join in the middle, especially during or just after a meal. That too however is just beginning to vanish.
>
> There is a rumour that Billy Crowe is going to get 56 Reserve Squadron ie. his majority – which I hope is well founded.
>
> I am going to do a lot of reading in the near future. 'A splash of sun, the shouting wind, the brave sting of rain, *and* the dreamy eyed hills, and *lots* of freedom, (also health) to enjoy them.' Ohh!

The weather improved on the last day of August and the squadron flew two patrols in the evening, A and C Flights taking off at 6 pm. The eleven SEs made for the patrol area of Houthulst Forest to Gheluvelt, and Maxwell, the A Flight commander, sighted a group of eight Albatri circling Moorslede at 12,000 feet. Looking up, Maxwell saw another formation of enemy scouts, four thousand feet higher, flying west. It was an obvious trap, the higher Albatri intending to attack the SEs out of the glare of the setting sun as they dived on the lower formation. This did not deter Gerald Maxwell. He knew that B Flight was in the vicinity and would keep the higher Albatri busy while A Flight dealt with their companions and he led his force down to attack.

Maxwell had stoppages in both guns and was chased back to the lines by a 'very good red nosed EA.' who kept on his tail, firing continuously. G.M. Wilkinson noticed his flight commander's predicament and shot the Albatros off Maxwell's tail, the enemy scout falling out of control. The remainder of the Albatri then cleared east. Their companions in the top layer had not come to their assistance, seeing somewhat easier prey in the shape of two French Spads. During their subsequent attack on these they were attacked by McCudden and Johnson, reinforced by the remainder of A Flight, who had climbed into the fight. While the SEs were fighting with these black and white Albatri, the initial group, now numbering seven and led by a red-nosed machine, joined in the action. Sloley of A Flight sent down one of the black and white Albatri in a spin, and Coote sent another down with clouds of blue-black smoke coming from it. The fight gradually died out and after a great deal of manoeuvring for position the enemy aeroplanes flew off east towards Armentières.

Arthur had shot at and driven down under control, three of the black-and-white scouts, but had been prevented from pressing home his attacks by the arrival of seven additional Albatri. When the enemy force broke off the combat, Arthur followed and, accompanied by two Nieuports and a Spad, flew parallel with the Albatri and a thousand feet lower in an attempt to induce them to attack. The German pilots either did not see or ignored the little force, and although Arthur stalled and fired up at one of their number – without result – they continued to fly towards Armentières, finally turning north-east, where Arthur left them and returned to Estrée Blanche. He wrote home the following night:

> Dearest Mums,
>
> No news at all. We had a show last night: first time since leave for me. Plenty of Huns about: we got 2 out of control, but as there were 25 Huns about and nobody else up apparently except about 9 of us the fighting was indecisive. My new machine was not going very well yesterday but I think it will be alright in time. Weather better but very hazy yesterday, today again overcast. We have been reading two very amusing books lately, one called 'Bachelor's Buttons' by Edward Burke, and one called 'Lost Diaries' by Maurice Baring, who is Trenchard's aide-de-camp. I re-enclose N's letter: how truely delightful it is. We had our first game of rugger last night, or rather night before. I believe I mentioned it in my last letter to Viv. Anyhow, most successful and we are trying to get up another tonight. I am temporarily in charge of B Flight now, the CO being on leave, and the real Flt Commander (one McCudden who came when Henderson left) being temporary CO and Barlow, who is senior to me, being on leave. Ping-pong is also going strong in the mess now.
>
> Best love to all three beloved. I am having a wonderful time.

Captain McCudden had joined 56 Squadron as B Flight Commander on 15 August and was to have a highly successful career while serving with the squadron. When he was finally posted to Home Establishment in March 1918 he had a total of 57 victories to his credit, all confirmed, and was acknowledged to be one of the finest patrol leaders in the RFC. An indication of his worth is that, during his leadership of B Flight, from August 1917 until March 1918, he led it in over seventy patrols for the loss of only four pilots.

When he took command of the flight it consisted of Arthur Rhys Davids, Leonard Barlow, Keith Muspratt, Verschoyle Cronyn and Maxwell Coote – as McCudden put it, 'as splendid a lot of fellows as ever set foot in France'. It is curious that out of the four who failed to survive the war, only one was killed in action, the remaining three losing their lives in flying accidents. Both Muspratt and Barlow were killed in 1918 when flight testing and lastly, McCudden himself, crashing fatally on 9 July 1918 while flying out to France again to take command of 60 Squadron.

August had been a successful month for 56 Squadron. Despite the bad weather it had been a month of heavy fighting and the squadron had claimed forty victories for the loss of eight pilots. On the ground the continual rain of the last weeks had transformed the terrain of the battlefield of Ypres into a morass, turning the ground fighting into attacks of a purely local nature. Plans were being made, however, for a resumption of the Ypres offensive just as soon as the ground had dried sufficiently and a heavy programme was laid down for the squadrons of the RFC concerned.

September was to be an even more successful month, for 56 Squadron in general and Arthur in particular. Besides adding substantially to his personal score, Arthur was to fight an action during the month that finally established him as one of the RFC's most successful fighter pilots.

The month started well for Arthur. Obviously refreshed by his leave he threw himself into the fighting with renewed determination. His first patrol, a special mission, flown with Maybery on the morning of 3 September, was uneventful, with no action of any kind, but in the evening he took off with his new flight commander on another special offensive patrol. Their orders were to patrol the Ypres Salient and fifty minutes after taking off Arthur, who had separated from McCudden soon after leaving Estrée Blanche, saw eight Albatros 'V' Strutters attacking the SEs of C Flight who were flying a normal evening patrol. One of the Albatri was hovering on the edge of the fighting, probably in the hope of picking off a straggler. Unseen, Arthur approached to within fifty yards. Ten rounds from each gun sent the Albatros down to crash near Houthem. In the event the credit for this Albatros was shared between Arthur and Richard Maybery, who had attacked it just before Arthur had appeared, but it was a good start to the month.

The next day McCudden, escaping from his duties as temporary CO, took B Flight off the ground after lunch. His orders were to escort the DH4s of 55 Squadron on a bombing raid to Audenarde, and after seeing the bombers safely back to the British lines, he led the flight back to the vicinity of Lille. While accompanying the DH4s on their outward journey, McCudden had seen several Albatros scouts gaining their height over the town, and he now went back to look for them, finally finding them at 16,000 feet, but flying east. Arthur was all for chasing the Albatri, 'Young Rhys Davids kept calling my attention to them, for he was all for chasing the Huns out of the sky altogether, and I had some difficulty in making him realize that bravery should not be carried out to the extent of foolhardiness,'[1] but the wily McCudden knew that before the SEs could catch them the Albatri would be a long way east of the lines and the flight would have to fight at a serious tactical disadvantage. Sure enough, the German force soon returned west and attacked the SEs over Becelaere.

Arthur tackled the highest of the enemy scouts, firing a whole drum of Lewis at it while he held the SE in a stalled position. The Albatros pilot dived steeply away towards Inglemunster, with Arthur in hot pursuit, but the excessive speed of the dive caused the SE to vibrate in an alarming manner and he was forced to pull out, climbing back and rejoining his companions over Polygon Wood before returning to base.

Arthur took no part in the morning patrol flown by B Flight on 5 September. His new SE, B525, had not been going well – he had borrowed Lieutenant Johnson's machine for the patrol on 3 September – and was being attended to in the squadron workshops. He wrote to Nesta, finishing with the time-honoured line which he knew she would appreciate:

5/9/17   56 Squadron.
Dearest Nesta,
    Many thanks for long letter. The fine weather has just come right for you, I hope. First of all please give Mrs Tait and Cassie my love and say I would wish I were with you too if I wasn't having such a priceless time here. In spite of the fine weather I am not frightfully busy as my machine is not functioning properly, but it should be alright by tonight. The day before yesterday (on somebody else's machine) I got my twelfth Hun. Poor beggar just

[1] *Five Years in The Royal Flying Corps*, J.T.B.McCudden. Aeroplane and General Publishing Co. 1918.

hit the ground at a perfectly appalling pace, but it was his own
fault, as he let me get right behind him and open fire without
deviating at all. Anybody that lets someone sit on his tail without
seeing him get there has no right to be there at all.

Muspratt, whose name you probably remember, and Maxwell,
who is one of the original four left in the squadron, have both just
got the MC wherefore band and much rejoicings tonight.

Sand and sea, sea and sand, O you lucky people! The bathing
place we used to frequent here is now quite impossible owing to
multitudinous Portuguese who use it as a bathroom. The place
reeks of them.

We have had two splendid games of Rugger so far, up on the
aerodrome with grass nearly a foot long and only 11 a side, but still
great fun and good exercise. Here endeth. 'oping you are in the
pink has it leaves me at present from your loving brother. Arthur.

In the evening of 5 September, Hoidge took out C Flight, Captain
Bowman the flight commander being on leave, and Arthur tagged
along to make up the numbers, flying SE5a A4563. It turned out to
be a most successful evening's fighting for him. Owing to engine
trouble, Taylor and Gardiner both dropped out and only Hoidge,
Maybery and Arthur reached the lines, crossing them north of Ypres
at 11,000 feet and patrolling to Moorslede. The three SEs came
under attack from a force of twelve black-and-white Albatri and,
finding the odds too great, they cleared to the west. They climbed to
13,000 feet and returned to the Roulers-Menin road, climbing all the
time. Eight Albatri were then seen, east of Roulers, but as the SEs
went into the attack Hoidge's engine began to give trouble and he
was forced to turn west to rectify it. On returning he found Maybery
and Arthur fighting the Albatri, assisted by Camels, Nieuports, FEs
and Bristol Fighters, which Arthur had led into the fight.

Arthur singled out an enemy scout and got in a good burst with
both guns at close range. The Albatros went down in a steep dive,
then began to spiral down with smoke pouring from its engine.
Arthur wasted no more time watching this Albatros, pulling down
his Lewis and firing twenty rounds into another, flying above him.
This Albatros, which had a red fuselage with a black band around it,
dived straight in front of Arthur's SE and he fired another burst with
both guns. The Albatros 'wobbled and went down steeply'. Arthur
zoomed away. Looking back he saw the enemy aeroplane had broken
up, the fuselage and one set of wings floating down in small pieces.

Arthur and Maybery were now isolated, with Arthur below. Arthur came under attack from three of theAlbatri, but he eluded these and made for the lines. Seeing a dull green Albatros with a yellow band round the fuselage, flying under some FEs, Arthur attacked it, but the enemy pilot, Vzfw Alfred Muth of Jasta 27, was no novice: he manoeuvred well and put some shots into the SE. Eventually, however, Arthur got above Muth, who rolled and went down in a dive. Arthur followed, firing all the time, and the Albatros 'staggered', went down vertically and finally crashed in a small copse a mile north east of Poelcapelle. Although he had disposed of three Albatros scouts in a short period, the engine of A4563 had been giving trouble for some time, owing to a faulty carburettor, and Arthur returned to Estrée Blanche. The next day he wrote to Vivien:

6/9/17   56 Squadron.
Dearest V,
    Just a hurried line for Muspratt to take home with him and post as he is going on leave. If the negatives have not been sent out yet, could you send them to K.K. Muspratt Esq. MC. 11 Madeira Rd Bournemouth, instead of out here, but send the enlargements here as soon as you can. I suppose its about time they were done.
    Yesterday I had a great show with old Maybery. I got 3 Huns – a record for one pilot in the squadron for one show. 1 broke to pieces in the air, 1 crashed and 1 out of control. That makes fifteen altogether.

The weather was still very changeable and no patrols were flown during the next two days. Major Blomfield had returned from leave on 9 September and Arthur's letter to Caroline, written during the afternoon, echoes the affection which nearly all the pilots, particularly the originals of London Colney, felt for Blomfield:

The CO returned from leave today, thank goodness. I love that man more and more every day. You will be pleased to hear Billy Crowe has been given 56 Reserve Squadron at London Colney as I hoped. We are all very bucked indeed – he so thoroughly deserves it. When I come home I should love to be an instructor under him. Yesterday no shows owing to low mist, though it was sultry. We had a comic game of Rugger against the men, very few of whom had even played the game before. We got awful hot, but still it was good exercise.

Vivien had evidently told Caroline of Arthur's sore throat and chest pains, which he had mentioned to her in his letter of 25 August. This was the Eton days all over again and Caroline had obviously written asking him how he was. He replied:

> You silly old angel worrying about my throat etc. It was alright again next day, and my pimpulae have also practically vanished. In fact I am in the pink as the AMs put it. Have been on a quasi show by myself this morning and am going on a proper one tonight. Best love. A.

The patrol mentioned in this letter left the ground at five in the evening, a combination of A and B Flights. The German aeroplanes were always out in force in the evenings and it was thought best to send out numerically stronger patrols of British fighters. Eleven SEs set out from Estrée Blanche but only six finally arrived over the patrol area. McCudden, Maxwell and Barlow had been forced to return with engine trouble, and Eric Turnbull and Potts had collided during a change of direction by Maxwell. Luckily the damage was slight and they both managed to land safely.

After losing Turnbull and Potts, A Flight attacked enemy scouts in the Menin road area but became separated in the action. Robert Sloley flew westwards to clear his guns, arriving over Houthulst Forest in time to see Arthur being pursued by two enemy scouts. Arthur had already been in a great deal of action. Taking over the leadership of the flight after McCudden's departure, he had attacked six Albatros 'V' Strutters over Gheluvelt, driving them east. He had then turned back to attack a lone Albatros over Polygon Wood. He closed with the German scout without being seen, but after only a few shots both his guns stopped. He almost collided with the Albatros and was forced to pull sharply away. He managed to get his Lewis gun working again but his Vickers was completely out of action owing to an air lock in the CC gear.

However, he rejoined the flight and it attacked a formation of eight enemy aeroplanes flying to the east of Polygon Wood. This action gained only a moral victory, the SEs driving the enemy down from 14,000 to 7,000 feet. The flight was then forced to clear to the west by the arrival of German reinforcements. Chased by two of these new arrivals, Arthur met Sloley over Houthulst Forest. Sloley passed over Arthur's SE and attacked the nearest of his two pursuers, causing it to dive away and turn east. Sloley was unable to follow as his guns again stopped, but Arthur dived after it. His first burst hit the Albatros in the cockpit and centre section; clouds of steam and boiling water poured from the top wing radiator of the Albatros and it went down to crash in the trees of Houthulst Forest.

Arthur then returned to the lines and attacked a two-seater about to cross to the British side. On seeing the SE5 the German pilot changed his mind and scurried eastwards. Arthur let him go, having seen a Rumpler returning from a mission over the British back areas. He fired a great number of rounds at this Rumpler, but it escaped by virtue of its superior speed.

Arthur then came under attack by two enemy scouts and they pushed him westwards towards his own lines. He then attacked an Aviatik, but his luck was out and this eluded him. He climbed to 13,000 feet, fired a red light to reform the flight and led it to attack a formation of seven Albatros 'V' Strutters at 9,000 feet over Moorslede. This fight was a long one, but although Arthur forced one of the hostile scouts 'right down', no decisive results were obtained. Arthur had now used all three of his Lewis gun drums and, his Vickers having been out of commission for most of the patrol, he returned.

In his next action, on the morning of 11 September, Arthur had an unnerving experience. After a brief skirmish with six hostile scouts over Houthulst Forest, – one of which glided down with its engine shut off – Arthur attacked another at 2,500 feet over Langemarck and while approaching 'end on' his Lewis gun slid down its slide and hit him on the head. Arthur turned away leaving the Albatros to McCudden. After replacing the Lewis gun in position and recovering from the blow, Arthur circled Polygon Wood, followed by Cronyn. Reaching 10,000 feet he saw his recent adversaries climbing north-west over Houthulst Forest and he attacked them from the east. The enemy pilots manoeuvred and co-operated well, however, and the SEs failed to gain any worthwhile result. Seeing Cronyn about to attack one of the Albatri which was a little apart from its Jasta comrades, Arthur followed, but as soon as Cronyn zoomed away after his first attack the Albatros pilot climbed towards Arthur, firing both guns, hitting the SE5 in the Vickers gun and centre section, holing the gravity petrol tank and causing all the petrol to escape. As Arthur later reported. 'I thought it advisable to leave the EA and return, especially as there were more EA approaching.' This was good shooting by the Albatros pilot and a narrow escape for Arthur.

In the usual evening patrol on 14 September, B Flight was in action with the pilots of Jasta 10 over Roulers. McCudden attacked Oberleutnant Weigand, hitting his Albatros DV in the engine and wounding Weigand, who nevertheless managed to land safely. Arthur attacked another of the Albatri – probably flown by Leutnant Groos. Hitting it from sixty yards' range he sent the Albatros down with smoke pouring from its engine. A Flight now arrived and, the Albatri having cleared east, the SEs combined forces and flew to Menin. Here they sighted a strong patrol of some twelve to fourteen red-nosed Albatros DVs coming from the east and, at 16,000 feet, with an height advantage of 2,000 feet over the British formation.

McCudden and Arthur flew under the enemy scouts and kept turning in an attempt to tempt them down to attack. The leader finally took the challenge and attacked Arthur. Albatros and SE5 fought for some time, Arthur observing that the enemy aeroplane was very smartly finished with a green fuselage and silver tail. The pilot of this Albatros was Leutnant Karl Menckhoff of Jasta 3, a German ace who was to score thirty-nine victories before being shot down and taken prisoner in July 1918. Menckhoff flew brilliantly, so well in fact that he ultimately outmanoeuvred Arthur and shot his SE through the petrol tank.

Petrol poured out over Arthur's feet and he zoomed for a little extra height before switching off his engine and gliding west. To his great relief Menckhoff made no attempt to follow him and he glided down to 6,000 feet over Comines. He then switched to his gravity tank, restarted his engine and landed at Bailleul. B Flight lost Lieutenant Crow from this patrol, shot down by Schmitt of Jasta 3, the Germans later dropping a note to say that he was dead.

A combination of B and C Flights led by McCudden and Bowman flew the evening patrol on 16 September. They saw a fair amount of action but only Barlow scored, shooting down an Albatros over Wervicq in his usual workmanlike manner. Arthur's engine was not going well and by the tone of his combat report he was unhappy about the entire patrol. He wrote home the next day and his letter again shows an unaccustomed note of asperity, a sign perhaps that his self-confidence had been badly shaken by having been shot down twice in the previous five days:

17/9/17   56 Squadron.
Dearest All,
    As I have two letters from Viv, two from Mother and absolutely

umph from Nesta all to answer I'm going to make a hash of it and leave you to fight it out which of you I have offended most.

First of all many thanks for writing pads, now in use. Secondly, I think V acted most wisely as regards the photos. Thirdly I want to know why the hell I get letters from May Smith, Viv and Nesta sympathizing with me about bronchial catarrh and double pneumonia or something. When I write home and say I have got a slight sore throat which lasts one day I don't want wild reports to rush around the country that I am in the last stages of collapse owing to lung trouble or God knows what. My chest has never been wrong since I have been out: I have never consulted the AMO: I merely took a few pills from the Medical Orderly, which is quite different. I'm not an anaemic baby, two years old with a flat nose and chronic whooping cough. In future I make no statement as to my health or ill health in my periodical letters.

The squadron flew no patrols for the next two days and a letter to Vivien on the 18th, although short, seems to show a slight indication of a return to his usual spirits:

18/9/17   56 Squadron.
Dearest V
    Only time for a short note. Enclosed you will find a cheque for £1.10.0. out of which you will buy yourself a *good* fountain pen, and take the rest for Mother's present. I am also sending her a book but that is quite outside – it is the poems of Maurice Maeterlinck which are quite thrilling if rather obscure.
    We are busy today buying furniture for our new hut.
                        Best love. A.

                                *

The Battle of the Menin Ridge Road opened on 20 September. A low wet mist covered the battlefield and failed to lift until about 8 am. C Flight took off just after lunch on the second offensive patrol of the day, with both Leonard Barlow and Arthur flying in place of its usual pilots. Bowman, who was leading the formation, was forced to return after half an hour with a leaking oil pipe and Barlow assumed command, leading the SEs into four engagements with hostile scouts, none of which produced a decisive result. As Arthur explained in his next letter home, the strong west wind made conditions difficult for the British pilots.

The west wind is a terrible drawback to Hun strafing as it makes it so easy for them to get away and so difficult for us to get back before we are sat upon by other Huns. In fact the conditions are ideal for the Hun and rather nasty for us. The same thing happens every day nearly – a rollicking west wind, gorgeous sun, and great brooding masses of clouds all making the same stately pilgrimage. I have done a fair amount of fighting but have had no startling results, but still I have been more or less doing my job. I shall be really sorry when I have to come home, if that comes off soon. With luck I may get another month or six weeks out here. Life still trés bong: would not change it for worlds. And last but not least heaps of happy returns of the 27th – I expect this will reach you about the 26th. I hope you appreciate the dazzling obscurity of that little book which ought to reach you about the same time as this.

B Flight having no patrol until the evening on 21 September, Arthur, Cronyn and Johnston took three Winchester 22s and went for a walk in the nearby woods to see if they could bag something for the pot, but Cronyn commented, 'The partridge seems far too wild to be able to get near enough to them for shooting with 22s. We must have disturbed at least a hundred in one hour's tramp.' A and C Flights had been out during the morning and although Maxwell and Wilkinson had each shot down a two-seater, A Flight had lost Arthur's friend Potts, whose SE was seen going down with its wings folded up.

McCudden and Bowman took out their flights in the evening, leaving Estrée Blanche at 4.45 pm. Cronyn wrote to his father:

I have never seen so many Huns before: there must have been about sixty altogether, and only about ten were two seaters. They were all very much afraid to attack us, and as the wind was very strong we didn't wish to go far over to attack them.

Three of B Flight went down after a pair of two-seaters, diving from 10,000 to 4,000 feet, 'so we had a bit of a drop.' Arthur caught his opponent at 4,000 over Geluwe and fired sixty rounds from each gun into it. His fire evidently either killed or wounded the observer as the rear gun stopped firing. A long column of smoke cascaded from the two-seater's engine and it glided east, smoke still pouring from it. Arthur let it go. His combat report gives no reason why he did so.

Possibly he felt the German crew had taken enough punishment and it was sufficient to send them down out of action. He had come so close to the enemy machine in his attack that he had been forced to zoom away to avoid a collision, and he now climbed and rejoined McCudden over Gheluvelt, patrolling about two miles east of the front lines. None off the enemy scouts in the vicinity seemed anxious to mix things with the two SEs and Athur turned for home. As he did so he saw an Albatros attacking an RE8 over Langemarke and he flew to the scene of the action as fast as he could He caused the Albatros pilot to break off his attack and retreat east. Arthur let him go. He had now been out for over two hours and he knew his petrol must be low.

No patrols were flown during the remainder of the day and people amused themselves in various ways. Another Rugby match was played in the evening, with Arthur Maybery and Gerald Maxwell playing a prominent part. Eric Turnbull, an English pilot, remembered these games with a certain amusement. Arthur's comment on the men not understanding the game too well also held true for the Canadians stationed at Estrée Blanche. They were used to playing American football and thought nothing of kicking the feet from under their opponents as they were running for the ball.

On 23 September no patrols were flown until the evening; but the evening fighting was to see a combat which has since become an epic in the annals of airfighting; a fight which would be the summit of Arthur's prowess as an airfighter and place him among the immortals of that relatively small band of men.

CHAPTER EIGHT

Werner Voss

The long summer and early autumn evenings over the Ypres Salient in 1917 saw a great deal of airfighting, full of variety and interest. James McCudden wrote:

> The Huns usually had as many machines up as we, and I have seen some colossal-sized formations fighting. The evenings were simply wonderful, as the fighting was usually very fierce and well contested....About thirty machines would all be mixed up together, and viewed from a distance it seemed as if a swarm of bees were all circling around a honey pot. Then perhaps one would notice a little speck start to go down, a trickle of flame would start behind it, and then grow larger, until the machine looked like a comet diving earthwards, leaving a long trail of black smoke to mark its line of fall. As one watched, it would hit the ground 10,000 feet below, and then would come a shower of burning debris, and a final large puff of flame. Or perhaps one machine would go down, turning round and round in an uncontrolled spin. Then another machine would dive away, flying on a zig-zag course so as to dodge his pursuer's bullets, after which it would zoom, and the second would follow, for all the world like a game of follow-my-leader. These are just incidents in a maze of others that happened every evening.[1]

The evening of 23 September was no exception. After a morning of cloud and ground mist the evening saw clearer weather and operations in the air became possible: a conformity to the almost general pattern of daily weather throughout the month. At 5pm McCudden and Bowman took their flights into the air and flew towards the front lines. McCudden led B Flight across the lines at Bixschoote and immediately noticed that there were a great number of machines in the air, both British and German. There seemed even more than usual owing to the thick cloud base at 9,000 feet,

---

[1] *Five Years in the Royal Flying Corps*, op cit.

compressing the combatants between its grey mass and the ground, effectively roofing the combat area. McCudden led Arthur, Jeffs, Cronyn, Muspratt and Young south from Houthulst Forest, the six SE5s silhouetted against the leaden sky and, flying at only 7,000 feet, a tempting target for the enemy anti-aircraft gunners.

Passing over Gheluvelt, McCudden saw an enemy two-seater from Flieger Abteilung engaged in artillery observation at 3,000 feet north of Houthem. McCudden dived, followed by the flight, and attacked the DFW. Leutnant Gustav Rudolph and unteroffizier Rudolph Franke were too engrossed in their work to see him and a burst from both McCudden's guns sent their DFW down in a vertical dive to crash south-east of the village.

McCudden reformed the flight and flew north, climbing back to 6,000 feet. Away to the east were clusters of little black specks: enemy aeroplanes moving swiftly , constantly changing direction. To the north were swarms of British machines: more SE5s, Camels, Pups, Spads, Bristol Fighters and, lower down, the artillery observation RE8s. Sighting a patrol of six Albatros scouts flying a little to the east, McCudden was about to attack them when he saw, just ahead of the flight, over Poelcapelle, an SE5 spinning down with a hostile triplane on its tail. 'The SE certainly looked very unhappy, so we changed our minds about attacking the six "V" Strutters and went to the rescue of the unfortunate SE.'[1]

The unhappy and unfortunate SE pilot was Lieutenant Hamersley of 60 Squadron. Two flights of 60 Squadron, led by Captain Keith 'Grid' Caldwell, were returning from a patrol. With A flight, having been reduced to two SEs - Hamersley and Chidlaw-Roberts - bringing up the rear. Hamersley, keeping an eye on a large formation of between twenty and twenty-five Abatros scouts, had seen what he thought was a Nieuport being dived on by an Albatros. Swinging across to attack the Albatros, Hamersley was surprised to see the 'Nieuport' turn towards him and he realized it was a German triplane. He put the nose of his SE down and opened fire. As he closed the range he zoomed and turned but the triplane pilot was already above him, coming in from the side and firing accurate bursts into his SE. There was a puff of smoke from the SE's engine and holes appeared along the cowling and the wings. Hamersley, realized he was in a hopeless position, threw the SE into a spin, but the German pilot followed him down, firing all the time, and

[1] *Five Years in the Royal Flying Corps*, op cit.

Hamersley had to execute an inverted dive to escape.

Chidlaw-Roberts had seen his companion spin away and had attempted to come to his rescue, turning to attack the triplane and firing a few shots at it from close range, The German pilot hardly paused in his pursuit of Hamersley. In seconds he was on the tail of Chidlaw-Roberts' SE and shot its rudder bar about so severely that Chidlaw-Roberts later commented: 'I retired from the fray and that is all I saw of it.'

Caldwell saw Hamersley going down with the triplane close behind, but McCudden and B Flight had now arrived and thinking six to one was pretty good odds in favour of the British pilots, Caldwell 'left them to it. We were more or less spectators and in my opinion there was little room to join in.'

McCudden and Arthur both dived to attack the triplane; McCudden from the right, Arthur from the left. The triplane pilot, Leutnant Werner Voss, Staffel Führer of Jasta 10, saw them coming and turned 'in a most disconcertingly quick manner, not a climbing or Immelmann turn', McCudden wrote, 'but in a sort of flat half spin.' Voss was now in the middle of the SE formation, who dived at him in turn, but he seemed unperturbed by the odds and made no attempt to escape from the action. McCudden wrote:

> By now the German triplane was in the middle of our formation, and its handling was wonderful to behold. The pilot seemed to be firing at us all simultaneously, and although I got behind him a second time, I could hardly stay there for a second. His movements were so quick and uncertain that none of us could hold him in sight at all for any decisive time.
>
> I now got a good opportunity as he was coming towards me nose on, and slightly underneath, and had apparently not seen me. I dropped my nose, got him well in my sight, and pressed both triggers. As soon as I fired up came his nose at me, and I heard clack-clack-clack-clack, as his bullets passed close to me and through my wings. I distinctly noticed the red-yellow flashes from his parallel Spandau guns. As he flashed by me I caught a glimpse of a black head in the triplane with no hat on at all.[1]

By now a red-nosed Albatros DV had arrived and joined in the unequal fight, although by this time Voss had already sent Cronyn

---

[1] *Five Years in the Royal Flying Corps*, op cit.

and Muspratt out of the fight. Cronyn had lost his pressure as he pulled out of his dive in his initial attack on the triplane. He later wrote to his father:

> In consequence my zoom was but a feeble climb. I take my hat off to that Hun as he was a most skilful pilot, but he did give me a rough passage. On seeing my feeble attempt, he whipped round in an extraordinary way, using no bank at all, but just throwing his tail behind him. He attacked me from the side and I had the opportunity of observing that he was one of the very latest design, being a triplane. He was at very close quarters and could hardly miss me. The bullets ripped all around me. I did not stick my machine down in an attempt to run, as I certainly would have done two months ago, but dived just enough to give me speed to turn under him and prevent him getting on my tail. The others were above, and I knew sooner or later they would drive him away, and the longer I stayed the better their opportunity to nail him. I do not know how many times I turned under him, I did not stop to count, but it seemed an eternity. He finally got too close for me, and I resorted in desperation to the old method of shaking a pursuing machine. On the completion of the second revolution of my spin, I flattened out, and to my intense relief the Hun was no longer following me. Nor had he escaped the others of the patrol, who were busily engaged in scrapping him.

Voss had now disposed of two of the four SE5s of B Flight which had initially attacked him.[1] After his attack on Cronyn, Voss had put bullets through the sump and oil pipe of Muspratt's SE, forcing Muspratt to dive away for the safety of the British lines. But Bowman and C Flight had now arrived on the scene and Voss and the red-nosed Albatros were now opposed by McCudden, Arthur, Bowman, Maybery and Hoidge, all highly experienced airfighters, some of the finest in 56 Squadron at that time. Bowman and his flight had been in action above the fight with Voss, Hoidge shooting down a green scout which had been attacking Maybery. Bowman led Maybery down into the Voss fight, while Hoidge, who had followed the green scout down, changed his Lewis gun drum before climbing back into the action. Maybery attacked Voss, but the red-nosed Albatros got on his tail, forcing him to do a climbing turn. He dived again at Voss,

---

[1] Jeffs and Young had left the flight earlier and took no part in the Voss fight.

but his Lewis gun stopped and both enemy pilots turned towards him, only to be attacked in turn by McCudden and Arthur.

As Arthur was attacking Voss the red-nosed Albatros took the opportunity to get on the SE's tail, but Maybery quickly came to Arthur's aid, firing his Vickers at the Albatros until he was forced to pull up over the top of it. It seems that, from this point on, Voss was alone in the fight, circling in the middle of the SE5s which were all firing as the chance arose. McCudden wrote with amazement that at one time the triplane: 'was in the apex of a cone of tracer bullets from at least five machines simultaneously.' Maybery simply reported: 'He seemed invulnerable'. Bowman later wrote:

We were then at about 2,000 feet and a mile behind the German front line. This left Voss alone in the middle of six of us which did not appear to deter him in the slightest. At that altitude he had a much better rate of climb, or rather zoom, than we had and frequently he was the highest machine of the seven and could have turned east and got away had he wished to, but he was not that type and always came down into us again. His machine was exceptionally manoeuvrable and he appeared to be able to take flying liberties with impunity. I, myself, had only one crack at him: he was about to pass broadside on across my bows and slightly lower. I put my nose down to give him a burst and opened fire, perhaps too soon; to my amazement he kicked on full rudder, without bank, pulled his nose up slightly, gave me a burst while he was skidding sideways, and then kicked on opposite rudder before the effects of this amazing stunt appeared to have any effect on the controlability of his machine. Rhys Davids was then on his tail. Whether or not, to have a crack at me, this flat turn of Voss's enabled Rhys Davids to get there I cannot say, but I should like to think so, as I doubt if any SE5 could have got on the tail of the triplane if Voss had not had his attention distracted; but Rhys Davids was there, with his prop boss almost on Voss's rudder. Rhys Davids was firing and Voss was flying nose down and straight for the first time in the whole scrap. Rhys Davids remained on his tail then turned away.

As Arthur turned away Voss made his fatal error: he also turned, directly into the path of the SE and slightly below. Arthur dived slightly and fired a whole drum of Lewis and a corresponding number of rounds from his Vickers into the triplane:

He made no attempt to turn until I was so close to him I was certain we would collide. He passed my right wing by inches and went down. I zoomed. I saw him next, with his engine apparently off, gliding west. I dived again and got one shot out of my Vickers; however I reloaded and kept in the dive, I got another good burst and the triplane did a slight right-hand turn still going down. I now overshot him (this was at 1,000 ft) zoomed and never saw him again.

McCudden and Bowman both saw the end of the triplane. McCudden had climbed above the fight to change a Lewis gun drum and looking down he saw Voss in the final moments:

. . . he was very low, still being engaged by an SE marked I, the pilot being Rhys Davids. I noticed that the triplane's movements were very erratic, and then I saw him go into a fairly steep dive and so I continued to watch, and then saw the triplane hit the ground and disappear into a thousand fragments, for it seemed to me that it literally went to powder.

Bowman recalled:

When near the ground the triplane turned over on its back and hit the ground in this position just our side of the lines. At no time was the angle of descent steeper than an ordinary glide-in to land.

Having overshot the triplane in his last attack, Arthur saw a red-nosed Albatros to the east of him. Whether or not this was the same Albatros which had earlier aided Voss is not certain, but evidence seems to suggest that it was piloted by Leutnant Karl Menckhoff, who had dealt so summarily with Arthur on 14 September. This time it was Menckhoff's turn. Arthur attacked, opening fire at a hundred yards range and holding down his triggers until only thirty yards separated him from the Albatros. He zoomed away. Looking back he saw Menckhoff spiralling down, his Albatros so severely damaged that he was forced to crash-land north of Zonnebecke.

In the 56 Squadron mess at dinner that night there was a great deal of speculation as to the identity of the enemy pilot who had flown and fought so magnificently. He was obviously one of the best German pilots and opinions varied as to whether it could have been Wolff, Voss, or even Richthofen himself. Arthur came in for enthusiastic congratulations, mainly from those pilots who had not taken part in the fight, for, as Bowman remembered: 'our elation was not nearly as great as you might have imagined. It was an amazing show on the part of Voss. I remember at the time feeling rather sorry that it had to end the way it did. Rhys Davids, I think, was genuinely upset.'

Perhaps Arthur sensed that here was the eternal and useless tragedy of war: that he had killed a boy, almost exactly the same age as himself; a boy who in happier times could have been a friend. Perhaps he also sensed a portent of his own fate.

At lunch the following day, General Trenchard heard of the fight and the death of Voss, and sent Maurice Baring to 56 Squadron to get details from the pilots involved, who were all loud in their praise of Voss for his matchless courage and flying skill. The fight stayed an indelible memory in Bowman's mind throughout his long life. Twenty-five years after the event, in the middle of another war, his remembrance of Voss's courage moved him to criticise the account of the fight given in the official history of the air war of 1914-1918.

I see that Voss is referred to as being 'dazzlingly elusive'. It sickens me to see what was an epic fight garnished with such journalistic garbage. The use of the word 'elusive' gives the impression that Voss was trying to escape from danger (see Oxford Concise); nothing is further from the truth.

In 1918 McCudden wrote:

. . . as long as I live I shall never forget my admiration for that German pilot, who single-handed fought seven of us for ten minutes and also put some bullets through all of our machines. His flying was wonderful, his courage magnificent, and in my opinion he is the bravest German airman whom it has been my privilege to see fight.[1]

McCudden's statement that Voss had put bullets through 'all our machines' was, if anything, understating the case. In his last action Voss had effectively shot down three SE5s and damaged three others. Cronyn's SE5 A4563 was to all intents and purposes a write-off. Muspratt had been forced to land at No 1 Squadron's aerodrome

---

[1] *Five Years in the Royal Flying Corps*, op cit.

with a bullet in his radiator which caused his engine to seize, and Maybery's machine had been hit in a longeron, necessitating its return to the depot for repair. Childlaw-Roberts' machine had been badly shot about and Hamersley's SE was unrepairable in 60 Squadron's workshops. In the brief flurry of that first encounter Voss had shot through the left-hand bottom engine bearer; two top planes and the centre section; spars, ribs, rudder and kingpost; the water jacket on the right hand side of the engine; radiator, propeller, CC gear, oil pipes, generator, and had put 'numerous holes in the fabric'. Hamersley had managed to land at No 29 Squadron's aerodrome, but he had been lucky to escape with his life: There was no doubt that Voss's marksmanship matched his flying ability and courage. Small wonder that many German fighter pilots of the day regarded him as their best fighter pilot, including Richthofen.

The triplane had crashed very near the front line and Voss was buried where he fell by a Lieutenant Kiegan 'without a coffin and without military honours, in exactly the same manner as all soldiers are buried in battle.'[1]

There was no rest for Arthur. The next day he was again in action, flying in the evening patrol. McCudden had been forced to return with a broken oil pipe and Barlow had led the flight across the lines at 11,000 feet. Over Passchendaele, at ten minutes to six, the three SEs – Leonard Barlow, Arthur and Reason – saw a pair of enemy two-seaters flying south-east over Houthulst Forest, but on their way down to attack these they saw two others under British anti-aircraft fire. These were evidently returning from a photo-reconnaissance over the British back areas and it was imperative that they were destroyed before they could return with their information.

Accordingly, the SEs switched their attacks. One of the enemy made off east, the other north, and Arthur attacked the latter, opening fire from a hundred yards and firing a whole drum of Lewis and a long burst of Vickers. His fire silenced the enemy gunner, the two-seater went down very steeply, and at 4,000 feet smoke and flames began to appear from the fuselage, which was soon burning furiously. Arthur zoomed away in time to see Barlow's two-seater spinning down to crash just south of the Forest.

Arthur now came under attack from six red-nosed Albatros 'V' Strutters, anxious to avenge the two-seater's fate, but he retreated under a patrol of DH5s. The Albatri had the advantage of height –

---

[1] Plum Farm, just north of Frezenberg.

Arthur was at 4,000 feet – and he was taking no chances. The enemy scouts finally made off and Arthur climbed to 6,000 feet. Ten minutes later he attacked an Albatros which was driving down a Naval triplane over Zonnebeke.

Arthur got in a good burst from close range, sending the enemy scout down, apparently out of control. The German pilot, however, was an old hand and when close to the ground he flattened out and flew east.

Arthur then flew to Langemarke and attacked another Albatros. He got into a good position on its tail, but he had a No 4 stoppage in his Vickers gun and a No 3 in his Lewis and was forced to break off his attack. He then rejoined Barlow.

Although there was a total of eleven Albatros scouts flying in two layers over Houthulst Forest, these persistently flew east and refused combat with the two SEs. Both these formations and several isolated Albatri were waiting for the opportunity to attack the British RE8s which were working in the area and were not inclined to waste time in unproductive combat with two SE5s.

Barlow again led the flight in the evening patrol the following day. Arthur flew in the patrol but he made no combat report so presumably saw no action, but Barlow fought a remarkable combat, shooting down three pilots of Jasta 10 in a matter of minutes. He engaged them – two Albatros DVs and two Pfalz D.IIIs – over Houthulst Forest, attacking the first Albatros head on. The Albatros, flown by Oberleutnant Weigand, went down in pieces and finally burst into flames: Weigand's second combat with 56 Squadron – McCudden had wounded him on 14 September – had proved fatal.

Zooming away from this attack, Barlow attacked one of the Pfalz, flown by Unteroffizier Werkmeister. The Pfalz went down in a slow spin and crashed at Stampkot. Werkmeister had joined Jasta 10 only two days previously and was buried six days later in the churchyard of St Joseph's Church. Barlow next turned his attentions to the other Albatros. He had time for only one quick burst before zooming away, for he had seen additional enemy scouts diving on him from the east. But it was sufficient. The Albatros continued to dive and was seen by Bowman to crash half a mile from the north-west corner of Houthulst Forest.

Arthur had written home that afternoon, telling Caroline of the fight with Voss:

25/9/17   56 Squadron.

Dearest Mums,

   Just a hurried line before going to the war to thank you ever so
much for the book and birthday letter, both of which turned up
yesterday! Never mind, two days early c'est rien n'est ce pas. I
enclose a telegram I got last night from the dear old general – all
for little me, after I had got my nineteenth Hun – a two seater who
burnt furiously all the way down. Three nights ago we had the
most wonderful fight. After the leader had got one two seater
crashed, six of us took on four Huns – two triplanes, their new
machines; one of another new type and one ordinary Albatros.
Maybery drove one triplane off, the other was the bravest man I
have ever seen and shot two of us about badly – Muspratt and
another, before I slew him. He is down in No Man's Land and we
do not know who was in it yet. My hat! he was equally a brave man
and brilliant pilot and had the devils luck in not being killed three
times instead of once. Meanwhile Voss, the great German star
after Richthofen, is down this side in the new type machine and
was one of the other two machines – we got all the other three
besides the second triplane. I got the great triplane and one other
– I thought an ordinary Albatros – and Hoidge – our PM a
Canadian who has now got 20 – or rather claimed 20 – got the
other. So Voss and the triplane are both to our credit, perhaps
both to me, but probably Hoidge's Hun was Voss. Still that will be
known soon. Must fly.

                    Best love   A.

This letter seems to imply that the squadron had not yet had the
news that it had been Voss flying the triplane, although they knew
that Voss had been brought down that evening. Arthur had been
congratulated at dinner for shooting down the *triplane* pilot who had
fought so magnificently and it seems strange that it was not obvious
from the outset that it must have been Voss in the triplane. But the 56
Squadron pilots had been told that Voss had been flying a new type
of machine and as far as they were concerned the green scout shot
down by Hoidge, which was a Pfalz D.III – called by the squadron
pilots at this time a 'Fokker biplane' – was also a new type. Why they
should have thought that the Pfalz pilot could have been Voss, and
not the pilot of the triplane, is hard to understand, in view of the
comparatively easy victory Hoidge had had over the Pfalz. In *Five*

Years in the Royal Flying Corps McCudden states that 'next morning [ie 24 September] we had a wire from the Wing saying that the dead pilot was found wearing the Boelcke collar and his name was Werner Voss. He had the "Ordre Pour le Mérite".

'Rhys Davids came in for a shower of congratulations, and no one deserved them better, but as the boy himself said to me, "Oh, if I could only have brought him down alive," and his remark was in agreement with my own thoughts.'

McCudden is known to have been extremely accurate, and demonstrably so, in his dates and factual information in his autobiography and it seems certain from this passage that when Arthur wrote to Caroline on 25 September he must have known that the triplane pilot had been Voss. The confusion in his mind seems to have arisen over the *identification* of the wreckage of the aeroplane at Plum Farm, which was known to have been flown by Voss. Was this the triplane, shot down by him, or was it Hoidge's green scout – the other new type?

Not until a report on the wreckage at Plum Farm had established that it was in fact the triplane, and he had received its rudder and compass as souvenirs, does it seem that Arthur was prepared to accept completely that the triplane pilot had been Werner Voss. Ironically, the official report on the wreckage, which also credits Arthur with the victory, is dated 27 October, but he seems to have finally accepted that he was Voss's victor after his letter home on 29 September.

With hindsight knowledge that Voss was the pilot of the triplane on the evening of 23 September, it is only too easy for air historians to be puzzled over the doubt, however slight, in Arthur's mind, but things were by no means always so certain in those days of conflicting reports and uncertainty. The triplane had crashed in an area of heavy and recent fighting and the ground forces had more important and pressing things to occupy them than reporting on crashed German aeroplanes as a matter of urgency.

Newall wrote on 25 September:

My Dear Rhys Davids.
  Once more my heartiest congratulations. I seem to write to you about once a fortnight on this subject, however I hope it may be my good fortune to continue doing so. There are still plenty of Huns waiting for it and I wish you the best of luck and an ever

increasing total to your credit.

It was Arthur's twentieth birthday on 26 September and he received many letters and presents from his family. One letter which survives is from his Aunt May and throws an interesting and informative light as to how his various exploits had been received; yet the line referring to the men of Wadhurst who had fallen in the war, 'not a bad list for a small place', has a chilling ring.

> Dearest Arthur,
>   Heaps and heaps of good wishes for Sept. 26 and many happy returns of the day. I don't know what to send you. Can you tell me of anything you specially want? No good sending useless and cumbersome things out to you in France. I was so delighted to hear of your bringing down 3 Huns in one flight lately. I was over at Chibbleswick when yr letter arrived, it quite bucked mother up. There is a very nice bit about you in last Monday's Times MC list – but surely you have brought down more, or rather destroyed more than 4 Huns? I am so glad to have the enlarged photo of you in your machine taken when you were here in June – it is excellent. What is that curious funnel sort of thing behind yr head? I have been down for a week at Wadhurst, our old home, and I took yr photo and showed it to lots of old folk, who were so pleased and interested. There is a bit about you in the Parish magazine too, put in by the Vicar's wife – badly worded I think, still it is a nice idea. 70 Wadhurst men have fallen, not a bad list for a small place.

Arthur was next in action on the morning of 28 September. The flight, led by McCudden, attacked five Albatros DVs over Houthulst Forest. McCudden shot the wings off one Albatros and Barlow drove another down. Arthur engaged several of the enemy scouts, but climbed to prevent an additional three or four Albatri, circling at a higher level, from joining the fight. Having dealt with this Albatros formation, the remaining SEs regained their height. Arthur rejoined them and they drove several formations of enemy fighters to the east of the Roulers-Menin road.

    After flying south to Comines, the flight again returned to the north of its patrol area and chased away a Rumpler over Houthulst Forest. This Rumpler was loosely escorted by a formation of Albatri, which scattered and flew east, but one came back west and Arthur 'dropped vertically' to attack it. However, he picked up so much speed in his dive that he completely misjudged his distance and overshot the enemy scout.

He was now down to 5,000 feet over Comines and, looking up, he saw five more Albatri flying above him. This enemy formation seemed completely unaware of his presence and he climbed, passed a hundred feet above them, and attacked the rearmost, opening fire with two cross shots at seventy yards' range, holding down his triggers until the enemy pilot turned into his line of fire. Two columns of smoke came out of the engine of the Albatros and it went down vertically. Arthur was now below the remaining four and he zoomed to regain his height; but they quickly scattered, making no attempt to avenge their comrade.

Arthur wrote to Nesta in the evening, thanking her for her birthday present:

28/9/17
Dearest Nesta, Just the briefest line which is all I have time for at present to thank you ever so much for the Robert Service. You really could hardly have hit upon a more apposite present. I am now simply deluged in lovely books with the result that boredom is merely non-existent: in fact my time is far too full. Which is just how it used to be and quite as it should be. You will probably have heard from Mother about the German star airman Voss having been brought down. Quite right, yours humbly at it again. How naughty I am. It is not absolutely certain, but almost: he landed this side and the machine is such a wreck we are not yet quite certain it was the one I shot down. My God, he was a brave man, and what is more an absolutely wonderful scrapper. I take off my mental hat to him. This morning I got my twentieth. I was so happy reading your dear letter. Goodbyeeeeeeeeeeee. Arthur.

He also wrote to Caroline, his Father and Vivien, unusually addressing his letter 'Dearest Three'. He dated this letter 29 September but his reference to his twentieth victory 'this morning' points to its being written on the evening of 28 September:

Weather has been splendid and the run total has been flying up - squadron total now being 195. Only five more and we shall have beaten Richthofen's squadron record - 200 of ours in 2½ months. I got my twentieth this morning. About Voss. I think it is now almost certain he was in the triplane I got. The machine is such a hopeless wreck that even now they are not certain absolutely whether it was a triplane or a biplane. Just think of poor little me having slain 2 damn fine fellows like Voss and Schaefer: I think I should be unpopular with the Baron's squadron if I ever got over there, considering they were his two right hand men. Anyhow, I take off my hat to Voss, he was the bravest fellow and the best scrapper I have ever met. The Huns have developed a pleasing trick of shedding their wings in the air. I think it is an excellent sign, by showing they are not so strongly built as they used to be. ie. more patchily turned out. We have got three in pieces today in 56 alone. Incidentally we have also got two more Bars to our MCs in the squadron, making four of them earned in the squadron and about half a dozen other MCs as well. I have hopes that I shall be staying out until the end of October, instead of coming home punctually after my six months as was at one time possible.

Arthur also wrote to a friend of Vivien who was apparently something of an expert on art. The first page of the letter is missing, so we have no means of knowing the identity of Vivien's friend, but Vivien had obviously sent Arthur his letter, knowing it would interest her brother. It throws an interesting light on Arthur's taste in painting, a subject he had as yet had no time to study:

. . . Viv was rash enough to send on to me with your parcel your letter to her – I know you won't mind me reading it – and it interested me immensely. I know so little about art that the opinions of an expert afford me (a) a pleasurable awe (b) a great hunger to know more. I am afraid I do not like the Dulac type much because it is so unrealistic and to me in all things the appeal comes from the harmony of fact and imagination. And out of the little I know, the Dulac school and also in a different way the old classical Italian madonna groups, are all imagination, whereas the Dutch landscape or portraits of country gentlemen are all fact. One startling exception has always stuck in my mind since I first saw it and that is Raphael's 'Pope Julius II' a picture of a dear old man in lovely red robes with big sombre eyes away in Heaven. Of the very few I know so far I love Edward Lear's Cretan and Greek mountains and Turner's great sunsets – both of which I know – at least I suppose Cretan and Greek mountains are not very far off the Alps, and I love Arthur Rackham's illustrations to my two volumes of the 'Ring' translated into English ie. Wagner's words to the 'Ring'. Also I like Holman Hunt. All of which is undoubtedly *dreadful* taste in the artistic eye, but there it is.

My present existence here is a delightful mixture of fact, which is the tiresome though somewhat amusing war, and imagination, which is the time I spend reading books and letters. I have discovered a Belgian worth considering – one Maurice Maeterlinck whose poems have been translated into very good English verse by one Miall. It is very obscure à la Blake, but quite thrilling.

Must stop now. Once more, many thanks. Arthur.

Arthur was rested on 29 September. At dinner that night there was a somewhat heated discussion as to which flight should fly the first patrol in the morning. During the day A Flight had scored three victories, bringing the squadron's total to 198 and each flight was anxious that it should have the honour of shooting down the squadron's 200th victory. It was, in fact, B Flight's turn of duty to fly the first patrol the next morning and, in face of much argument, McCudden stuck quietly but firmly to his guns, insisting that B Flight it should be.

In the event it served no purpose. Although B Flight took off at 7.45 it was an hour and a half before they sighted any hostile aeroplanes, enemy territory having been almost completely obscured by a thick ground mist. Although McCudden attacked five Albatri over Houthem, driving one down to 9,000 feet, he was unable to force a decisive result. The flight returned to Estrée Blanche having scored nothing and cursing the weather.

During the rest of the day a large number of 'special missions' were flown: Maybery, Hoidge, Gilbert, Muspratt and Barlow all took off alone during the day in attempts to win the elusive two victories needed. But it was a combined patrol of A and C Flights in the early evening that brought the desired result. Maybery shot down a Pfalz D.III to crash west to Roulers at 5 pm, and Gerald Maxwell shot down an Albatros out of control half an hour later for the squadron's 200th victory.

When darkness fell at Estrée Blanche that evening the entire squadron went out onto the aerodrome. At the word of command from Major Blomfield, the squadron's entire stock of Very lights were fired up into the night sky, the red, green and white lights illuminating the surrounding countryside. Dinner that night was a gala affair. The food was excellent, the band in fine-form, and there was 'much speechmaking'. The pilots went to bed well pleased with the successes of the day; elated and proud of their squadron's record.

CHAPTER NINE

Final Days

Arthur was now at the very zenith of his career as an airfighter. The news of the fight with Voss spread rapidly throughout the RFC and his name was soon a byword in the squadron messes. There were several other highly successful pilots in 56 Squadron, of course, but there was something about this goodlooking boy, little over a year away from Eton, with his easy charm and boyish ways, which captured the imagination of all who came in contact with him. In him, 56 Squadron considered they had another Ball; perhaps even more so, for he had an appreciation of strategy and tactics which Ball, for all his brilliance, had lacked. Charles, the squadron's engineering officer, remembers:

> Rhys Davids was a very fine classical scholar, and so he was a marvellous judge of people. That's what classical scholarship is all about – people. What Rhys Davids could do that nobody else seemed able to do was to weigh up what the Germans were going to do next. He seemed to have a genius for weighing up what the particular German squadron commanders from the different aerodromes would do. Over and over again he would say to McCudden, 'Now come on, Mac, tell 'em we should go up at half past eight in the morning, not half past seven. What old so and so (and here he would name the German commander at such and such an aerodrome) would do in view of the situation is to have his people here' – naming a town – 'and we should be here at that time with height to dive on them out of the sun.' Mac would go and see Blomfield. Blomfield would say, 'Who says so? Rhys Davids? Oh, certainly, go on and do it.' Do you know, Rhys Davids was nearly always bang on right. Such men as McCudden and Blomfield would listen to what Rhys Davids, the classical scholar, had to say about what he thought was in the minds of the enemy. Well, that's one of the things that classics is all about – people's minds and what they will do or think.

Several glimpses of Arthur in 56 Squadron at this time have come

down to us through the eyes of his contemporaries. At the celebration
dinner for his DSO, his eyes bright and his whole face lit up with the
joy of living, secure in the knowledge of his popularity with his
comrades, and their respect and approbation, he laughed so much
that Eric Turnbull remembered: 'He simply slid under the table, still
laughing. He hadn't been drinking or anything. It was sheer boyish
exuberance and good humour'. 'Beery' Bowman always referred to
him as a 'wonderful boy' and Charles laughed when he recalled:

> I used to tick him off for his furious diving, which made his wings
> all loose, but he would laugh and tell me that it was my job to see
> they stopped on. You know, he always stammered after a fight,
> but when he landed after the Voss fight he stammered so badly
> that we couldn't understand him at all, he was so excited.

That stammer, such an overwhelming problem in his early teens,
was now relegated to its proper perspective: who could possibly care
that this boy, 'hero of half a hundred fights', should stammer in
excitement after landing from a fight for life two miles above the
earth. Maurice Baring wrote:

> He was longing for the war to be over so as to go up to Oxford. He
> told me he always carried a small volume of Blake's poetry in his
> pocket in case he should come down on the other side. He also said
> to me one day. 'The Buddhists have got a maxim, "Don't be
> stupid". That's all that matters in life.' He was passionately fond
> of books and poetry, and his mixture of scholarship, enthusiasm,
> fun, courage, skill and airmanship made one feel that if these were
> the sort of pilots we had, whatever else might happen, we should
> never be beaten in the air.[1]

Although neither was aware of it at the time, Arthur and Maurice
Baring were related, Caroline and Baring being cousins.

*

October 1917 started badly for 56 Squadron. During the evening
patrol on 1 October the squadron lost one of its most promising
pilots. A and B Flights had left Estrée Blanche at 4.30 pm, B Flight
later attacking a trio of enemy two-seaters. McCudden and Arthur

[1] Op cit page 172.

became separated from the rest of the flight in the attack, so they regained their height and flew north, sighting a formation of seven black-and-white Albatri, led by a black-and-white Pfalz, over Westroosebeke. They flew under these, tempting them down to attack, as they knew Maxwell and A Flight were in the vicinity. As to plan, the Albatri came down on McCudden and Arthur, and Maxwell and his flight came down on the enemy. Before long the SE5s were reinforced by a formation of Bristol Fighters, the black and white Albatri by more of their kind, and a 'real dogfight' began.

In the general confusion, McCudden looked round and saw an SE5 'circling inside four Albatros scouts, and as I glanced I saw a Hun, who was turning inside the SE at twenty five yards range, shoot the SE's left wings off and the British machine went down in a spin with one pair of wings left. It was poor Sloley, who was, as usual, where the Huns were thickest.'[1]

Arthur was also in trouble. Looking round again, McCudden saw:

Another SE in amongst four black and white Albatroses. This SE was fighting magnificently, and simply could be none other than Rhys Davids, for if one was ever over the Salient in the autumn of 1917 and saw an SE5 fighting like Hell amidst a heap of Huns, one would find nine times out of ten that the SE was flown by Rhys Davids.[2]

McCudden dived to Arthur's assistance, followed by Gerald Maxwell, and for the next few minutes 'fought like anything, but the Huns were all very good and had not Maxwell and I gone to Rhys Davids' assistance when we did, I think the boy would have had a rather thin time.' After a time the Albatri broke off the combat and cleared east. McCudden and Arthur flew south and attacked a pair of two-seaters east of Zonnebeke. Both SE pilots got in good bursts at these aeroplanes, but they achieved no result, other than to force them east of the lines. The SEs then attacked a lone two-seater flying at only 200 feet over Polygon Wood. McCudden had a shot first, but 'he took not the slightest notice.' Arthur then dived and attacked and although McCudden could see Arthur's tracers 'splashing all over the Hun', the two-seater merely flew on, ignoring their attacks. McCudden commented bitterly: 'I believe the brute was armoured.'

[1] Op cit page 184.
[2] Ibid page 184.

Arthur was credited with one of the black and white Albatri from the earlier fight as out of control and another was awarded to B Flight as a shared victory.

Next day Barlow led B Flight in its customary evening patrol, taking off at 4.30. C Flight was also out and, almost from the very outset, were kept in a bad tactical position, Bowman caustically remarking: 'Driven out of the sky twice.' B Flight then joined their comrades and managed to bring the enemy into closer combat. Muspratt, outnumbered by three enemy scouts, was rescued by Arthur, who dived to his aid, driving the enemy pilots away. During this combat both Arthur and Muspratt reported having seen a Fokker triplane, or triplanes, amongst the enemy scouts. Arthur wrote: 'Saw two Fokker Triplanes with no dihedral, large extensions, Nieuport tail, Fokker rudder and Martinsyde shaped wings, engine probably rotary. Climb appeared good.'

These reports of Arthur and Muspratt are extremely interesting. Air historians have always accepted that, with the loss of the two prototype Fokker triplanes on 15 September[1] and 23 September, no other triplanes were at the front until Jagdstaffel 11 received six Fokker triplanes 'about the middle of October.'[2] From the evidence of British combat reports, by 56 Squadron and other squadrons, it is apparent that additional triplanes were in service by the beginning of October 1917, or even at the end of September. Maybery's sighting of another Fokker triplane, in addition to that flown by Voss, on the evening of 23 September, is rather vague and inconclusive, but Arthur's description of those met on 1 October is unambiguous and accurate.

Arthur wrote to Vivien that evening:

We got our two hundredth Hun last night: great festivities, band, champagne, bust up dinner and speeches. Maybery got the 199th – his 13th or 14th – and Maxwell the 200th – about his 13th too.

For some curious reason they have given me a DSO.

Enorm haste.   Best Love.   Arthur.

Newall had written the evening before:

[1] Oberleutnant Kurt Wolff of Jasta 11 was shot down while flying Fokker triplane FI 102/17 on 15 September 1917. Voss was killed in FI 103/17.
[2] *Fokker: The Creative Years*, A.R. Weyl. Putnams.

My Dear Rhys Davids,

Once more my many congratulations. You have earned your DSO thoroughly and have made a very great name for yourself.

The very best of luck to you in the future and many more Huns and honours.

The weather was now bad, stopping all flying for the next two days. On the first day of enforced rest Arthur played rugby, cutting his knee and spraining his elbow, and next day, deciding on less strenuous pursuits, he went with Gerald Maxwell, Keith Muspratt, Maxwell Coote and Bert Johnston in the squadron tender to Le Touquet. Long trips in the almost unsprung Leyland tenders could hardly have been comfortable, especially for young men accustomed to covering distances in a somewhat quicker fashion. After flying a completely uneventful patrol the following day, 5 October, Arthur sat down in the evening by the mess fire – an ingenious contraption, designed by 'Georgie' Hoidge, who had been an architect before the war – and wrote to Caroline.

5/10/17

Dearest Mums,

Many thanks for the budget dated 30th. I re-enclose various components. Did you see all the comic nonsense in the Daily Mail about our nameless hero and all the rest of it? My hat, the squadron was furious about it, it was so wildly exaggerated and journalese. From Beach Thomas's account one would think that I was the only one there, which is of course absurd. I have just got the compass and rudder off the wrecked machine. Day before yesterday was our first dud day for a long time and we had a game of Rugger, good fun but resulting in a cut elbow and a sprained wrist both of which are well on the way to recovery. Yesterday was again dud and we went to . . . a neighbouring seaside resort for the day – fairly amusing but for a 3½ hours drive back in cold rain. Today we had a show at 9 which was the first real cold one we have had for months. Winter is starting at last. Am writing in front of our great open fire in the mess. Have had a delightful letter from Urquhart the Balliol history don. Last push seems to have been good.

Best Love   Arthur.

The weather again stopped flying the following day and that evening the squadron held a large dinner party to celebrate the award of a

DSO to Arthur, Barlow's second Bar to his MC and a Bar to McCudden's MC. Friends from other squadrons were invited and after drinks in the ante-room everybody went into dinner at 8.30 to the strains of 'Old Comrades' played by the squadron orchestra. Major Blomfield sat at the head of the table; above his head the squadron's Honours Board, on which each officer's name and decorations were in black and gold letters, the growing list headed by Albert Ball's Victoria Cross. After dinner, speeches were called for. First to speak was Eric Turnbull. Then Arthur was clapped to his feet. He began by saying how pleased and honoured he felt to have been awarded a DSO, but he felt that he must express his appreciation of their daily enemy, the German pilots and observers who fought with such courage and tenacity. Perhaps he was asking for an unprecedented toast, but he would like all to rise and drink to 'von Richthofen, our most worthy enemy.' All present rose, with the exception of one non-flying officer, and drank the toast, and after speeches from Barlow and McCudden all adjoined to the ante-room for the remainder of the evening.

As Arthur had commented in his letter, the weather was now becoming cold and the pilots woke every morning to the welcome sound of rain. On one such day of enforced but welcome rest, Maurice Baring came to lunch, bringing with him the artist William Orpen, who was in France to do a series of paintings for the War Office. Orpen recalled that the squadron had made a circular saw for cutting firewood in the coming winter and that Baring, as ADC to General Trenchard, was called upon to cut off the end of a cigar in the 'official' opening of the new saw. After being smoked a little the cigar would then be mounted in a specially made glass box and displayed in the squadron mess. The ceremony was a great success. Baring made a fine speech, cut the cigar to the accompaniment of the cheers of the assembly, and was then given the first log to cut. This done, Baring then took off his cap and cut this in half, to the great delight of the pilots, with whom this great man of letters, undoubted genius and lovable English eccentric, was a great favourite. When Baring further warmed to his task and took off his tunic, intending it should suffer the same fate as his cap, he was carried away from the saw by the laughing pilots. Orpen commented:

It was a great day. I remember Maurice saw me back to Cassel about 1.00am after much ping-pong and music. I never saw any squadron in France that was run nearly so well as 56 under

Blomfield, nor any Major loved more by his boys.[1]

Although present, Arthur made no mention of these happenings in his next letters home, as he would have done a few months previously. He had now been in France for six months and there is no doubt that he was due for, and needed, a rest. With one or two exceptions his letters at this time are short, almost terse, with none of the enthusiasm and exhilaration of the earlier letters. His letter to Vivien dated 8 October and naming the last four of the original pilots still remaining with the squadron, shows his state of mind. With the exception of Hoidge, Arthur was the last of those pilots who had flown out from London Colney in April to be posted back to Home Establishment.

> Dearest Sister,
> Just a 'urried note to thanks awfully for box and letter. You will know by now all about Voss etc. I have got his rudder and compass as trophies.
> There are four original pilots of the squadron left – Hoidge (C) Maxwell (now Flight Commander of A Flight) Barlow and self (B). Maxwell and Barlow go home day after tomorrow, Hoidge and I stay on for about a fortnight or three weeks more. Blomfield of course came out with us but he is CO and not a pilot.
> Best love Arthur.

A letter to Caroline, written a few days later, starts with an impatient first sentence which would have been unthinkable a few short months before.

> 10/10/17
> Dearest Mums
> Your last letter received with further recriminations about something.
> No news. Dud weather continuous till this afternoon when it cleared up and some of us did a show – not me. Have been out to dinner and lunch at various places: last night with dear old Straker. Mail very bad lately.
> Am disagreeing violently with old Marc Aurel. He is a Buddhist in some ways, N'est ce pas?

Arthur fought his next combat during a morning patrol on 11

[1] *An Onlooker in France 1917-1919*, William Orpen. Williams and Norgate 1921.

October. Despite the rain and low clouds, nine SE5s – a combination of C and B Flights – left Estrée Blanche at 6.15 am and an hour later attacked a mixed patrol of Albatri and Pfalz D.III over Zonnebeke. Arthur circled with an Albatros for some time until the German pilot attempted to escape in an evasive spin. Arthur followed, firing both guns, and the Albatros steepened its spiral and went down with a great deal of smoke pouring from its engine. This victory was confirmed by Lieutenant Gardiner of C Flight. This was a costly combat for 56 Squadron. For the one Albatros shot down by Arthur, Preston-Cobb was shot down and killed and Cunningham fatally wounded.

During the early afternoon, Keith Muspratt collected SE5a B31 from the depot and it was allocated to Arthur. He had flown B525 almost exclusively since it had been issued to the squadron on 23 August and it was now passed on to a new pilot, Captain Fielding-Johnson.[1]

Arthur was not to fly in action again for another nine days. Some of this inactivity on his part was due to getting B31 ready for the war and some to adverse weather conditions, but there is also no doubt that Blomfield was resting him as much as possible before he was due to go home, either at the end of the month or the beginning of November. Two of Arthur's letters to his aunts at this time show a slightly more relaxed frame of mind, no doubt attributable to his rest:

> The rain has come at last with a vengeance and we are having a slack time – comparatively. I am so sorry for the poor fellows in the infantry who are doing their best to do the impossible and make an advance in the appalling mud. I am so glad you enjoy your visits to Chipstead: to me, Mother and Father in their little cottage form an almost Homeric sphere where the advantages of civilization so called are so happily blended with the more sensible advantages of lack of civilization.
>
> You can't think how I appreciate your letters to me. I shall come and stay with you, with Vivien perhaps, one of these heaven blest days. We would play chess and I should read books to you and we could discuss them. What a dreadful shame it is that you cannot read to any great extent. I waste an appalling lot of time here in playing cards instead of reading.
>
> My best love always yrs affectionately. Arthur.

[1] After passing through the hands of three more pilots, B525 was finally 'retired' to 2 ASD as 'unfit due to age' on 2 February 1918.

Another letter, written two days later, shows a lack of patience with the Londoner's lack of morale under the air raids and the reason why he had not yet been posted home:

> Have been very busy lately getting a new machine into order for the war. Weather continues dud and v cold up high when fine. I do not think I shall get home till the first or second week in November, as the squadron has just got a lot of new pilots and they don't want to get more than necessary just at present.
>
> London seems to be in a dreadful state about the raids. So far as my little sphere goes, we are all disgusted at the lack of moral courage displayed. Fancy going and sleeping out on a common for fear of being bombed when the chances are literally about 70,000 to 1 against being hurt. I hope they will stop talking about the rotten 'morale' of internal Germany.

In a letter to Caroline on the same day he seems to have recovered his spirits a little, almost to the old level, but the date of his coming home is still of obvious importance to him. Despite the rest he was plainly tired; he had not written to Vivien for some time and this letter to his mother has scribbled on the back: 'please send to V.':

> 14/10/17
> Dearest Mums,
>
> Blades (razor) arrived all safe very nice and OK. Many thanks. Also large budget from Viv and a delightful letter from Nesta. I wonder why it is that Nesta is such a wonderful letter writer. The inconsequent way she tells things in my favourite style of metaphor is too delightful for words. I am also so frightfully pleased that she is developing so the love of history and literature. In fact the dear girl seems to be rather prosperous at school.
>
> I have had delightful letters from J.F.C. and a boy friend at Eton about the DSO. I got *seven* letters one day and four the next! I have been very busy lately as I have got a new machine and it has had to be got ready for work – clear decks for action so to speak. Time in fact very full up.
>
> Shall be out here now to the end of the month at least, probably coming home in the second week of November at a guess.
>
> I remembered Auntie's birthday somehow.
>
> Best love to the dear man. A.

Four days later he wrote again. He was now more relaxed and seems to have an inkling of Blomfield's plan to rest him as much as possible, probably using the rugby injuries at the beginning of the month as a partial excuse. Coming home was still in the forefront of his thoughts, however.

Of course I'm afraid there is absolutely no hope of my being at Bab's wedding if it is on the 20th of *this* month. I will write tonight and congratulate. If it is next month I might just be home in time. Nothing further about my probable date of return since last letter. . . I had my picture painted yesterday Zeus! – by one W Orpen ARA (major attached staff) – a quaint quick little Irishman who was most charming. I am sitting ¾ full face wearing a flying cap and my burberry over my shoulder falling down at the side to show my wings and silly medals. I don't think it is frightfully good but then I'm no judge.[1] It – the picture – belongs to the government as he has a job painting things for Govt, and if it approves of it will be sent home and reproductions taken. They have been keeping me on the ground rather more than necessary, I think, lately during these intervals of fine weather. I have not been to the war for a week. Football wounds progressing slowly but steadily – nearly OK now.

Best love to all. Arthur. Have heard from V and N.

Arthur had gone to Cassel on 1 October to have sketches made for the Orpen portrait. Orpen wrote:

General Trenchard and Maurice Baring chose two flying boys for me to paint, and they sat for me at Cassel.[2] One was 2nd Lieutenant A.P. Rhys Davids, DSO, MC, a great youth. . . The first time I saw him was at the aerodrome at Estrée Blanche. I watched him land in his machine, just back from over the lines. Out he got,

---

[1] After Arthur's death, when Caroline first saw the painting, she wrote to Nesta. 'Oh Nesta! it's *beautiful*, so far far finer than any photo – and much more like. Vivien, at first viewing, was not so impressed, but later wrote. 'It certainly grows on you. Painting him like that with the cap on has made his face look so absurdly long, but I was more reconciled when I discovered that quarter smile: an expression in which he just seems to be sucking in his cheeks, so as not to laugh, and saying: "Lord, what futile rot this all is." He was so different in different moods that one wants 4 (views) to get him at all.'

[2] In the courtyard of the Hotel Sauvage.

stuck his hands in his pockets, and laughed and talked about the flight with Hoidge and others of the patrol, and his Major, Bloomfield (sic). A fine lad, Rhys Davids, with a far-seeing clear eye. He hated fighting, hated flying, loved books and was terribly anxious for the war to be over, so that he could get to Oxford. He had been Captain of Eton the year before, so he was an all-round chap and must have been a magnificent pilot.

Arthur at last managed a letter to Vivien on 19 October. After discussing the bill for the photographs taken at Bekesbourne, he again touched on his being rested and the Orpen painting:

Not much news here. I have been kept on the ground lately in the fine intervals: today was very misty and cloudy but no rain, so we had quite a lot of aerodrome flying and also an excellent game of football.

The day before yesterday I went and had my portrait painted by one Major Orpen ARA who is attached to HQ Staff out here for purposes of painting various pictures connected with the war. Isn't it comic? He did me wearing my flying kit, a flying cap and burberry, sitting down in a chair and looking nowhere. I didn't think it was like me, but then I'm no judge.

. . . you can address me DSO if it amuses you, put it before the MC. Has the present turned up. I have been wearing your excellent socks all day. Don't be silly about boring letters. 'Da Capo' in the same strain if you please.

Neither Maybery (now on leave) or Muspratt have yet Bars to their MCs but Maybery will soon get one or a DSO. Two others in our Flight have got 1st and 2nd Bars to MC – one my Flight Commander – names would not interest you. Ball didn't get the DSO in the squadron – got it in 60 last year. The ribbon of the DSO is about the nicest ribbon going I think.[1] You will gather from these disjointed remarks that your letter is beside me now.

Despite these distractions, the war was still relentlessly continuing and it claimed Arthur again on 20 October. B Flight took off in the morning and caught an enemy two seater over Wervicq at 12,000 feet. All the flight had a shot, with Arthur firing short bursts of Lewis

[1] Light Blue. Red. Light Blue.

– his Vickers had jammed – across the two-seater's bows before zooming away to avoid two of his comrades who were also attacking. The enemy machine went down in a steep spiral, but under control. Arthur, down to 5,000 feet, found that the engine of B31 would not pick up due to loss of pressure in the dive, cutting off its petrol supply. He pumped up enough pressure to restart his engine and rejoined the other SEs. The flight saw no more action, and Arthur commented in his combat report that enemy activity seemed below normal.

Wing Headquarters telephoned the squadron just before midday on 21 October and asked them to intercept three enemy two-seaters flying south from Calais. McCudden, Keith Muspratt and Arthur said their goodbyes to Gerald Maxwell and Leonard Barlow who were just leaving in the squadron car for Home Establishment, and took off to look for the enemy. McCudden took the SEs towards Calais, had a look at DH4 and then turned away, continuing to climb. Arthur and Muspratt returned to Estrée Blanche and told Marson that they had left their flight commander stalking a friendly DH4, but McCudden finally caught a Rumpler after a long and careful stalk of nearly an hour and shot it down to crash near Mazingarbe. This special mission was the last patrol Arthur was to fly with McCudden and his friend Muspratt. McCudden left on leave on 23 October and Arthur took command of B Flight in his absence. The previous evening he wrote to Caroline. It was his last letter to her:

22/10/17
Dearest Mums,

Heaps of thanks for enormous budgets of today and also letter which came on the 20th.

About that photo of self and little Thais – if you want any more prints I am afraid they must be copied off the prints you have as the owner of the negative has sent it home and cannot be certain of getting it back for at least a fortnight.

I think I shall have another photo taken when I come home. Our first 2 men went home yesterday after great send off – leaving now only two in the squadron who came out with it. The Major is also leaving us shortly, probably to get a Wing at home. (ie. be a Colonel) The other one left besides me[1] has taken over the vacant post of Flight Commander so I am now the only original flying

---

[1] Hoidge.

officer. Good old Father. I am glad he seems to be full of life.

You never told me whether the Maeterlinck has turned up yet. The Beethoven lecture has not reached me. It did not come in the same parcel as the Quest Review, did it? I like your article in latter immensely though it is still a bit too technical for me to understand thoroughly. But I know what you are driving at.

All my love. Arthur.

PS. I have got a new bus merely because my old one was getting a bit stale – not in the least shot about. New one v. good.

Caroline did not share Arthur's enthusiasm for Maeterlinck's verse. She wrote:

The Maeterlinck verse: what shall I say, what can I say about these languors of the soul? The translation gives the atmosphere amazingly well. But they are too pathetic in tone and matter to appeal to me much. One such poem or two I could tolerate a man writing, esp. the first, with its final outcry for air and freedom – but to write 33 of these 'glaucous sobs' is a dementia, as if so sane a mind as M's worked off periodical crazy fits by writing one each time. But to have read them is none the less interesting. . .

But oh! my heart, how slowly go these last weeks of your term of war! Come soon! Mother.

This letter was dated 28 October.

*

On 27 October, the weather, which had practically stopped all war flying for the previous four days, improved enough for patrols to take off in the morning. Captain Hoidge, now leader of A Flight on Maxwell's posting to Home Establishment, led his new command across the lines to escort a formation of DH4s of 25 Squadron to bomb both Roulers railway station and Abeele aerodrome. Having seen the bombers safely back across the British lines, the flight sighted a large formation of enemy machines over Menin. Three of the SEs had returned with engine troubles, but Hoidge, Eric Turnbull and Harmon attacked the enemy formation, chasing the German machines east. Frustrated by continual gun jams, none of the SEs obtained a decisive result.

The next patrol left Estrée Blanche at 10.40: Captain Bowman leading Jarvis, Muspratt, Slingsby, Coote, Maybery and Arthur.

The SEs were a mile south west of Roulers when Bowman sighted two formations of enemy fighters – two Pfalz D.IIIs a thousand feet below the SE5 formation, and six Albatros DVs above them. Leaving the rest of the flight to deal with the Albatri, four of the SEs dived on the Pfalz. Bowman attacked the nearest, firing forty rounds from both guns. The Pfalz went down in a 'quick spiral'. Bowman followed it down to 1,000 feet but failed to get into position for any more shots. He accordingly climbed back into the fight between the SEs and the Albatri. The enemy scouts cleared east before Bowman could get into the action and he reformed the remainder of the flight and climbed back to 11,000 feet. Arthur was not with the formation. He had last been seen diving east after one of the Albatri.

Three SE5s failed to return to Estrée Blanche from this patrol. Maybery later telephoned to say he had landed safely at Bailleul, and Slingsby had force landed near Poperinghe, but there was no news of Arthur. At first there was no anxiety. It was generally felt that 'it would have to be a damned good Hun to get RD.' He would ring later to say he had landed at another aerodrome, or had a forced-landing somewhere. But as the day progressed, and no news came, it became obvious that he was down on the enemy side.

The squadron had not suffered such a heavy blow since the loss of Ball – perhaps not even then. His fellow pilots felt, or made a pretence of feeling, that he was safe; a prisoner of war, and no doubt reading Blake, a volume of whose poetry he always carried while flying: an antidote to the boredom of captivity, he had so often said.[1]

Keith Muspratt wrote home:

You will be sorry to hear we lost Rhys Davids on the 27th. No one knows what happened for certain but I was on the show and there were very few Huns and what there were were very half hearted. Rhys Davids is a great loss to the squadron and the Flying Corps. He and I have been together so long that it comes as a great shock, but we all hope he is alright and I myself feel confident that he is.

On 29 October the squadron gave a farewell dinner for Major 'Dickie' Blomfield. Maurice Baring was a guest and wrote: 'Everything was the same except Rhys Davids was not there. We kept up the pretence of saying we were certain he was a prisoner and would soon escape.' Baring had heard that Arthur was missing on

[1] Vivien had given Arthur this small volume of Blake for Christmas 1916.

the afternoon of 27 October and he remembered that Arthur had told him at their last meeting that he felt certain he would be killed. Many pilots had this uncanny prescience of their own deaths. McCudden, returning to France after his last leave, gave his sister Mary his medals for safekeeping in a way which left her in no doubt that he knew he would not return. Mannock also had no illusions that he would survive the war, almost predicting the manner of this death. Serving pilots seem to have sometimes had a curious knowledge of which of their comrades were destined to be killed. 'Grid' Caldwell, the New Zealander who served with such distinction in 60 Squadron and later commanded 74 Squadron, in a letter written over sixty years later, commented on a pilot, later killed: 'We all knew he'd go west, he had that look about him.'

Major Blomfield, about to relinquish command of 56 Squadron, had the unenviable task of writing to Arthur's parents. It must have been a doubly sad blow for him that one of his last acts while still in command of the squadron, a squadron he had done so much to nurture and bring to fruition as one of the finest in the RFC, was to write of the death of one of its original members; a boy he had so much admired and for whom he had felt a deep affection.

28/10/17   56 Squadron.
Dear Mrs Rhys Davids

It is with very greatest regret that I have to inform you that your Son – 2Lt. A.P.F. Rhys Davids DSO MC did not return from an offensive patrol over enemy territory yesterday morning (27/10/17). The formation with which he was attacked a hostile formation and in the fight which ensued became split up and therefore I have no definite information as to what actually happened to your Son, who was last seen by two other members of the formation fighting with his usual dash and gallantry. I sincerely hope that he was unable to get back to our lines through some trouble with his machine and that the worst that has befallen him is a forced landing in enemy territory and being a prisoner in German hands. Messages are being dropped today, and every effort will be made to asertain his fate and to inform you immediately.

Of his personal bravery and skill as a pilot it is needless to speak, the decorations he had won speak for themselves.

His loss is felt by myself and by every officer and man in this squadron for he was held in the highest regard by everyone.

All his kit and trophies are being sent to you per Cox's Shipping Agency with the exception of the rudder from Lt Voss's machine – and if you would like this, and will let me know, I will arrange to have it delivered to you. Please accept my very sincere sympathy in the anxiety and suspense which this must cause you.

Yours sincerely.
R G Blomfield
Major,
Commanding No.56 Squadron.
Royal Flying Corps.

This letter from Blomfield held a ray of hope that Arthur might be alive and a prisoner, but it brought an agonized response from Caroline Rhys Davids.

3rd November 1917   Cotterstock.
How Lane.
Woodmansterne.

Dear Major Blomfield.

I am sorry my beloved son left the commanding officer, to whom he was so greatly attached, so terrible a task as that of the letter you sent us. It was too much like an obituary notice to leave us much room for hope. It was a glorious finish, though some of the squadron must feel bad indeed that they were not there to rescue.

I never expected when he wrote to say he was staying beyond his six months that we should get him safe back. I should be glad if you can tell me just why he stayed on after mid-September and why he was allowed to do so. Was it because he wanted to make up for those first three weeks when his accident prevented his beginning scrapping?

His was really a most valuable young life, so full of high gifts, firm pure purposes and a winning personality, that it was worth straining a point and compelling him to come back to relative safety against his will. And he was all we had!

Thank you, do not send home rudders of fallen Huns. I could not bear to see them.

Some day I shall hope to meet and thank you for your regard for Arthur.

Sincerely yours,
Caroline Rhys Davids.

This letter was not received by Blomfield until 20 November and he made haste to reply, writing the following day.

21/11/17
Dear Mrs Rhys Davids,
    In reply to your letter of the 3rd. There is no fixed period for a pilot to serve overseas.
    In the case of your Son I gave him the opportunity of going home early in September and again in October but he preferred to stay on with the view of running his Flight whilst his Flight Commander was on leave. I am quite sure he was very happy with us. No-one – outside his own family – feels his loss more than I do; but you can rest assured that everything possible in every way was done for him.
                                    Yours sincerely.
                                    R.G. Blomfield.

The months following the date Arthur was posted missing were to impose an almost intolerable strain on the entire family and Caroline in particular. She refused to give up hope that her son was still alive. She had written to Vivien after receiving the long-dreaded telegram:

31/10/17
My Darling,
    My long expected news has come at last – not the worst – as yet – I felt his luck could not last over this postponement and have been more depressed about him this month than ever, tho' I would not say one word to him to worry. I did beg him a month ago not to outstay what one calls his luck – a matter really of probabilities. I've so looked for such a mail that we've gone on today quietly at work as usual and said no word.

The remainder of this short letter is taken up with domestic affairs and family news. Caroline was obviously hopeful that Arthur was still alive, despite the fears expressed in her letter to Blomfield, written a few days later, and throughout November 1917 she and Vivien made many enquiries in an attempt to discover if Arthur was a prisoner of war. Lady Margaret Leighton, whose son Richard had been shot down and captured in August 1917, while also serving in 56 Squadron, wrote to give hope and encouragement:

It always takes from 4 to 8 weeks to get any news of a missing RFC officer. Your son being such a splendid pilot is almost sure to have landed all right. The SE5 machines (which your son would be flying) are very good for landing – my son fell 12,000 feet and only had his arm broken and his head badly cut from the fall.

In response to this letter Caroline asked how Lady Leighton had first heard the news of her son's capture. Lady Leighton replied that she had contacted a Mrs Livingston at the Board of Works, that she had also received a telegram from the Crown Princess of Sweden – 'the Duke of Connaught had sent her a wire for me' – and that she had heard from her son on 28 September, nearly six weeks after he had been reporting missing. She also advised Caroline to write to Arthur care of Stammlager Wahn as she believed that letters were forwarded from there. Caroline wrote several letters to this address:

Dec 3 1917.
Hallo! Hallo! are you there? Best Beloved, are you there? Oh me! is this telephone any good? Will my voice ever reach? Is there a Beloved Son somewhere at the other side of this miserable world to answer? Shall I ever see another word in his handwriting – can he write – from whom I have never yet been absent for one week without a letter or news of some sort – shall I ever see him again. Where is God's name is Wahn? Sinister word! It means illusion.

The sixth week has begun since you, my sweetest Arthur were missing; lost sight of tackling 2 Huns – another rumour, tho' Alan Storey says pursuing low one you had shot down. Engine trouble, all say. Barlow came here to enquire. It has all been one long ache. But Father keeps well and brave and sisters write cheerfully. Vivien rushed home to see us, but we sent her back. Nesta is longing to send books and things to 'somewhere in Germany'. The RFC Prisoner's Fund is ready to dash off provisions. Cox's, the World, is waiting for news of Arthur. He sits looking at me from the mantelpiece with 'Don't worry Mother' written above. Hallo, hallo! are you there, boy of my heart? Are you there?
Mother.

This letter, full of a mother's anguish, was followed by another on 21 December. This letter was more normal in tone and content, talking to Arthur as if he were definitely safe in captivity, giving him details of the family Christmas and plans to sell Cotterstock. On Christmas

Day 1917 Caroline wrote again, another chatty letter, full of family news and ending:

> As soon as I do hear at last from or of you – we have even enlisted the King of Spain to enquire, as he has done for others – we will begin sending you things – be sure tell all you want.
>
> Oh my dearest, if I could only picture you at last where you really are. Mother.

But these hopes were dashed on 29 December when a letter from the War Office stated that a German aeroplane had dropped a message in the British lines to say that Arthur was dead, and in early January 1918 Vivien received a letter from a friend in the Central Prisoners of War Committee. Although they had no positive news from their agent in Copenhagen, who was enquiring through the Berlin Red Cross, a rumour had been heard that Arthur's name had appeared in a German newspaper as being dead:

> This news, of course, is not accepted officially here until it comes from Berlin, but unfortunately I must say that this sort of news is often correct. When once his name appears on a German list as having been killed, I shall then hope to be able to trace where he died, whether he was killed outright, and where he is buried. The German Red Cross is extremely well organized and when one approaches them in the right way they certainly are most kind in giving us information.

There was no further news after this, and on 2 March 1918 Caroline wrote to Blomfield's successor, Balcombe-Brown. An angry and hurt letter.

To the CO 56 Squadron RFC BEF.   March 2 1918
Dear Sir,
    I have only lately heard that Major Blomfield, your predecessor, is promoted to a post in the USA and I have only now found courage to send you a letter of enquiry that costs me so much to write; I was in too great an agony of mind to do so before.
    Concerning the fate of my only and utterly beloved son Lieut. Arthur Rhys Davids DSO MC and late of your squadron, we have received, since early in November *absolutely no news* save the CO's and WO's messages: 'missing' October 27, and the latter's letter

of December 29, that German airmen had dropped apparently the baldest announcement – two months later, that is – of death: no burial place, no relics.

I have also heard that his kit is at Cox's and have written to ask the WO for a permit to get it, and so far have no reply.

Not a soul of those who knew him and were on patrol with him that day – October 27 – have sent us a single word, either of what they last saw of him, or of sympathy to us or of tribute to their comrade! Is this usual in the RFC? I hear such different stories concerning infantry officers who have fallen. I know that his few best friends either had preceded him on leave, or have themselves become missing. eg. Muspratt, Barlow, Maybery. But surely others must have seen something of him during that fatal flight. I only heard the formation got broken.

Think what we have been suffering for over four months – the blind darkness, the silence – has no one in 56 the least imagination what it has all cost us? In Arthur was centred our happiness [lines here missing, apparently cut off the bottom of the letter. Author] It makes me think he must in some way, after his swiftly earned fame, have disgraced the squadron at the end. What am I to think?

Yours very truly
Caroline Rhys Davids.

Balcombe-Brown replied to this letter:

56 Squadron RFC
BEF 14th March.

Dear Mrs Rhys Davids,

I have just arrived back from leave to find your letter of the 2nd March here. It is a difficult and unpleasant one to answer and I have never before had such a letter written to me.

I can quite understand your agony of mind in losing your only son and beg to offer my heartfelt sympathies. At the time he went missing I did not write because it was only my second day in the squadron and Major Blomfield was still in command for another day or two, but we all felt terribly grieved and hoped for the best. Practically all of us have lost brothers and close relatives in the war so we can imagine slightly what it is like.

No word was received of your son till about 2 months later, when a message was received from a German airman saying he was dead. I'm afraid you expect far too much of them if you require full particulars of his burial place and relics. The list they very kindly drop for our information would be altogether a very complex affair were they to give all the information one would naturally like to have regarding missing officers.

I am sorry that none of the officers on that ill fated patrol wrote. The commanding officer's letter is usually written on behalf of the sqdn and that letter should supply all the available details as it is the CO's job, in my opinion, to question all the officers and find out whatever he can about the fight. In this case it was a very severe fight during which each pilot was engaging singly either one or more of the enemy. All that was known was that your son went down in his usual recklessly brave manner too low. He was last seen to be all right and it was presumed that being so low he would return to our lines and climb up again, but he must have encountered some more machines later while still low down and attacked them.

To conclude, because no one from this squadron except the ex-CO has written to you, that your son has fallen *in*gloriously does not seem to me to be reasonable of such a son, surely you can't for a moment entertain such a thought. I have heard of Cols and even Generals and often Majors getting either the DSO or MC (once) for nothing at all, but if a youth who is a Sec Lieut wins the MC once, and then again and then gets the DSO you need not worry over whether he died gloriously or ingloriously because one would be the natural way for him to die, and for such a man the other way of dying would be non-existent.

During the months while waiting for news of him there were a number of us who were indeed upset. By the time news did come Capt. Maybery had just gone missing otherwise, of course, he would have written.

At the moment there is hardly an officer who was in the squadron with your son. I knew him before when in England and played golf with him and of course I was always in touch with his doings in this sqdn before I came to it.

I am not going to say much about what I thought of him because I have already written at length, but one thing I have always said is this. There are three officers I know whom I consider the bravest and unfortunately the most reckless in the RFC. Those three have done more towards winning our supremacy of the air than any 15 other pilots put together. But the brave and reckless sooner or later when taking on heavy odds 'stop a bullet' because it needs *superhuman skill to avoid it in the end*. The three pilots I refer to have now all been killed. They should all have had the VC. They are

Captain Ball VC DSO^2 MC

2Lt. A.P.F. Rhys Davids DSO MC^2

Capt. R A Maybery MC^2

Apologies for this letter.

Yours sincerely

R Balcombe-Brown.

Earlier in March, Maurice Baring had written to Caroline:

March 4.   Air Ministry Hotel Cecil.

Dear Mrs Rhys Davids,

Will you forgive a complete stranger writing to you? I have today received a photo of the picture Orpen did of your son and I may say I was instrumental in this being done as I took Orpen to your son's squadron and arranged for the sitting. I don't know that the picture is very like him, but his brother pilots told me that was what he looked like just before he went up into the air. I was very fond of your son – I saw him often and we talked of many things; but I always feared he was of those to whom the Gods give their fatal love. However, the last time I saw him he said to me. 'there is only one thing in the world that matters and that is "Don't be stupid"'. He showed me a small copy of Blake's poems he used to carry about 'in case I come down over the other side. The only thing I should hate would to be a prisoner,' he said once. He was looking forward to Oxford after the war, passionately looking forward to it, and would have given up, I think, all his exploits for a term at Oxford. I thought I had got used to hearing that people and friends and companions were missing, but when I heard your son was missing the blow seemed as unexpected, the wound as sharp, as fresh and as inexplicable as ever and I felt once more a novice in sorrow. He was incomparably gallant and gay and it is worth all the war to have been for some moments under the reflection of his spirit and his example. I am very proud to think that he honoured me, as I think he did, with his friendship and his confidence. Forgive me if I ought not to have written. I can't help writing.

Yours sincerely.

Maurice Baring.

To receive this letter only two days after her own to Balcombe-Brown must have been a great comfort to Caroline, and she wrote to Baring, thanking him for his kind thoughts. He replied four days later:

March 8 1918   Air Ministry Hotel Cecil.
Dear Mrs Rhys Davids,
    Thank you so much for your letter. I have been longing to write to you ever since Oct. 27 when I heard he was missing. I took Orpen to the squadron on Oct.12 and we spent the whole day there – such an enjoyable day. Your boy said that he and Muspratt (do you know him) had been translating the Gospel of St. John into plain language – that was the only way, he said, to understand the Gospels. He was reading Euripides too. His hut was full of books of poems. He was fond of a book called 'Bachelor's Buttons' and he enjoyed Mrs Meynell's latest book which I had sent him. J C Squire, the editor of the New Statesman, who knew of him through me, sent him some books. He liked a story I wrote called 'Orpheus in Mayfair' and talked about it a lot. He said machinery – oil tanks, cylinders etc bored him very much. I don't know whether it did. At dinner, talking about Oxford after the war, he said 'well I don't suppose I shall go, as I am sure to be killed.' That day the sitting with Orpen was arranged. On October 24 I dined there again. That was the last dinner I had when he was there. On October 29 I dined there again for Blomfield's farewell dinner and he was not there. Bowman, one of the Flight Commanders, said to me. 'Wherever he is he would like us to go on just as usual, but sometimes it is very difficult.'
    There has never been any news except the message, has there? They hoped at first that he was perhaps all right as his machine was not seen to crash and they thought he had perhaps had a forced landing or that his engine had got a bullet in it.
                            Yours sincerely.
                            Maurice Baring.

It was shortly after this letter that Caroline discovered that she and Baring were cousins. Subsequent letters from Baring were always addressed 'Dear Cousin.'[1]

[1] Baring was the fourth son of Edward, Lord Revelstoke. Revelstoke's mother and Caroline Rhys Davids' mother were sisters.

On 18 March 1918 the War Office officially confirmed Arthur's death.

C.2.Casualties. 144544/2.   WAR OFFICE
                                                   LONDON SW1.

Madam,

I am commanded by the Army Council to inform you that the message reported from the base as dropped in our lines from a German aeroplane, stating that Second Lieutenant A.P.F. Rhys Davids, DSO MC Royal Flying Corps Special Reserve, is dead, has been further considered.

In view of this report and the lapse of time since Second Lieutenant Rhys Davids was reported as Missing, the Army Council are now regretfully constrained to conclude that he was Killed in Action on 27th October, 1917.

I am to express their sympathy with you in your bereavement and to add that publication will be made in the official casualty list.

I am to say that for military reasons it is not considered desirable that allusion to the message dropped from a German aeroplane should be made in any obituary notice inserted in the Press

I am,
Madam,
Your Obedient Servant.

This was the final blow to Caroline's hopes that Arthur might still be alive. All the newspapers now carried the story of his exploits and death – the *Daily Sketch* published his photograph on the front page, calling him 'Eton's Boy Airman' – and letters of condolence poured into the family home. Apart from those from family and friends, these letters range from those of importance and position in the land and its armed forces, to letters from more humble people who had known Arthur. Agnes Green, the family's old cook from the days of Nalanda in Forest Hill, wrote:

I think of the time when he used to creep down the kitchen stairs at Nalanda Forest Hill while I lived in your service and just tapped at the door. 'Please Cookie may I come in and watch you grind the eggs up?' Also the first day he went to school, saying he would fight. I said, 'but Boysey, you mustn't fight'. He said. 'You see

Agnes, I shall and fight the big boys too.' I little thought then what a brave heroic fighter he would become in later years. Our dear little Arthur.

The agony dragged on for Caroline and Professor Rhys Davids; Vivien and Nesta, with the resilience of youth came to grips quicker with the finality of Arthur's death. Towards the end of March, Vivien wrote to Nesta.

Mother seems much better and cheerier, much more as she used to be. She certainly gets bad times, but on the whole she seems calmer and more gay. She laughs heartily now at jokes and makes them. Father I'm a little worried about. He is his own quietly cheery self to all outward respects but he seems to have less vitality – he seems constantly tired. . . The Kit has come and Mother and I unpacked it. Fums Up was in the pocket of one of his coats so I've got it.

Caroline's good spirits were deceptive. She suffered frequent periods of 'black despair' and she wrote to Nesta in May 1918 'the dreadful heartache goes on getting worse.' Her love for her daughters and interest in their lives and ambitions helped to allay the pain of Arthur's death a little, and in June 1918 she turned for a short time to Spiritualism. She was convinced she was in touch with Arthur through automatic writing and this gave her a great deal of comfort. Caroline Rhys Davids was an erudite, highly intelligent woman, far removed from the stereotype of the neurotic, self-deluding and easily duped women preyed upon by many fraudulent mediums in those war years of great distress for so many. She practised automatic writing with Arthur, completely on her own, with startling results, and it pulled her through this darkest period of her life.

In 1918 Vivien joined the WRAF, being finally accepted on Armistice Day, 1918. She served in France and, after the armistice, in Cologne with the Army of Occupation. After she had returned to England she received a letter from T.B. Marson, the former Adjutant of 56 Squadron.

22/5/19.
Dear Miss Rhys Davids,
    I have just seen Major Paul who has seen you several times in Cologne and he told me you would like to hear from me with any

news of your brother. I could tell you so much of him that I am doubtful where to begin, but when I feel most inclined to blame the fate that cut short a career that held every promise of brilliancy and usefulness I always think of a conversation in which he compared the termination of the careers of great characters on the World's stage. He took two examples – Jesus Christ and that very brave fellow officer of his of whom he and I were so rightly proud, Albert Ball vc. Death, he said, was the only fitting and suitable ending to such careers which were only finished and made complete by the deaths each respectively sought and found. I realized at the time he had stated a great truth and one which I now firmly hold his own death bore out. In 1917 all the Western Front knew and admired Ball's successor – the boy from Eton – and all mourned his death. I always put Ball, your brother and Maybery in the same class. They were all VCs and they all gave their lives – and I always feel knew they would have to give them. I loved them as if they had been my own sons. My wife and children were so fond of your brother, of whom they saw a lot at Bekesbourne, and often still talk of him. My little girl of ten has never forgotten him and often so wishes he would come back. I do hope that when you are in London you will come and see us, and my wife would be delighted to hear from you or write to you. I am at present Private Secretary to Gen Trenchard and am very busy – but will write again if I may.

Yours very sincerely.

T.B. Marson. Capt.

In March 1920, Caroline presented the rudder of Voss's Fokker Triplane to the Imperial War Museum. The rudder had been brought back from France by Gerald Maxwell in July 1918. In October 1920 the Secretary of the War Office wrote that he was forwarding the effects of 2nd Lieutenant A.P.F. Rhys Davids, which had been received from Germany through 'diplomatic channels'. 'No information is forthcoming regarding the circumstances of their recovery'. He enclosed an inventory.

Treasury Note Case

Cheque for 5 Francs.

Letters.

1 Franc.

Of Arthur's friends in 56 Squadron, Richard Maybery was next to be killed, on 19 December 1917. Only two members of B Flight – McCudden's 'as splendid a lot of fellows as ever set foot in France' – survived the war: Maxwell Coote and Cronyn. Leonard Barlow and Keith Muspratt were both killed while test flying: Barlow in February and Muspratt in March 1918. And finally, in July 1918, the great McCudden, now a VC, also lost his life in a flying accident.

Professor Rhys Davids died in 1922 in his eightieth year. Caroline succeeded him as President of the Pali Text Society until her own death in 1942. Neither Vivien nor Nesta ever married. Nesta died in 1973 and Vivien in 1978.

Arthur Percival Foley Rhys Davids has no known grave. There is for him no 'corner of a foreign field that is for ever England'. His only memorial in France is his name engraved on the Air Services Memorial at Arras. Perhaps his favourite poet, William Blake, had written his epitaph many years before.

> And thou, Mercurius, that with wingèd brow
> Dost mount aloft into the yielding sky,
> And thro' Heav'n's hall thy airy flight dost throw,
> Entering with holy feet to where on high
> Jove weighs the counsel of futurity;
> Then, laden with eternal fate, dost go
> Down, like a falling star, from autumn sky,
> And o'er the surface of the silent deep dost fly:[1]

Or did Agnes Green, the family cook from Nalanda, who so vividly remembered the little boy shyly tapping at her kitchen door, put it, in her own simple way, more succinctly:

> Our dear little Arthur. Great acts like his will ever remain in England's history.

---

[1] An Imitation of Spenser. William Blake.

Postscript

No details were ever learnt of the circumstances of Arthur Rhys Davids' last fight and death. Because of this T.B. Marson believed that the SE5 had been completely destroyed by a direct hit from an anti-aircraft shell. The fact that Arthur's personal belongings were returned to the family after the war disproves this theory. Recent research has shown that Rhys Davids was almost certainly shot down by Leutnant Karl Gallwitz. Gallwitz, at that time acting Staffelführer of Jasta Boelcke, claimed a 'Martinsyde' – a type the German fighter pilots often confused with the SE5 at this stage of the war – at Polterrjebrug, just over a mile north-west from Dadizele, at 12.08 German time (11.08 British time). This claim of Gallwitz fits for both time and location the loss of Rhys Davids on the morning of 27 October 1917. The area in which the crash took place was very near the front line during the Third Battle of Ypres in the October and November of 1917, and the grave site may well have been totally obscured during the heavy fighting in the area during the battles for the Passchendaele Ridge, just as the grave of Voss had been a month earlier. Arthur Rhys Davids and Werner Voss both lie in complete obscurity, a little under five miles apart.

APPENDIX

Appendix

Aerial Victories of Arthur Percival Foley Rhys Davids. DSO MC and Bar.

Date	Type	Classification	Location	Remarks
May 23	Alb.D.	Out of control	E of Lens.	
May 24	Single seater	Out of control	S of Douai	Shared with B Flight.
May 24	Two Seater	In Flames.	Gouy-sous-Bellone.	
May 24	Two Seater	Out of control	Sains.	
May 25	Two Seater	Destroyed	Flers. Lens/Douai Rd.	
May 26	Alb.D	Out of control	Gouy-sous-Bellone.	
June 4	Alb.D	Destroyed	W of Moorslede	Jasta 28. Possibly Lt. Dickinson's victory.
June 7	Alb.D	Out of control	Westroosebeke	
July 12	DFW.CV	Forced to land	Brickfield	DFW CV 799/17. Fl/Abt.7 Ltn Mann and Uffz Hahnel both POW. This DFW was later given the British classification G 53.
July 12	Fokker DV.	Out of control	E of Roncq	
July 13	Alb.D	Out of control	Over Menin/Roulers Rd.	
July 17	Alb.D	Out of control	Over Menin/Roulers Rd.	
July 21	Alb.D	Out of control	Polygon Wood	Shared with B Flt.
Sept 3	Alb.D	Destroyed	Near Houthem 150 yds W of Ypres/Comines Canal	Black and White colour Shared with Maybery.

Date	Aircraft	Result	Location	Notes
Sept 5	Alb.D	Out of control	E of Menin nr Moorseele	
Sept 5	Alb.D	Destroyed	E of Menin nr Moorseele	
Sept 5	Alb.D	Destroyed	1 Mile NE of Poelcapelle	Possibly Vzfw Alfred Muth Jasta 27.
Sept 9	Alb.D	Destroyed	SE end of Houthulst Forest	
Sept 9	Alb.D	Driven down	Moorslede	
Sept 14	Alb.D	Out of control	E of Menin/Roulers Rd	Possibly Ltn Gross Jasta 10.
Sept 23	Fokker Triplane	Destroyed	NE of Ypres Salient.	Ltn Werner Voss Jasta 10.
Sept 23	Albatros D.	Forced to land.	NE of Ypres Salient	Ltn. Karl Menckhoff Jasta 3.
Sept 24	Two seater	Destroyed in flames.	S of Houthulst Forest.	
Sept 28	Albatros D.	Out of control	Nr Comines.	
Oct 1	Albatros D.	Out of control	Nr Westroosebeke.	
Oct 1	Albatros D.	Out of control	Nr Westroosebeke.	
Oct 11	Albatros D.	Out of control	Beceleare	Shared with B Flt.

INDEX

Index

Index